Corporate Complicity in Isr

CORPORATE COMPLICITY IN ISRAEL'S OCCUPATION

Evidence from the London Session of the Russell Tribunal on Palestine

Edited by Asa Winstanley and Frank Barat

Foreword by Alice Walker

PlutoPress
www.plutobooks.com

First published 2011 by Pluto Press
345 Archway Road, London N6 5AA

www.plutobooks.com

Distributed in the United States of America exclusively by
Palgrave Macmillan, a division of St. Martin's Press LLC,
175 Fifth Avenue, New York, NY 10010

British Library Cataloguing in Publication Data
A catalogue record for this book is available from the British Library

ISBN   978 0 7453 3160 7   Hardback
ISBN   978 0 7453 3159 1   Paperback

Library of Congress Cataloging in Publication Data applied for

This book is printed on paper suitable for recycling and made from fully managed
and sustained forest sources. Logging, pulping and manufacturing processes are
expected to conform to the environmental standards of the country of origin.

10   9   8   7   6   5   4   3   2   1

Designed and produced for Pluto Press by Chase Publishing Services Ltd
Typeset from disk by Stanford DTP Services, Northampton, England
Simultaneously printed digitally by CPI Antony Rowe, Chippenham, UK and
Edwards Bros in the United States of America

For Inas and Leo

Contents

List of Figures

Acknowledgements

Thanks to Alice Walker for very kindly writing an inspirational foreword. Thanks to Roger van Zwanenberg and everyone at Pluto. For invaluable help with transcripts, many thanks to the following people: Hilary Aked, Florent Barat, Andrea Becker, Roger Briottet, Hilda Dunn, Eleanor Kilroy, Herve Landecker and Dena Qaddumi. Hilda Dunn kindly translated the parts of the closing session that were originally spoken in French.

For organisation of the London session of the Russell Tribunal itself thanks go to: Joanne Crouch, Jeanne Mortreux, Harry Fear, Ewa Jasiewicz, Stuart Platt, Susan Worsfold, Leah Borromeo, Kasia Lemanska, Kristian Buus, Hocine Ouazraf, Bea Martinez, Eva Ortigosa, Camino Simarro, Nicole Ochando, Paul Collins, Andrew Sanger, Shubhaa Srinivasan, Nathanael Corre and all the fantastic volunteers that helped during the three days.

For their overall contribution to the tribunal, thanks to: Pierre Galand, Stéphane and Christiane Hessel, Virginie Vanhaeverbeke, Daniel Machover and Eric David. Thanks to the International Organising Committee and all the jury members, experts and witnesses that made the tribunal an event to remember.

Foreword

Alice Walker

'Nothing is Stronger Than a Circle Which is Why, as Black Elk Teaches us, Everything Tries to Be Round'

Thoughts on the Russell Tribunal by Alice Walker

In many of my talks to young people, to women, to peace activists, I advocate that in these times of planetary disasters and instability people everywhere should gather together in circles of friends, in each other's homes, on a regular basis, to talk through the fears and challenges with which we, as a world, are faced: more frightening events at this time than at any period in human history. It is time to circle, I advise, with the hope that eventually our diverse circles will engage each other, merge and organically transform the earth.

I think of the Russell Tribunal as one of these circles, perhaps the most important, though its members may consider themselves strangers to each other. That they are not strangers is evident by their appearance, as a group, to take on the tribunal's exacting and highly essential work: to cast the light of conscience on the behaviours of powerful interests and destructive players in the world community. This is a duty that calls out to those who understand how important it is to end our common silence about abuse and atrocities committed in our names, and who also realize that we must be determined in our efforts to care for the maligned and traumatized and oppressed of the earth. That this caring signifies our awareness of membership in the same clan, the same family. The family of humankind of which any oppressed person is the brother or sister, the mother or father, the child or grandparent that is, at one point or another of our lives, also our own self.

It has been an honour to be invited to join the present session as part of a jury hearing testimony on international corporate complicity in the destruction of the Palestinian people, who, since I visited Gaza a year and a half ago, have become part of the earth's peoples to whom I have felt duty bound to show up for. What has happened to them has happened to countless others. Including my own tribes: African, Native American, poor European immigrant. It is because I recognize the brutality with which my own multi-branched ancestors have been treated that I can identify the despicable, lawless, cruel and sadistic behaviour that has characterized Israel's attempts to erase a people, the Palestinians, from their own land. For isn't this what the US military was ordered to do to the 'Indians' of America? Did not the British burn out communities of Scots and horrifically oppress the Irish? Did not wealthy and powerful Whites, generally, for a time, rape, kill, capture and/or enslave Africans? And are not some of their descendants, at this very moment, stealing and confiscating African and Indian and poor White land, and harming people, using many of their ancestors' ancient tools of brute force and deceit?

It grieves me that I am unable to be in this circle of brave and compassionate people on this occasion because of a mundane yet tenacious visitor: the flu. Which condition, as I recover, I can almost consider absurd. Since college I have admired the pacifist Bertrand Russell, the founder of the tribunal and also Jean-Paul Sartre and Simone De Beauvoir, early members. James Baldwin, as well, a person of such laser-like intelligence and moral integrity, that it would have been a joy to sit in his symbolic chair.

But the tribunal will go on: because it is a living part of all of us. That part that knows what is right. That part that really does not appreciate wrong. That part that is not blind. Not deaf. The part that hears the cries of others in distress because those cries echo our own internal expressions of shame, horror, dejection and despair.

The Russell Tribunal is rare and precious and glorious, because it reminds us to act for ourselves, to follow our own conscience. To join with our fellow humans who are also awake. Or at least beginning to stretch and yawn. It is a treasure that makes the world not only more safe, but infinitely richer.

I bow to its belief in justice, fairness, international standards of decency and law. The ability of humans to acknowledge and defend what is right and to do the work of holding the light in a world that seems at times to be sliding inexorably into the darkness. All that is ever needed to challenge that darkness is one light. May each of us, following the tribunal's example, be that light, however small and flickering, wherever we find ourselves.

POSTSCRIPT: THE FIRST DAY OF SPRING, 2011

And when we bring our flickering candles together, what happens?

Like much of the world, I watched with intense hope and emotion the unfolding of the Egyptian Uprising that began 25 January 2011.

Would the people stand their ground in the face of a cruel dictator's efforts to frighten, batter, torture and destroy them? Would they look at the bodies falling around them and, sickened and afraid, fade back into the shadows? Shadows with which all oppressed people are familiar: the backstreets of non-belonging, non-being; the dark corners of being hungry, insufficiently housed and clothed; the dim corners of being denied education and therefore intellectual stature and light; the literal dungeons of underground torture chambers.

There were moments when it was almost unbearable to watch the Egyptian people's sincere and principled revolt that has, by its example of peacefulness and dignity, transformed and renewed the spirit of creative resistance around the globe. I did watch and listen, however, to every sight, every sound, relying especially on the guidance of a young Egyptian-American broadcast journalist, Sharif Abdel Kouddous, who was inspiring in his courageous determination to do justice to the unfolding drama of the Egyptian people in perhaps their finest hour, and who is a member of the astonishingly thorough and savvy team of journalists and producers at Democracy Now! in the United States. Many times I could not hold back tears of joy, to see so many people, sick of their own oppression, get off their knees, climb out of the shadows, and rise.

I felt I knew them. Their willingness to sacrifice themselves for the future of their children, culture and country felt familiar to me. I have seen this same courage among African Americans, in our struggle for dignity and equal rights; I have seen it in the lives of Native Americans, whose long struggle not only to free themselves but also Mother Earth from aggression and defilement has been a life-enhancing example for me. The images of people praying, singing, weeping, suffering, dying; these are now, thanks to the people of Egypt, relics to be referred to, touched, reviewed, cherished, to give us strength for the road ahead.

I think of events like this uprising as 'a human sunrise'. My faith is always in the people and in our ability to create this. In that spirit, I offer poems. For it is poetry that – like music, dance, theatre, and art – generally can send us beyond the edge of our fear. These poems encourage us to look deeply into what kind of world it is we wish to construct, as we rightfully demolish the old one.

I wrote the first three poems decades ago to commemorate what can happen when hope is lost and a revolution in the making begins, for whatever reasons, to sour. The soured revolution is unfortunately common; mistrust, greed, internecine squabbling and warfare usually produce it. Also the age-old dilemma for the masculine of what to do with the feminine after political change is made and woman clearly intends to remain by man's revolutionary side. Then too, there is the revolutionary leader who loses the way and turns a wrathful face to the people, that frightens them into backwardness and submission.

It is well, I think, to consider these things and to recognize them as they are happening.

THE QPP

The quietly pacifist peaceful
always die
to make room for men
who shout. Who tell lies to
children, and crush the corners
off of old men's dreams.
And now I find your name,
scrawled large in someone's
blood, on this survival
list.

HE SAID COME

He said come
Let me exploit you;
Somebody must do it
And wouldn't you
Prefer a brother?
Come, show me your
Face,
All scarred with tears;
Unburden your heart –
Before the opportunity
Passes away.

ENDING

I so admired you then;
before the bloody ending
of the story
cured your life
of all belief.

I would have wished
you alive
still. Or even
killed.
Before this thing we got,
with flailing arms
and venomous face
took our love away.

*　　*　　*

A soured revolution is one of the saddest disasters that can befall
humanity. For it comes after so much hope, and suffering, and loss.
So much pain and sacrifice. So much dashed belief, in ourselves and
in others who have appeared so beautiful and magical, brave and
compassionate to us.

What can help prevent it? That is what is considered in the
following poems, written in response to the unfolding of uprisings
and revolts in Tunisia and Egypt and the Middle East generally,
but in many other parts of the world as well. Parts of the world
that remain unseen and therefore uncared about by much of the
global community.

'BLESSED ARE THE POOR IN SPIRIT (FOR THEIRS IS THE KINGDOM OF HEAVEN)'

Did you ever understand this?
If my spirit was poor, how could I enter heaven?
Was I depressed?
But now I see the power
of editing;
and how a comma, removed or inserted
with careful plan,
can change everything.
I learned this, anew, when a poor young man
in Tunisia
desperate and humiliated
set himself ablaze
and I felt uncomfortably warm
as if scalded by his shame.
I do not have to sell vegetables from a cart as he did
or live in narrow rooms too small for spacious thought;

and, at this late date,
I do not worry that someone will
remove every single opportunity
for me to thrive.
Still, I am connected to, inseparable from,
this young man.
Blessed are the poor, in spirit, for theirs is the kingdom of heaven.
Jesus. (Commas restored).
Jesus was as usual talking about solidarity: about how we join
    with others
and, in spirit, feel the world the same as them.
This is the kingdom of knowing the other as self, the self as
    other;
it is this challenge, overcome, that transforms grief into
peace and light.
I, and you, might enter the heaven
of right here
through this door.
In this spirit, knowing we are blessed,
we might remain poor.

TO CHANGE THE WORLD ENOUGH

To change the world enough
you must cease to be afraid
of the poor.
We experience your fear as the least pardonable of
humiliations; in the past
it has sent us scurrying off
daunted and ashamed
into the shadows.
Now,
the world ending
the only one all of us have known
we seek the same
fresh light
you do:
the same high place
and ample table.
The poor always believe
there is room enough
for all of us;

the very rich never seem to have heard
of this.
In us there is wisdom of how to share
loaves and fishes
however few;
we do this everyday.
Learn from us,
we ask you.
We enter now
the dreaded location
of Earth's reckoning;
no longer far
off
or hidden in books
that claim to disclose
revelations;
it is here.
We must walk together without fear.
There is no path without us.

OUR MARTYRS

When the people
have won a victory
whether small
or large
do you ever wonder
at that moment
where the martyrs
might be?
They who sacrificed
themselves
to bring to life
something unknown
though nonetheless more precious
than their blood.
I like to think of them
hovering over us
wherever we have gathered
to weep and to rejoice;
smiling and laughing,
actually slapping each other's palms

in glee.
Their blood has dried
and become rose petals.
What you feel brushing your cheek
is not only your tears
but these.
Martyrs never regret
what they have done
having done it.
Amazing too
they never frown.
It is all so mysterious
the way they remain
above us
beside us
within us;
how they beam
a human sunrise
and are so proud.

For the Egyptian people 11 February 2011.

*   *   *

I will never get over the fact that human beings are sometimes willing to die for each other, for their dreams, and for a future that is only dimly imagined. Nothing moves me more deeply than this sacrifice; it makes me wonder, often, if this isn't part of the reason we are born, to recognize ourselves in others, in the planet itself: in grass and trees and children and turtles, and to die for all of it, that all of it, of us, might live.

In any case, my response to the human sunrise is always the same, as shown by this poem:

MAY IT BE SAID OF ME

May it be said of me
That when I saw
Your mud hut
I remembered
My shack.
That when I tasted your

Pebble filled beans
I recalled
My salt pork.
That when I saw
Your twisted
Limbs
I embraced
My wounded
Sight.
That when you
Rose from your knees
And stood
Like women
And men
Of this Earth –
As promised to us
As to anyone:
Without regrets
Of any kind
I joined you –
Singing.

'The QPP', 'He Said Come' and 'Ending' are from *Revolutionary Petunias*, © Alice Walker, 1973.

'Blessed are the poor in spirit (for theirs is the kingdom of heaven)', 'To Change the World Enough' and 'Our Martyrs' are © Alice Walker, 2011. 'May It Be Said of Me' is © Alice Walker, 2009.

Poems from *The World Will Follow Joy: Turning Madness Into Flowers* (a work in progress) © Alice Walker, 2011.

Introduction

Asa Winstanley and Frank Barat

The Russell Tribunal on Palestine is an international people's tribunal created to address governments' unwillingness to stop Israel's violations of international law. It was established in the spirit of the Tribunal on Vietnam set up by Bertrand Russell in the 1960s.

The tribunal's aim is emphatically *not* to examine the question of Israel's guilt – in terms of illegal occupation of Palestinian and other Arab territories, war crimes and other violations of international law. Israel has already been proven guilty several times over by international legal rulings, famously including the International Court of Justice's 2004 advisory option against the Israeli apartheid wall in Palestine.[1]

In his presentation to the tribunal, barrister Paul Troop made an especially valid point in relation to the case of activists who took direct action against arms manufacturers EDO/ITT and Raytheon. During trials of the activists he defended, 'witnesses for the companies in both cases denied that they were supplying weapons to or assisting the Israeli military' (see Chapter 5). So instead of trying to deny Israel had been involved in war crimes, lawyers acting for the arms companies attempted (unsuccessfully) to distance themselves from Israel. Israel's guilt is by now clear to the whole world.

So the starting point of the tribunal was always that Israel is guilty. The question is: what can we as citizens do about it? The emphasis of the Russell Tribunal is on how to seek legal remedies in courts (both national and international), and how to campaign effectively. As well as noted human rights lawyers, many of the experts who gave presentations to the tribunal were activists and campaigners, so legal support for their work was examined.

Each of the tribunal's international sessions deal with different aspects of the complicity of governments, international organizations and corporations in the ongoing occupation of Palestinian territories and violations of international law by Israel. The London session's focus was on corporations.

In the words of Jean-Paul Sartre, speaking of the tribunal on Vietnam, 'The legality of the Russell Tribunal comes from both its absolute powerlessness and its universality.'[2] The tribunal has no legal status, and draws its strength from the will of citizens who wish to put an end to the impunity that Israel enjoys while denying the Palestinians their most basic rights.

Members of the International Support Committee of the Russell Tribunal on Palestine include Nobel Prize laureates, a former United Nations Secretary-General, two former heads of state, other personalities who have held high political office, representatives of civil society, writers, journalists, poets, actors, film directors, scientists, professors, lawyers and judges. See the website for a detailed list: <www.russelltribunalonpalestine.com>.

THE BARCELONA SESSION

On the weekend of 1–3 March 2010, the first international session of the Russell Tribunal on Palestine was held in Barcelona. It looked at the ways the European Union and its member states are complicit in the ongoing occupation of Palestinian territories by Israel, and its violations of international law.

Testimonies by 21 experts and witnesses over the two days looked at the right to Palestinian self-determination; the closure of the Gaza Strip and 'Operation Cast Lead' (Israel's deadly 2008–09 assault on Gaza); illegal settlements and the plundering of natural resources; the annexation of East Jerusalem; the wall built through occupied Palestinian territory and the EU-Israel economic association agreements and military cooperation. After deliberation, the jury issued its conclusions in an international press conference. These texts are available on the website.

The conclusions of this first session emphasized the shortcomings of the EU and its member states in implementing international and European law. Copies were sent to all European heads of government and foreign ministers; to the presidents of the European Commission and Parliament; to the United Nations, Israel, the Palestinian Authority and the Arab League.

THE LONDON SESSION

The London session of the Russell Tribunal is the subject of this book. The second international session took place in London on 20–21 November 2010, with the jury's preliminary findings presented at a press conference on Monday the 22nd (see Chapter 7). It examined the complicity of multinational corporations in Israel's violations of international law.

Twenty-eight experts and witnesses gave detailed presentations to a jury of notable human rights figures. They examined specific corporations involved in Israel's occupation and colonization of the occupied Palestinian territories (the Gaza Strip and West Bank – the latter includes East Jerusalem). The tribunal also shed light on systems that allow companies to aid illegality, and showed how states and international organizations can be held accountable for such actions.

The jury focused on three main questions: which Israeli violations of international law are corporations complicit in? What are the legal consequences of the activities of corporations that aid and abet Israeli violations? And what are the legal remedies available and what are the obligations of states in relation to corporate complicity?

The corporations examined were invited to participate and submit their views. They were Veolia, Cement Roadstone Holdings, Ahava, Dexia, EDO/ITT, Caterpillar, G4S, Elbit Systems, Carmel-Agrexco, SodaStream and PFZW.

Only Veolia, PFZW and G4S submitted replies to the tribunal. All three replies were carefully considered by the jury before deliberation. The replies show that these corporations were aware of their involvement in violations of international law and acted knowingly. All three of these responses are reproduced in Appendix 2.

THE JURY

The final composition of the jury for the London session of the Russell Tribunal on Palestine was as follows:

- *Stéphane Hessel*, France. Member of the French resistance during the Second World War, co-editor of the Universal Declaration on Human Rights, former ambassador of France to the UN, and honorary president of the Russell Tribunal on Palestine.
- *Mairead Corrigan Maguire*, Northern Ireland. Nobel Peace Laureate 1976.
- *John Dugard*, South Africa. Professor of international law and former UN Special Rapporteur on Human Rights in the occupied Palestinian territories.

- *Lord Anthony Gifford QC*, UK. Barrister and Jamaican attorney-at-law.
- *Ronald Kasrils*, South Africa. Veteran of the anti-apartheid struggle, writer and activist, and former government minister.
- *Michael Mansfield QC*, UK. Barrister, and president of the Haldane Society of Socialist Lawyers.
- *José Antonio Martin Pallin*, Spain. Emeritus judge, Chamber II, Supreme Court, Spain.
- *Cynthia McKinney*, USA. Former member of US Congress and 2008 presidential candidate for the Green Party.

ABOUT THIS BOOK

We present in this volume a collection of the written submissions that the experts and witnesses provided to the tribunal. Based on these papers, each gave a presentation during the weekend in London. The papers are reproduced here in the order the speakers presented over the course of the two days. After each talk, the jury took some time to ask questions on more specific aspects of the presentation. After some of these papers, we have included transcripts of the most pertinent answers to the jury's questions (along with a few transcripts of extra comments where relevant). The full videos are available to watch on the Russell Tribunal website.

Chapter 6 is a transcript of the last part of the London session, in which the jury recalled several witnesses for further questioning and Stéphane Hessel gave a summing-up. The book concludes with the jury's closing statement, presenting its interim findings.

It is our hope that this book will prove useful in the fight against Israeli war crimes, occupation and apartheid. The London session of the Russell Tribunal on Palestine brought together a unique collection of dedicated activists, lawyers and human rights figures. Over the course of the weekend, these experts highlighted a great number of possibilities for campaigning and legal action against companies based in Europe and North America for their complicity in Israeli war crimes. Please use this book as a tool to take concrete action against them.

> 'We have seen great things happen in our time and we shall see more: never despair.'
>
> Anthony Gifford QC

1
The Legal Framework Relevant to Corporate Conduct

International Law and the Complicity of Business in Human Rights Abuses

Hocine Ouazraf

The debate over the complicity of transnational corporations in violations of human rights and international humanitarian law (IHL) and, in particular, war crimes and crimes against humanity, has in recent years begun to attract renewed attention. The responsibility of multinational companies for complicity in the violation of human rights and IHL, especially in areas of armed conflict, required a response from the international community and the formulation of a judicial framework within which to supervise the conduct of multinationals. The obligation to avoid any involvement in violations of human rights and IHL is clearly set forth in the 1999 United Nations Global Compact, which was adopted at the initiative of the secretary-general at that time, Kofi Annan. Principle 2 of the pact stipulates that 'Businesses should make sure that they are not complicit in human rights abuses.'

While it is not binding, that text makes it possible to identify some major trends that can clarify the various forms which may be covered by the idea of complicity. The commentary on this principle clearly establishes a typology for various types of complicity in the following terms:

> Direct Complicity occurs when a company knowingly assists a State in violating human rights. An example of this is where a company assists in the forced relocation of peoples in circumstances related to business activity. Beneficial Complicity suggests that a company benefits directly from human rights abuses committed by someone else. For example, violations committed by security forces, such as the suppression of a peaceful protest against business activities or the use of repressive measures while guarding company facilities,

are often cited in this context. Silent Complicity describes the way human rights advocates see the failure by a company to raise the question of systematic or continuous human rights violations in its interactions with the appropriate authorities. For example, inaction or acceptance by companies of systematic discrimination in employment law against particular groups on the grounds of ethnicity or gender could bring accusations of silent complicity.[1]

For example, it will be up to the tribunal to consider the cases of such businesses as Caterpillar, Volvo and Daewoo and to see whether they are complicit in violations of human rights committed by the Israeli authorities in the Palestinian territories. The bulldozers which those companies supply to the state of Israel are used in the wholesale destruction of Palestinian homes, schools, orchards and olive groves. In recent years, thousands of Palestinians have seen their homes destroyed with the direct support of Caterpillar, Volvo and Daewoo. Such conduct constitutes a violation of the most basic rules of IHL. The interdiction on the destruction of civilian dwellings is taken from the Fourth Geneva Convention of 1949 relative to the protection of civilians in time of war and, in particular, Article 53, which provides as follows:

> Art. 53. Any destruction by the Occupying Power of real or personal property belonging individually or collectively to private persons, or to the State, or to other public authorities, or to social or cooperative organizations, is prohibited, except where such destruction is rendered absolutely necessary by military operations.

Furthermore, those three businesses are involved in the construction of the West Bank wall by supplying construction material. In its advisory opinion of 9 July 2004, the International Court of Justice stresses that the construction by Israel, the occupying power, of the wall in occupied Palestinian territory, including in and around East Jerusalem, and the associated regime, violate the international obligations which are incumbent upon it. Furthermore, through the construction of the wall, Israel ignores its international obligations under the relevant treaties. According to the Court, '... the construction of the wall has led to the destruction or requisition of properties under conditions which contravene the requirements of Articles 46 and 52 of the Hague Regulations of 1907 and of Article 53 of the Fourth Geneva Convention.'

The construction of the wall has imposed substantial restrictions on the freedom of movement of the inhabitants of the Occupied Palestinian Territory as guaranteed under the International Covenant on Civil and Political Rights, Article 12, paragraph 1, which states that 'Everyone lawfully within the territory of a State shall, within that territory, have the right to liberty of movement and freedom to choose his residence.'

An important and significant step was taken in August 2003 with the adoption by the Sub-Commission on the Promotion and Protection of Human Rights of a text concerning norms on the responsibilities of transnational corporations and other business enterprises with regard to human rights. Companies are enjoined in the following manner not to render themselves guilty of complicity in violations of human rights and IHL:

> 3. Transnational corporations and other business enterprises shall not engage in nor benefit from war crimes, crimes against humanity, genocide, torture, forced disappearance, forced or compulsory labour, hostage-taking, extrajudicial, summary or arbitrary executions, other violations of humanitarian law and other international crimes against the human person as defined by international law, in particular human rights and humanitarian law.

The commentary on this article makes absolutely clear what is meant by 'the complicity of companies'. It forcefully stresses as follows:

> (a) Transnational corporations and other business enterprises which produce and/or supply military, security, or police products/services shall take stringent measures to prevent those products and services from being used to commit human rights or humanitarian law violations and to comply with evolving best practices in this regard.
> (b) Transnational corporations and other business enterprises shall not produce or sell weapons that have been declared illegal under international law. Transnational corporations and other business enterprises shall not engage in trade that is known to lead to human rights or humanitarian law violations.[2]

The significance of this text lies essentially in the fact that it contains principles that are directly derived from international law and major human rights-related international conventions. In other words, it merely confirms the existing law and demands that it should be applied to company activities.

The Russell Tribunal on Palestine will consider the case of the French company Veolia, which is directly involved in the construction of a tramway to link Jerusalem to West Bank settlements, and will examine its contribution to the violation of one of the most fundamental rights of the Palestinian people: the right to self-determination. The pursuit by the Israeli authorities of an aggressive colonisation policy in the West Bank violates numerous provisions of international law and, in particular, of IHL. Indeed, under Article 49, paragraph 6, those settlements are illegal, and contravene the principles set forth in this article, which stipulates as follows: 'The Occupying Power shall not deport or transfer parts of its own civilian population into the territory it occupies.'

Those practices, which are forbidden by the Fourth Geneva Convention and aim to change the demographic character of the Palestinian population, have been condemned on several occasions by the United Nations Security Council and General Assembly. On 8 December 1972, General Assembly resolution 2949 (XXVII) recalled the prohibition on the modification of the physical character or demographic composition of the occupied Arab territories in the following terms:

> Declares that changes carried out by Israel in the occupied Arab territories in contravention of the Geneva Conventions of 12 August 1949 are null and void, and calls upon Israel to rescind forthwith all such measures and to desist from all policies and practices affecting the physical character or demographic composition of the occupied Arab territories ...

The involvement of Veolia in constructing a tramway line that links the settlements to Jerusalem directly reinforces the infrastructure of the Israeli occupation.

In 2005, the wish to clarify and expand the concept of the complicity of companies led the United Nations Secretary-General to appoint Professor John Ruggie of Harvard University, as Special Representative of the Secretary-General on the Issue of Human Rights and Transnational Corporations and other Business Enterprises (hereafter referred to as the Special Representative). The report which the Special Representative submitted in 2008 unquestionably constitutes a considerable advance in the discussion of the activities of multinationals and their consequences for human rights and IHL. The responsibility borne by companies with respect to human rights is emphatically confirmed. The report states as follows:

> 23. The corporate responsibility to respect human rights is the second principle ... Because companies can affect virtually all internationally recognized rights, they should consider the responsibility to respect in relation to all such rights, although some may require greater attention in particular contexts. There are situations in which companies may have additional responsibilities – for example, where they perform certain public functions, or because they have undertaken additional commitments voluntarily. But the responsibility to respect is the baseline expectation for all companies in all situations.[3]

In order to carry out this mission of respect for human rights, the report refers to the idea of 'reasonable diligence', which obliges every company to evaluate the potential risk of human rights violations to which it is exposed as a result of its activities and, where possible, to cease those activities. Reasonable diligence revolves around three principles which the Special Representative summarises in the following terms:

> Companies should consider three sets of factors. The first is the country contexts in which their business activities take place, to highlight any specific human rights challenges they may pose. The second is what human rights impacts their own activities may have within that context – for example, in their capacity as producers, service providers, employers, and neighbours. The third is whether they might contribute to abuse through the relationships connected to their activities, such as with business partners, suppliers, State agencies, and other non-State actors. How far or how deep this process must go will depend on circumstances.[4]

The Russell Tribunal will have to consider whether the Belgian bank Dexia, which is accused of financing the construction of West Bank settlements, has shown disregard for the obligation of 'reasonable diligence'. The implantation of settlements has been condemned on several occasions by the United Nations Security Council.

In resolution 446 (1979), the Security Council notes that the colonisation of occupied Arab territories has no legal validity and

> ... calls once more upon Israel, as the occupying Power, to: abide scrupulously by the 1949 Fourth Geneva Convention, to rescind its previous measures and to desist from taking any action which would result in changing the legal status and geographical nature and materially affecting the demographic composition of the Arab territories occupied since 1967, including Jerusalem, and, in particular, not to transfer parts of its own civilian population into the occupied Arab territories.

Is it possible to maintain that the Belgian banking group Dexia, through economic involvement in illegal activities linked to settlement, ignored the obligation of 'reasonable diligence' and was complicit in the sense meant by the Special Representative in that it supported the process of colonising the Palestinian territories?

The Special Representative devotes particular attention to areas of armed conflict. He calls for more systematic recourse to the sanctions which are taken by the Security Council against companies that are implicated in the arms trade, with a view to ending the flow of arms towards areas of armed conflict. He refers to a report of the United Nations Secretary-General which recommends that this principle should be applied to companies that have helped to kindle certain conflicts, particularly in the Congo, Sierra Leone and Liberia. In that regard, the Secretary-General noted in 2008 that:

> Arms embargoes can be effective in reducing conflict by preventing new outbreaks of fighting, if they are properly monitored and enforced and violators held responsible. Monitoring of compliance by expert groups is an important component in ensuring the effectiveness of sanctions regimes. However, greater attention must be paid to implementing the recommendations of such monitoring groups ... .[5]

It is not always easy to establish legal complicity. In order to carry out that task, the Special Representative advocates reasoning by analogy with the principles of international penal law. If the *ratione personae* competence of the international criminal tribunals for the former Yugoslavia and Rwanda only concern natural and not legal persons, the jurisprudence of those two tribunals with regard to complicity in such international crimes as war crimes and crimes against humanity makes it possible to extrapolate principles that go well beyond the complicity of natural persons *stricto sensu*. In 1998, for example, the Court of First Instance of the Tribunal for the Former Yugoslavia maintained the following: '... the Trial Chamber holds that the *actus reus* of aiding and abetting in international criminal law requires practical assistance, encouragement, or moral support which has a substantial effect on the perpetration of the crime.'[6]

This passage appears to echo the 1996 version of the International Law Commission draft code of crimes against the peace and security of mankind which, in Article 2, paragraph three (d), provides that an accomplice is someone who 'Knowingly aids, abets or otherwise assists, directly and substantially, in the commission of such a crime, including providing the means for its commission.'[7]

Furthermore, analysis of the jurisprudence of national criminal tribunals makes it possible to deduce the existence of an international obligation on the part of companies not to be complicit in international crimes. In fact, several domestic courts have felt compelled to make statements on cases of complicity linked to multinational companies. As the Special Representative underlines:

A number of domestic jurisdictions allow for holding legal persons, including companies, criminally liable for at least some international crimes. Provided these jurisdictions also have aiding and abetting liability, it will generally be possible to criminally prosecute companies for aiding and abetting such crimes.[8]

The action taken in the Belgian courts in 2002 against Total on the basis of the Belgian Law of Universal Jurisdiction of 16 June 1993, as amended by the law of 10 February 1999, albeit inconclusive because of an unduly restrictive interpretation by the Belgian Court of Cassation of certain provisions of that Law,[9] none the less illustrates the position of the Special Representative on the existence of international obligations on companies and, in particular, the obligation not to be complicit in international crimes. In Belgium, plaintiffs relied on the law of 1994/1999, which allows the Belgian courts to refer to cases relating to crimes of genocide, crimes against humanity and war crimes, in order to denounce the complicity of Total in certain crimes against humanity that were committed by the Burmese authorities. That case makes it possible to draw certain lessons as to the existence of international obligations on the part of multinational companies. In this case, a company was accused of complicity in human rights violations, which means that the rules of international criminal law also cover legal persons, not just natural persons. The Total case that was brought before the Belgian courts demonstrates that when transnational companies ignore their international obligations, they may be held criminally responsible.

Similar cases have been brought before the French and American courts.[10] The Unocal case, involving an American partner of Total in Burma, also makes it possible to conclude that multinational businesses have international obligations. The proceedings that were taken in the United States against that American partner of Total were based on the Alien Tort Claim Act, American legislation from 1789 which authorises persons of foreign origin to take civil proceedings in respect of a reprehensible act committed on their own territory. The grievances of the Burmese plaintiffs were largely identical to those of the Burmese plaintiffs who were taking action in the Belgian courts. Albeit the proceedings undertaken against Unocal did not result in a firm judicial decision, it made it possible, as did the Total case in Belgium, to construct an argument aimed at demonstrating the existence of judicial elements that involve the responsibility of multinational enterprises. In fact, in 2002, an American court that based itself directly on the jurisprudence of the International Criminal Tribunal for Rwanda and the International Tribunal for the Former Yugoslavia concluded that Unocal had been complicit in the violation of human rights in Burma. That decision clearly affirms that, on the one hand, Unocal made a significant contribution to the violation of human rights in Burma and, on the other hand, had acted knowingly, with the knowledge, in particular, that its involvement at a Burmese construction site would help to uphold human rights violations committed by the Burmese authorities. Those two cases show that criminal or civil proceedings can be brought against multinational companies for their involvement as accomplices to war crimes and even crimes against humanity.

Hocine Ouazraf is a political scientist specialising in international law from Belgium.

*   *   *

Redress for Palestinian Victims of Human Rights Abuses in the Courts of England and Wales[11]

Richard Hermer QC

This paper would not have been possible without the input of Andrew Sanger of the University of Cambridge who provided the tribunal with the first draft of this document based upon his careful and erudite researches. Although all errors are mine, he should be considered as co-author. RH

INTRODUCTION

The tribunal have asked me to consider whether, and if so how, English law could provide remedies to victims of human rights abuses by reference to a number of specific examples. Whilst I remain happy to talk about these examples at the hearing, I hope I can be forgiven for thinking that it is likely to be of greater assistance to the tribunal if I provide an overview of the basic components of English law in so far as they relate to redress and accountability for victims of human rights abuses.

This paper considers civil law remedies.[12] As I will explain in detail below, there are two broad categories of English civil law that could be utilised to assist victims, namely public law and private law. Public law regulates the behaviour of the state and other public bodies and permits judicial review of the legality of their actions. It is confined solely to the actions of UK public bodies; there would be no possibility of bringing a claim directly against the state of Israel or any Israeli public bodies (such as the IDF), because they enjoy immunity from suit before the English courts.[13] Similarly, no action could lie against Israeli diplomats based in London because they enjoy diplomatic immunity. A public law challenge would therefore focus upon the legality of the acts and omissions of UK public bodies in so far as they have impacted upon Palestinian victims. As we explain below, some attempts to utilise public law in the context of Israel/Palestine have not been successful but there still remains the possibility of successful challenges if formulated on an appropriate basis.

In contrast to public law, private law regulates the relationship between private entities, be they individuals or large corporations. The bedrock of English private law is tort law, premised upon the recognition in law of a 'civil wrong' committed by one private entity on another and giving the victim the right to redress. In this paper, we consider how tort law might be utilised to permit redress for victims of human rights abuses in circumstances in which it is alleged a multinational corporation (MNC) has been involved.

One other basic tenet of English law is worth highlighting at the outset, namely the status of international law. England and Wales are dualist legal systems, by which we mean domestic law has primacy over international law – the latter is only of direct effect in circumstances in which Parliament has expressly incorporated it into domestic law. Thus, whilst the United Kingdom has ratified a very large number of international conventions, which bind this country on the international stage, relatively few of them have been incorporated into domestic law. Thus, the status of unincorporated international law treaties in both public and private law claims is relatively limited: they cannot be relied upon directly by a claimant but rather they are of persuasive impact, not least because domestic law will often be interpreted on the basis that it is deemed to be consistent with international law.

PUBLIC LAW

As stated above, public law claims, brought by way of an application for judicial review, are challenges to the legality of the acts and omissions of public bodies. The law adopts a liberal definition of who amounts to a public body; for example, the following would all be amenable to judicial review:

- Government bodies – for example, government ministers, departments and agencies, local authorities, health authorities, the police, prisons, schools, courts, tribunals and regulatory and supervisory bodies.
- Private bodies that are authorised by Parliament and/or that carry out a 'public function'.

The grounds for challenging decisions by way of judicial review are where it can be shown that a decision was:

- Without legal authority/outside the power of the public body.
- In pursuance of an improper purpose.
- In violation of the proper exercise of discretionary powers (for example, fettering of discretion, use of discretion for a purpose for which it was not intended and/or taking irrelevant

factors into consideration or failing to take into consideration all relevant factors).
- Irrational or contrary to the rules of natural justice – that is, fairness.
- In violation of the Human Rights Act 1998.
- The Act requires public bodies to act in a way that is compatible with the European Convention on Human Rights; a failure to do so creates a free-standing statutory ground of challenge. The Act also requires all domestic legislation to be interpreted in a way that is compatible with Convention rights; thus the Act potentially affects all of the legal bases underpinning the public body's powers and duties.
- In violation of European Community Law/European Convention on Human Rights.

We now examine how public law has, or can be used, in relevant cases and the issues that arise. We do so by assessing first what we term 'direct challenges' to government policy in respect of Israel/ Palestine, and secondly by more 'indirect challenges', a term we explain below.

DIRECT CHALLENGES

There have been two judicial reviews brought before the English courts that have sought to directly challenge the United Kingdom's government policy in respect of Israel/Palestine.

The first in time was *R (Saleh Hasan)* v *Secretary of State for Trade and Industry*,[14] which was a request to scrutinise the Secretary of State's decision to grant export licences for weapons used by Israel in violation of international humanitarian and human rights law. The second case was *R (on the application of Al-Haq)* v *Secretary of State for Foreign and Commonwealth Affairs*,[15] which was a claim against the UK government claiming it had failed to adhere to its international law obligations vis-à-vis Israel. Both cases failed and although in each case the facts are relatively specific, the general thrust of the courts' approach was a reluctance to interfere with the government's handling of foreign affairs. This judicial reticence was clothed in the legal terminology of justiciability.

The courts held the following: it is beyond the competence of courts to evaluate the conduct of a state in relation to its foreign affairs except in exceptional circumstances; a court will also not evaluate the conduct of a foreign state.[16] Here the courts repeated their refrain from earlier cases: they would not interfere with foreign policy decisions unless the rights of individuals were crucial to the decision – see, for example, *CND* v *Prime Minister*, a case seeking a declaration that a second UN Security Council authorisation was required before war with Iraq could be lawful and *Abbassi* v *Secretary of State of Foreign Affairs*, a case seeking to compel the UK to seek the release of a national held in Guantanamo Bay.

In *Al-Haq* the court noted three exceptions: (1) where the breach of international law is 'plain and acknowledged' (*Kuwait Airways*[17]) or 'clear to the court'[18] (*Abbasi*[19]);[20] (2) there is legislative authorisation (*Gentle*[21]);[22] or (3) the issue arises in the context of ensuring a fair trial in England and Wales.[23]

A further difficulty facing those who wish to challenge UK policy in respect of foreign affairs is demonstrating that they have sufficient 'standing' to mount a challenge. In *Al Haq*, the court cast doubt on whether a non-UK NGO had a sufficient standing to bring a claim before the English court in respect of domestic foreign policy.

In the *Al-Haq* case, the court deferred to the executive (it is not for the court to determine the foreign policy of the UK nor is it for the court to determine whether another state has committed a violation of international law; thus, a court will only consider a 'violation of international law' if it has already been sufficiently confirmed by the executive (that is, state practice). In *Hasan*, the court deferred to the legislature (that is, the UK Parliament already exercised a sufficient level of oversight of arms-export licensing, rendering the claim unnecessary; further, given the sensitive nature of the material, it is preferable for Parliament to view it rather than through unguarded publication).

LESS DIRECT CHALLENGES

Direct challenges raise constitutional issues relating to the separation of powers in England and Wales; the court considers that some roles are best filled by the executive or Parliament. Therefore, less direct challenges may be more successful, for example, where government loans or facilities are provided to a corporation that assists in the violation of human rights in the OPT, and the public body has guidelines or a published policy that sets out its intention not to facilitate human rights violations. In this situation, a public law challenge could be used to force a public body to adhere to its own voluntarily adopted standards.

Public Procurement

This could take place through public procurement law, which regulates public body purchases of contracts for goods, works or services. Although the law is designed to open up the EU's public procurement market to competition and to ensure the free movement of goods and services, it may be possible to use it to include human rights obligations in the tendering process. During the oral evidence given to the Joint Committee on Human Rights, it was explained that 'The Government told us that departments and other public sector bodies can "take steps to exclude firms with a poor human rights record from tendering and where relevant ensure that appropriate human rights issues are covered in the contract".'[24]

Examples of using public procurement practices to encourage good business practice in relation to human rights include the US state and city 'anti-sweatshops' legislation that requires all corporations which supply products to any public body not to have acquired those products either domestically or internationally where poor labour standards have been applied.[25] Indeed, under the Public Contract Regulations 2006 in England and Wales, a contracting authority may (i) exclude an economic operator (that is, corporation) from bidding for a contract or (ii) reject a bid where it is found that the corporation has committed an act of grave misconduct in the course of business.

However, though there is nothing in the EU Public Procurement Directive that prohibits public authorities incorporating human rights principles into their purchasing practises, the only issue currently being examined by the UK government is that of equality.[26] The new Equality Bill contains the power for central government to impose specific equality duties on public authorities in relation to public procurement.

PRIVATE LAW CHALLENGES: THE LAW OF TORT

Until relatively recently, tort law was often overlooked as a relevant vehicle for human rights claims. In the past few years however, and partly inspired by the use of tort claims under the Alien Tort Claims Act (ATCA) in the US, a series of claims in the UK have demonstrated that private law is capable in certain circumstances of offering an effective mechanism for redress for victims of human rights abuses.

The key question for the tribunal is the extent to which private law claims could be utilised to hold those responsible for human rights abuses in Israel/Palestine to account. In light of the fact that tort law does not permit claims to be brought against the Israeli state (because they enjoy absolute immunity even for gross violations of human rights[27]), the real question is whether private bodies (such as corporations) who are complicit in the machinery of the Occupation can be held liable.

The jurisprudential basis for civil claims in the UK is quite distinct from the US. There is no English equivalent of the ATCA; the foundation of a claim is grounded solely in common law rather than statute. English law provides nothing as grand as a cause of action premised upon a breach of international law; rather, any claim must be based upon previously recognised and long-established torts. For example, claims against a company for complicity in torture are not based upon a breach of CAT [the Convention Against Torture], or upon a tort of 'torture', but would rather be pleaded under the long-established tort of trespass to the person. Further (and generally helpfully), English tort law does not have geographical limits; the court is not confined as a matter of principle from examining whether a tort was committed by reference to the boundaries of the UK – a tort is a tort. The constraints apply not so much as a matter of substantive law but more as a consequence of English procedural law, which imposes restrictions on foreign claims by notions such as jurisdiction and choice of laws, as well as discrete difficulties in English company law in pursuing claims against corporations for the acts of their subsidiaries. These constraints fall to be examined.

JURISDICTION

Torts Committed by UK Companies

In order to found a claim against a corporation, it is essential that the jurisdiction of the English court be established. In real terms, that means demonstrating that the Defendant is 'domiciled' within the jurisdiction.

The rules for the establishment of jurisdiction stem from European Union treaty law. The common EU rules on jurisdiction and enforcement of judgments in civil and commercial matters stipulate that any company with its registered office in the UK, *or* if it has no registered office, which was incorporated in the UK, *or* with its central administration or principal place of business in the UK; can be sued in UK courts.[28] The UK courts have a general power to stay proceedings on the grounds that some other forum is more appropriate for determination of the proceedings (the *forum non conveniens* principle) but in *Owusu* v *Jackson*,[29] the ECJ[30] held that the Brussels Convention precluded a court in a member state from declining jurisdiction conferred on it pursuant to that convention on the ground that a court in a non-contracting state would be a more appropriate forum. This is because: (i) the Brussels Convention is mandatory and no exception is provided in it for the doctrine of *forum non conveniens*; (ii) legal certainty was a specific objective of the Convention and the doctrine of *forum non conveniens* undermined the predictability of the rules on jurisdiction, and (iii) the doctrine of *forum non conveniens* affected the uniform application of the rules on jurisdiction, as only a limited number of states had a similar doctrine (the UK and Ireland).

Following this ruling, it is likely that the court will accept claims (indeed they must) where the Defendant is domiciled in England or Wales. A court will only not hear a claim in these situations:

- where proceedings have already been commenced between the same parties on the same subject matter in another jurisdiction;
- where the parties have contractually agreed that the courts of another state should have jurisdiction over the dispute;
- where there is a particularly close connection between the dispute and another jurisdiction of the type which ousts the exclusive jurisdiction of EU member states under Article 22 of the Convention; for example, in relation to rights in land and specific technical matters of company law.

Torts Committed by Non-UK Companies

UK courts may accept jurisdiction over a defendant outside the UK in relation to a tort where damage was sustained within the jurisdiction or the damage resulted from an act committed within the jurisdiction.[31]

However, foreign parties with no connection with England could be brought into proceedings in England if the English court has jurisdiction over one potential defendant. A defendant outside the UK may be joined into proceedings in England against a defendant who is the subject to the jurisdiction of the English courts with the court's permission – even if the overseas defendant would not otherwise be subject to the jurisdiction of the UK courts – if:

- there is a real issue to be tried between the claimant and the first defendant;[32]
- the overseas defendant is a 'necessary and proper party' to the claim,[33] *and*
- the claims can conveniently be disposed of in the same proceedings.[34]

However, it has been suggested that, in view of the fact that they no longer have power to stay proceedings on the ground of *forum non conveniens*, the courts may be more likely to refuse permission to join overseas defendants where injustice would result.

APPLICABLE LAW

Whenever a claim is brought in respect of torts that occurred overseas, the court will be asked to consider whether the law of the foreign country applies to determine the dispute or whether English law should govern the matter. If, as is more often the case, foreign law is applicable, then the court will apply foreign law basing itself upon the legal analysis provided by the parties' foreign law experts. This can sometimes be important where the foreign law does not recognise the 'torts' that give rise to the claim.

Civil law claims in relation to torts occurring overseas are subject to the provisions of the EC Rome II Regulation,[35] the provisions of Part III of the Private International Law (Miscellaneous Provisions) Act 1995 (PIL(MP)A) and common law rules.

If the event giving rise to damage occurred on or after 19 August 2007, then the rules contained in Rome II apply; however, the PIL(MP)A applies in areas not governed by Rome II.

If the event giving rise to damage occurred after 1 May 1996 but before 19 August 2007, the rules contained in (PIL(MP)A) apply.

If the event giving rise to damage occurred prior to 1 May 1996, then the common law double actionability rule applies: a claim must be actionable both under the law of the forum state (the UK) and under the law of the state where the damage occurred for a tort to be actionable in UK courts.[36]

Rome II Regulation

Rome II applies in all conflict of laws proceedings relating to civil or commercial matters[37] brought in the UK, whether the event/damage occurred in an EU member state or another country: it is only relevant that proceedings are brought in a member state.[38] Article 4 provides the general rule for tort claims[39] and comprises three elements: a general principle, an exception and an escape clause:

- General Principle: the applicable law will be the law of the country in which the damage occurred and irrespective of the country or countries in which the indirect consequences of that event occur.[40]
- Exception: the general principle is displaced where the Claimant and Defendant share a common habitual residence[41] at the time when the damage occurs.[42]
- Escape Clause: if it is clear that the tort is manifestly more closely connected with a country other than that indicated by applying the general principle, the law of that country will apply.[43] Note that this provision is similar to s.12 of the PIL(MP)A (discussed below), although some commentators have questioned whether the standard of 'manifestly' is higher than 'substantially' (see below). Article 4(3) specifically refers to a pre-existing relationship, such as a contract, being relevant to the assessment. Other relevant factors will be similar to those relevant for s.12 including: the parties; the event giving rise to the damage; and the consequences of that event.

Choice of law by agreement: it is possible for parties to choose the applicable law in their case by agreement entered into after the event giving rise to the damage has occurred.[44]

The scope of the 'applicable law' includes: the basis and extent of liability (for example, who may be liable); defences (grounds of exemption) or limitation (for example, contributory negligence) and any division of liability; the existence, nature and assessment of damages;[45] vicarious liability; entitlement to compensation (for example, who gets damages), *and* limitation periods. Where Rome II does not apply, Part III of the PIL(MP)A 1995 will apply.

Part III of the Private International Law (Miscellaneous Provisions) Act 1995

The PIL(MP)A contains a general rule, a rule of displacement and exceptions. General Rule: the law applicable to issues in tort is the law of the country where the events constituting the tort occur.[46] If the facts relevant to elements of the tort occur across different jurisdictions (for example, where a transnational corporation is based in the UK, but the injury, death, or damage is sustained in another jurisdiction, such as Israel), the general rule[47] is that the applicable law will be that of the country where the injury, death, or damage was sustained.

There is a residual category – 'any other case' – where the applicable law will be the law of the country in which the most significant element(s) of the relevant events occurred.

Rule of Displacement: the general rules may be displaced under s.12 if the courts consider that in all the circumstances, '… it is substantially more appropriate for the applicable law for determining the issues arising in the case, or any of those issues, to be the law of the other country.'[48] The courts will take into account factors relating to the parties, to any of the events that constitute the tort in question, or to any of the circumstances or consequences of those events.

There is little case law on what might make displacement 'substantially more appropriate'. Lord Wilberforce in the pre-PIL(MP)A House of Lords case, *Boys* v *Chaplin*,[49] explained that a foreign rule could not be rejected on grounds of public policy or some general conception of justice. Consideration must be given to whether the foreign state whose law is to be displaced has an interest in applying the law in the particular circumstances, having regard to the interest that rule was devised to meet.

Conflict with UK public policy: English courts will not apply the standard rule (s.11), and therefore overseas law, if it conflicts with principles of public policy. For example, UK courts will not give effect to foreign law that breaches international law, international human rights law, the European Convention on Human Rights, or if it amounts to an international crime.[50]

This might well be an important exception where many of the acts/omissions complained of might be lawful under Israeli law (for example, demolition of homes, construction of the wall, and so on), but unlawful under international law.

Practical Problems

Invariably, practical problems arise in trying to apply the aforementioned provisions on applicable law, including ascertaining where exactly the conduct that gives rise to a tort claim took place; for example, construction and work on the wall occurs on Palestinian land, but Israel regards this land as its own. Similarly, Israel has annexed East Jerusalem onto its territory but it is still regarded as part of the occupied Palestinian territories.

Given the conduct that often occurs on occupied Palestinian territory, whether the applicable law is that of Israel or that of Palestine (which may be Israeli law, Jordanian/Egyptian law, British Mandate law, or Palestinian law).

THE CORPORATE VEIL AND THE ACTS OF SUBSIDIARIES

A significant issue in litigation of this nature is establishing liability for the UK parent company for the acts and omissions of its subsidiary based overseas. This is because companies rely upon the notion of the 'corporate veil', a long-established principle that treats subsidiaries as wholly separate entities (for the purpose of liability) from their parent company – even when they are wholly owned subsidiaries.

Under UK law, every company is treated as a separate legal person; this legal personality cannot be bypassed in order to attribute its rights and responsibilities to its shareholders or parent company.[51] A veil will not be pierced just because justice requires it or because of a purely economic reality.[52] The corporate veil will only be 'pierced' in very limited circumstances and there is no precise test for 'veil-piercing'.[53] Following *Adams* v *Cape Industries*, the court will only pierce the veil where a statute or contract permits a broad interpretation to be given to references to members of a group of companies, or if the company is a sham or façade (the so-called 'fraud exception'[54]). Liability may also be established if it can be demonstrated that a corporation is an authorised agent with the authority or capacity to create legal relations on behalf of the parent corporation[55] (although this is not technically 'piercing the corporate veil').

In *Ngcobo and Others* v *Thor Chemicals Holdings Ltd*,[56] the English parent company of a South African mining company that made mercury-based products was sued in tort in England for the mercury poisoning of workers at a factory in South Africa. The court pierced the corporate veil to allow an action against the parent company in light of the active role the parent company had played in the design, transfer, operation and monitoring of the factory, as well as the decision not to review and update the factory's health and safety policies.

Joseph has also suggested that

> … a court will often be willing to pierce the corporate veil in circumstances where the shareholder(s) exercise extreme control over the relevant company, and the considerations of justice and policy mandate that the shareholder(s) should bear the burden of a wrong perpetrated by the company, rather than the person(s) who have suffered from that wrong.[57]

Of course, each element of this proposed test requires some evaluation and their application will therefore vary according to each particular fact situation.

A number of cases in the UK have also sought to sidestep the issue of the corporate veil by seeking to argue for the existence of a 'parent company responsibility' that identifies reasons why in a particular case the risks of damage to the victim would have been so apparent to the Defendant that a distinct duty of care arose. The English courts have yet to determine this issue at a trial but the principle has been accepted at interlocutory hearings[58] in many cases; indeed, very significant claims, premised on this concept, have been settled by Defendants.

FUNDING AND COST EXPOSURE

In general, the unsuccessful party pays the successful party's costs as well as their own. State funding for legal representation in civil claims is available through the Legal Services Commission but only for claimants with very limited assets and both merits and cost/benefit requirements must be satisfied. Furthermore, the legal aid is unlikely to be granted to fund cases where the applicable law of the substantive claim is not that of England and Wales, particularly where the Claimants are not UK residents.

In reality, most claims are funded by Conditional Fee Arrangements (CFAs) whereby the costs are borne by the Claimant's lawyers and can only be recovered in the event that the claim succeeds. The most significant (and welcome) difference between a CFA and the US 'contingency fee' is that in the former, legal costs are payable by the losing Defendant rather than out of the victim's damages. The costs of litigating complex tort claims, particularly those involving numerous victims can be immense. Thus far in the UK only one firm, Leigh Day & Co, have undertaken large-scale claims of this nature. They have achieved very considerable successes.

BRIEF OUTLINE OF TORT LAW PRINCIPLES

To establish civil liability, it will often be necessary (this will vary depending on the tort, for example, fault liability as compared to strict liability) to consider the following:

1. Whether the harm has been inflicted contrary to an interest of the victim protected by law

- What harm has occurred? What law?
- Did the corporation provide the principle perpetrator of the harm with the means to carry out the harm?
- Is there a duty of care? What is that duty?

2. Knowledge of risk

- Did the company know, or would a careful and responsible company in the same circumstances have known, that its conduct posed a risk of harm to the victim's interest?
- Either in its own conduct or, in the context of a joint venture, would a responsible company have foreseen the risk that harm could occur as a consequence of its partner's conduct? Did the corporation undertake risk assessments?
- The character of the product or service and the character of the corporation/state/organisation using the product should be examined; generally, the more a product or a service is apt to be used to infringe human rights, the more suspicious a provider will need to be. The law will most likely not consider that a company providing multi-purpose generic products/ services ought to have foreseen that third parties would be the victims of human rights violations (though check for special circumstances).
- Look for tailor-made or adapted goods/services to meet specific circumstances, such as operating in conflict zones.

3. Precautionary measures

- Considering the risk of harm identified in (2), did the company take the precautionary measures a responsible company would have taken in order to prevent the risk from materialising?

- Did the corporation undertake a proper risk assessment on the potential use, misuse, or unintended consequences of a product or service given the potential buyer and the area where the product/service may operate?
- Did the corporation negotiate conditions to safeguard human rights for parties affected by its activities or the activities of a joint partnership that it is involved in? Did it obtain an undertaking?
- Did the corporation try to identify who might be the potential victims? Did it identify civilians?

4. *Causation*

- Did the corporation's conduct contribute to the infliction of the harm?
- Was the provision of the goods or services a factual element in the chain of causation? If yes, was it a *legal* cause, that is, was it sufficiently integral to the chain of causation that it was foreseeable that the harm suffered would occur as a result?
- Examine the relationship between corporations, and corporations and the state. Consider the nature of the good/service in question: have goods/services been tailored for a specific purpose that involves the perpetration of harm?
- Examine the specific acts of the corporation: if the corporation were not involved, would the same harm (or even harm at all) have occurred?

EXAMPLES

BP Lawsuit – Colombia

In July 2005, a group of Colombian farmers instituted proceedings in the English High Court against BP Exploration Company (Colombia) alleging that the construction of an oil pipeline by OCENSA (a consortium led by BP) caused severe environmental damage to their land; *and* that BP, while not directly involved, benefited from the activities of paramilitaries employed to guard the pipeline.

BP argued that it already made compensatory payments to the farmers and any lawsuit against BP should take place in Colombia. In June 2006, BP and the farmers met for mediation and eventually settled. BP paid out monies and agreed to establish an Environmental and Social Improvement Trust Fund for the farmers.

In December 2008, a new group of farmers filed a Particulars of Claim and this case is still ongoing. As a result of BP's activities, it is being accused of negligence in failing to effectively mitigate the environmental impact of its construction, which the claimants state was their responsibility as Project Operators. BP denies that it owes any relevant duty of care to the claimants stating that it 'did not design, construct or operate the pipeline' and was 'at no stage responsible for its maintenance'.

Trafigura – Ivory Coast

Trafigura, a British oil company, was accused of dumping lethal toxic waste near Abidjan, the commercial capital of the Ivory Coast, in 2006. Trafigura brought a cheap consignment of oil and pumped the toxic sludge, which was left over from selling the oil, onto a ship and then left it at 18 different sites on the Ivory Coast. This was the largest group claim in English legal history and it was settled two weeks before the trial date, with the company agreeing to pay compensation to the victims whilst maintaining its denial of responsibility.

British Mining Corporation – Peru

Protesters filed a claim in the High Court in London against a British mining corporation after they were detained and illegally tortured at an opencast copper plant that the firm is seeking to develop in the mountains of northern Peru. The claim is against the British parent company for the acts and omissions of a Peruvian company that it wholly owns via a Cayman Island subsidiary. Allegations include firing teargas at protesters and the subsequent detention of 28 people, who were hooded, beaten with sticks, whipped and subjected to noxious substances.

The law firm bringing the High Court case, Leigh Day, obtained a freezing injunction requiring the company to keep at least £5 million of its assets in the UK.[59]

THIRD-PARTY RIGHTS UNDER CONTRACT

As a general rule, the courts recognise the common law doctrine of privity of contract, and will not hold a third party liable for breaches of contract between other parties. There are exceptions to this doctrine that may apply in the case of an individual seeking to bring an action for breach of contract against a TNC parent company. It may also enable third-party employees to claim the benefit of contractual terms, which exclude or limit liability between a subsidiary and parent of a TNC.[60]

THE OECD GUIDELINES FOR MULTINATIONAL ENTERPRISES

The OECD Guidelines for Multinational Enterprises (Revised Version)[61] provide voluntary principles and standards that governments adhering to the guidelines encourage international businesses to comply with, wherever they are trading and operating, and covering employment and industrial relations, human rights,[62] environment, information disclosure, combating bribery, consumer interest, science and technology, competition and taxation.[63] Governments that have signed up to the guidelines are required to establish National Contact Points (NCPs) that promote the guidelines and consider allegations that the conduct of a corporation is inconsistent with the guidelines. The guidelines do not legally bind corporations and as such are not a substitute for national or international law; they represent supplementary principles and standards of conduct of a non-legal character.

The UK NCP[64] is made up of officials from the Department for Business, Innovation and Skills (BIS). There is also a Steering Board[65] that monitors the work of the UK NCP and provides it with strategic guidance. The UK NCP has also worked with the Foreign and Commonwealth Office (FCO) to provide guidance to British Embassy staff overseas on the OECD Guidelines so that they can assist UK companies operating overseas.

The procedure for the UK NCP is as follows:[66] if a complaint involves the operations of a UK-registered corporation or its subsidiaries, it can be filed with the UK NCP by filling out the appropriate complaints form.[67]

There will be an initial assessment, which involves a desk-based analysis of the complaint, the corporation's response and any additional information provided by the parties. The UK NCP will decide whether further consideration is warranted.

If a complaint is accepted, the UK NCP will offer conciliation/mediation to both parties with the aim of reaching a settlement agreeable to both. If this fails or if the parties decline the offer, the UK NCP will examine the complaint in order to assess whether it is justified.

If a mediated settlement is reached, the UK NCP will publish a Final Statement with details of the agreement. If the UK NCP has examined the complaint, it will prepare and publish a Final

Statement setting out whether or not the Guidelines have been breached and, if necessary, recommendations to the corporation as to future conduct.

If the Final Statement includes recommendations, it will specify a date by which both parties are asked to update the UK NCP on the corporation's progress towards meeting these recommendations. The UK NCP will then publish a further statement reflecting the parties' responses.

PROPOSALS FOR REFORM

Although in recent years much conceptual work has been done on holding corporations to account for violations of human rights and other international law obligations, the central problem still remains: a lack of concrete, effective remedies for victims.

Strengthening Home State Protection: Extraterritoriality

There are numerous proposals suggesting the UK develop its domestic law so that it can make parent companies directly responsible for: (i) their actions overseas, (ii) the actions of their subsidiaries, or (iii) the actions of those in their supply chain, where human rights violations cannot be remedied in the states where they take place. However, several broad criticisms have been made of these proposals, focusing on issues of legitimacy, sovereignty, economic competitiveness and cultural hegemony. The UK government opposes such extraterritorial action.[68]

Strengthening Home State Protection: Steps for the UK Government

There are a number of proactive steps that the UK could take to further accountability of corporations incorporated in or operating from the UK, including:

- Providing clear guidance and support for business on human rights issues. Outline a specific framework of human rights policies/guidelines for corporations operating at home and abroad.
- Incorporating human rights obligations in public procurement and public investment policies.
- In the Netherlands, certain forms of support are not given to corporations who cannot prove they comply with the OECD Guidelines. In Norway, statutory ethical standards are applied

to certain actions of public bodies, especially in relation to public investment.

- Introduce a clear reporting mechanism that allows the government, consumers and other stakeholders to test business performance against voluntarily accepted standards. Introduce reporting standards to ensure (i) consistency in reporting and (ii) that specific and detailed information is provided on corporations' impact on human rights.

- Readdress and reform the government's approach to Export Credit Guarantees. For example, deny or set a probation period for corporations trying to secure export credit if they have received a negative final statement from the UK NCP. Introduce mechanisms whereby individuals aversely affected by projects supported by export credit guarantees can raise their grievance.

- Revisiting the Companies Act 2006 with the purpose of expressly including human rights responsibilities (and that such requirements should apply to all corporations) and that UK corporations should be required to conduct a human rights assessment of its activities.[69]

- Change the general approach towards investment to include a human rights ethos. For example, a practice similar to the UK and EC Codes of Practice was introduced for companies investing in South Africa during apartheid, which required annual reporting on conduct and employment practices in South Africa.

- Scrutinise the role of institutional investors – for example, pension funds and fund managers – who have the power to influence activities of corporations operating overseas. Examine the long-term risk to shareholdings posed by irresponsible behaviour and associated allegations of human rights violations.

THE PROTECT, RESPECT AND REMEDY FRAMEWORK

Professor Ruggie, the UN Secretary-General's Special Representative on human rights and transnational corporations and other business entities, has made numerous recommendations under his 'protect, respect, remedy' framework, including the state duty to protect against human rights abuses by third parties, including businesses; a corporate responsibility to respect human rights *and* the need for individuals to have effective access to remedies for breaches of their human rights.[70]

In June 2008, the UN Human Rights Council approved the framework and extended the mandate of the Special Representative until 2011.[71] Professor Ruggie has been asked to provide practical recommendations to assist states in protecting human rights from abuses involving corporations and to enhance the possibility of remedies for victims. In his most recent report, dated 9 April 2010,[72] Professor Ruggie focuses on operationalising his three-tiered framework. It is pragmatic in nature and sets out much of the evidence Ruggie and his team collected in the previous twelve months in anticipation of his final report, which was published in the spring of 2011.[73] Specific reference is made to arguments by states that certain investment treaties may prevent them from enforcing human rights obligations against corporations and the need for states to proactively create a 'corporate compliance with human rights' culture. Ruggie makes it clear that his goal is to 'provide companies with universally applicable guiding principles for meeting their responsibility to respect human rights, recognizing that the complexity of tools and processes companies employ, will necessarily vary with circumstances'.[74]

INTERNATIONAL REGULATION OF CORPORATIONS OPERATING IN CONFLICT ZONES

In his April 2009 report, Professor Ruggie singled out the operation of businesses in conflict zones as an area where international action is particularly needed. Corporations need clear guidance on when and how to operate in conflict zones with clearly demarcated zones of 'legal risk'. The UN Special Representative has convened a working group on business and human rights in conflict zones. The UK government is participating in this working group, which aims to clarify further the risks associated with business in war zones or high-risk areas of conflict and the appropriate responses of home states.

UN World Court on Human Rights

Professor Manfred Nowak, the UN Special Rapporteur on Torture, has called for the creation of a UN World Court on Human Rights, which would offer remedies based on the breach of individual rights by states, intergovernmental organisations and transnational corporations.[75]

International Treaties

Professor Ruggie believes that an international agreement is unrealistic in the current climate. Peter Frankental of Amnesty International believes that it is unlikely to happen in the next decade. This is not a pessimistic forecast.

CONCLUSIONS

Public Law Claims

English law does provide the possibility of redress for acts and omissions of UK companies complicit in human rights abuses in Israel/Palestine. Such actions are however only likely to be viable in certain, very carefully defined, circumstances.

With all of the case examples, it may be possible to demonstrate to public bodies that they should not be contracting with or in any way assisting these corporations as (a) it is likely to be contrary to their voluntary codes of conduct/guidance, and (b) it is contrary to the government's obligations to promote and protect human rights. It may also be possible to submit a claim to the UK NCP for mediation and/or investigation and a final statement.

Private Law

English tort law develops on an 'incremental basis' and thus only carefully constructed cases, based on good facts, are likely to succeed – the maxim 'bad facts make bad law' very much applies.

A claim for damages against a UK company which provided goods and services that it knew (or should have known) would be used in a manner that would cause the claimant (or a class to which the claimant belonged) damage/loss, particularly personal injury, may succeed where it can be shown that damage was caused. The fact that the acts were those of the Defendant's subsidiary need not be a bar to recovery in every case.

Whilst this paper sets out the general framework applicable to such claims, each would have to be examined very carefully upon its particular facts.

Richard Hermer QC, of Doughty Street Chambers, is a barrister in the fields of domestic and international human rights law.

TRANSCRIPT OF JURY Q&A: RICHARD HERMER QC

Michael Mansfield QC: Richard, may I just kick it off in a way from what I said in opening, to try and take concrete examples rather than the principles. How the principles might apply. And there are really two issues I want to take up with you. One relates to the objection that is taken in America, as well as here, about dabbling in foreign policy by the courts – that's one.

But I'm going to start with the private law situation of a company, like Caterpillar, but I am going to use one that I hope you are aware of, and others will be aware of; this is a company called Elbit. Now Elbit is one of the largest weapons manufacturers, and it manufactures not only weapons but electronic systems. It has been complicit in the building of the wall, complicit in the building of surveillance materials, complicit in the building of drones, sometimes called Hermes drones.

Now, let's again take a very – again – concrete example: if you are living in the Occupied Territories and you have been injured by a drone that has been manufactured – and this company has manufacturing bases within the United Kingdom, one of which I understand is at Lichfield. Now, would a Palestinian have recourse to the English courts in tort to do something about a situation in which injury has been caused by a drone manufactured by that company?

Richard Hermer QC: The answer is they would have access to the court if it could be demonstrated that Elbit were domiciled within this jurisdiction, within England or Wales, that as of right you can bring a claim for them. So let's say we have a victim, a Palestinian victim of that drone attack. They would bring a claim for their injuries, or if they were killed, their estate would bring a claim for their injuries and the English court would entertain it because jurisdiction had been established. What one would then have to go on to show, is firstly that their losses were caused by that drone that was manufactured by a company domiciled here. Actually forensically not always very easy. They would also have to show that Elbit was acting unlawfully, essentially, by providing that drone to the Israeli government.

Now there it would become a question of foreseeability. Was it foreseeable – not that they would provide it and it would be used – but was it foreseeable that they would provide it and it would be used in an unlawful way? Because the courts here will not say that every use of every weapon is unlawful. But if you are going to use it in an unlawful way – so for example in an unlawful military incursion or to attack a civilian population in a way that is contrary to international law – then it would be certainly arguable.

What – I will just give this as an example to reflect the complexity often of these cases because there are no simple answers – what would be said by Elbit is that they provided these arms in accordance with a export license approved by the government. And they would rely upon case law saying – which wasn't developed in the field of arms – that when you provide something in accordance with your own home state's regulations, then you can't be in breach of duty of care. Now that is case law developed on different facts and I'm not convinced it would be applicable here; there would certainly be an argument about it here.

But the short answer to your question is yes. That's the type of case that *could* be developed, and the caveat is with a whole host of layers of complexity. Nevertheless, that is the type of case, and it is quite a good example of a case because there are many cases which are so compelling on their facts where what has happened to the victim is just so awful but they just don't actually result in good legal cases. And the difficulty for human rights lawyers, as you all know as well as anybody, is that when you are trying to develop the law you want to do it on the best facts possible, because bad facts create bad law for human rights lawyers.

MM: A subsidiary to that really is asking you – you used the word 'domiciled'. What would make Elbit domiciled in the United Kingdom in order to make them eligible?

RH: If they had their registered office here, for example.

MM: Right. But if they didn't have a registered office?

RH: Well, if the factory that was producing the drones or the missiles was a factory here, that's sufficient.

MM: Right. Second point which I started with, and then I will hand over to others – and that is this question of government policy. Namely that courts here, and elsewhere as it happens, will not interfere with issues that could be said to relate to foreign policy. Now, is there any prospect – as it seems to me just a matter of logic and common sense – that actually this is confusing policy issues about who you are going to help as opposed to dealing with clear human rights violations?

RH: There's a much better position here than in the [United] States. In the States, a whole host of important human rights cases have been closed down simply because they touch upon issues of foreign relations. To give you an example, Binyam Mohamed – one of the Guantánamo detainees – has been bringing an action in California against Jeppesen [*Binyam Mohamed et al. v Jeppesen Dataplan Inc.*] who were a company who arranged the rendition flights, and that has been closed down by the Appeal Court, the Ninth Circuit, in the States, because they received a witness statement from a General Hayden telling them that this was just far too sensitive – end of story. In this country, the courts are much more robust – not in the field of public law: there the courts have been very careful to say you can't bring challenges that tell the government what they can and cannot do on foreign relations. But in the realm of private law when you want to bring a case against a company, there the courts are very robust. There they might be called upon to make findings about other countries' international law positions – it doesn't really bother the courts here. And they do it every day, for example, from an immigration perspective, when you're trying to stop someone from being returned to a country with a bad human rights record. The courts here are happy to do it and I don't think that would present a major problem for these types of cases.

MM: Right. Anyone else? Yes: John.

John Dugard: I would like to ask a question about the principle of *forum non conveniens*. There is a recent decision in Canada involving a Canadian company which did business with one of the settlements in Israel. An attempt was made to bring a case in Canada against this particular Canadian company. And the Canadian court held that it was 'more convenient' for the case to be heard in Israel rather than in Canada despite the fact that the Israeli courts have refused, consistently refused, to pronounce upon the legality of the settlement endeavour. I've seen your paper where you say that this is no longer a problem in the United Kingdom. Is that absolutely clear?

RH: Can I explain how we got to this point? *Forum non conveniens* – that's the argument that defendants would always deploy to say you can't bring your case in England when it's to do with what is going on in the DRC, or Israel/Palestine, wherever, because it is much more convenient, since the acts and omissions took place in that other country, not in England, so you should deal with them there. So the principle of *forum non conveniens* was always an argument we faced, and a very big argument.

It is mainly gone for two reasons. Firstly because a case was brought (again by Leigh Day who I mentioned has been bringing cases of this nature in this country) on behalf of a large group of Southern African miners who had all contracted asbestos, and they brought it against the headquarters company in the UK. And the *forum non conveniens* argument was taken and run all the way along by the defendants saying you have to have this in South Africa, you can't have it in London. What the House of Lords, our highest court – what was then our highest court – held was that even though South Africa was the most convenient forum, because the claimants could not get justice in that country, because it was still in the early post-Apartheid days, there was no system for dealing with thousands of claims, class actions, because legal aid wasn't available – so because justice couldn't be done there, jurisdiction could be established in London.

So that was a major step forward. But what actually has really made this issue beyond argument in many cases is the decision of the European Court of Justice looking at the regulations that bind European countries. And in a decision in a case that actually had nothing to do with human rights – about travel package rules for holidays in Jamaica – they held that once a defendant is domiciled in a member state, then you can establish jurisdiction against it as of right, irrespective as to where the wrong was committed. So for example in the Trafigura case [*Motto & Others* v *Trafigura*], there was no argument about jurisdiction where there would have been an enormous argument years before that. In the Peru case I mentioned [*Guerro & Others* v *Montericco & Another*], no argument about jurisdiction, because even though the acts and omissions occurred in a mine in a very remote part of Peru, the headquarter company which is the one that is being sued [is] registered in London. So that has actually enormously assisted in this type of human rights litigation.

*   *   *

Principles and Mechanisms to Hold Business Accountable in US Courts

Yasmine Gado

This brief is a summary of Section 5 of the Badil group's Working Paper No. 11, 'Principles and Mechanisms to Hold Business Accountable for Human Rights Abuses: Potential Avenues to Challenge Corporate Involvement in Israel's Oppression of the Palestinian People', authored by Yasmine Gado and published in December 2009. YG

Set forth below is a general overview of the legal framework relevant to corporate conduct under US law as applied to corporations conducting certain economic activities in the Occupied Palestinian Territories (OPT) or with the Israeli government or military. It should be noted that pro-Israeli bias in all branches of US federal and state governments make it unlikely that the efforts described below would be successful. Private lawsuits against Israeli defendants and their corporate aiders and abettors have to date established only negative precedents.

COMPANIES PROVIDING ARMS AND REPRESSIVE INFRASTRUCTURE

Private Claims

With respect to US or foreign (including Israeli) companies providing arms and repressive infrastructure to Israel (hereafter 'military contractors'), if the Israeli government/military uses the products and services purchased from these companies to commit war crimes, or gross human rights abuses that constitute crimes,[76] then the following private claims may be pursued by victims.

Alien Tort Claims Act

First, Palestinians (but not US citizens) may sue the company for damages in US courts under the Alien Tort Claims Act for aiding and abetting war crimes and extrajudicial killing. Some US courts currently require that the plaintiff prove the corporation knowingly provided substantial assistance to the perpetrator (the IDF) of the war crimes (the 'knowledge standard'). Others require that the plaintiff prove the corporation provided the assistance for the purpose of commission of the war crimes (the 'purpose standard'). The purpose standard is almost impossible to meet since companies are almost always driven by a profit motive, not by political (or racist) designs.

The family of Rachel Corrie, an activist crushed to death by an IDF officer using a Caterpillar bulldozer, and a number of Palestinians who suffered death, bodily harm and property damage through demolitions with a Caterpillar bulldozer brought this ATCA claim against the company. They lost on political question grounds (discussed below).

Torture Victim Protection Act

Secondly, both Palestinians and US citizens can sue the military contractors for aiding and abetting extrajudicial killings under the Torture Victim Protection Act (TVPA). Because of ambiguity in the statute's language, US courts are divided as to whether corporations may be sued under the TVPA or just the company's officers; some do allow a suit against the company itself. The statute requires that the killings must have been approved under the law of a foreign nation or under the authority of a foreign official. US courts have applied this statute against persons who aided and abetted the violation. Unlike the ATCA, the TVPA requires that plaintiffs first exhaust any 'adequate' remedies available under Israeli law; the plaintiffs should argue that this remedy is inadequate because Israeli courts have proven their bias in cases involving Palestinian human rights (the plaintiffs in the Caterpillar case brought a TVPA claim as well).

RICO Civil Claim

US citizens (and Palestinians with jurisdiction through ATCA or TVPA) may sue the military contractors under the Racketeer Influenced and Corrupt Organizations Act (RICO) to recover for *property* loss or damage. RICO makes it unlawful to form an enterprise to engage in extortion and 'racketeering activity', including murder and robbery, and allows victims to sue for property damage. The plaintiffs in the Caterpillar case brought a RICO claim, alleging that Caterpillar and the IDF formed an illegal enterprise engaged in a pattern of murder, robbery, extortion and physical violence because of Caterpillar's manufacture, design, financing, sales, servicing and training of the IDF with respect to its bulldozers, knowing they were being used for home demolitions and killing of civilians.

It is unsettled whether RICO applies to conduct committed outside the US. Because the case against Caterpillar was dismissed, this issue was left decided. In RICO claims against other corporations challenging the commission of crimes or human rights abuses overseas, US courts have taken the approach that the RICO statute applies where (a) the crime had an effect within the US (such as giving the company a competitive advantage), or (b) the company's conduct in the US (such as transfer of technical or financial assistance) directly caused the plaintiffs' injuries overseas.

Traditional Torts

US citizens, and Palestinians who have gained access to US courts through an ATCA or TVPA claim, can add claims against the military contractors for negligently or recklessly harming the plaintiffs or their property and for intentional torts such as wrongful death, battery (a harmful bodily contact), assault (fear of an imminent battery) and infliction of emotional distress. If a company sells goods or services to a third party which uses them to commit crimes that cause the plaintiff to suffer mental or bodily harm or loss of or damage to property, and this harm is foreseeable to the company (due to the third party's history of criminal conduct vis-à-vis the plaintiffs, for example), then the company is liable for (a) *negligently* harming the plaintiff (because it disregarded a foreseeable risk), (b) *recklessly* harming the plaintiff (because it ignored an obvious unjustifiable risk), and (c) *intentionally* harming the plaintiff *assuming* it was substantially certain the company's acts would result in harm to the plaintiff.

Shareholder Breach of Fiduciary Duty Claim

Under US corporate law, shareholders (of any nationality) can sue the directors of the military contractors on the grounds that by approving or condoning the aiding and abetting of war crimes or gross human rights abuses, they breached their duties of care, loyalty and good faith to the company and its shareholders and caused them to suffer a loss. These cases are difficult to win unless the shareholder can prove the directors acted in bad faith (that is, knowingly took illegal action) or were grossly negligent in failing to prevent the company's involvement in illegal actions.

DEFENCES

Corporate defendants facing the above claims[77] can raise the following defenses: (a) that the case raises a political question committed to another branch of government such as a foreign policy issue ('political question doctrine'), (b) that the case involves questioning an act of a foreign sovereign state within its territory ('act of state doctrine'), (c) that the court is not the appropriate forum to decide the case due to the location of the evidence and witnesses, the burden on the court or the defendant ('*forum non conveniens*'), or (d) that the US court lacks jurisdiction because (x) the company does not do significant business where the court is located, or (y) the defendant is a parent or subsidiary of the offshore corporate entity that caused the plaintiff's harm and is shielded (by the corporate form) from liability for the overseas entity's conduct.

The biggest hurdle for plaintiffs in cases against corporate aiders and abettors of Israeli perpetrators is the political question defence, which was the defence Caterpillar used successfully to defeat the plaintiffs' claims. The court found that the US pays for the bulldozers purchased by the IDF and that deciding the case involved questioning US foreign policy. To avoid the outcome in *Caterpillar*, plaintiffs should sue companies that are not receiving assistance by the US government to conduct their activities in the OPT and are as far as possible unconnected with US government activities there. However, the military contractors still have a strong argument that a decision in the plaintiff's favour would necessitate a court finding that the Israeli government/military is committing war crimes or gross human rights abuses which would interfere with the executive's conduct of foreign relations.

To the act of state doctrine, plaintiffs can reply that because Israel is acting outside its sovereign territory (in the OPT) and because a violation of fundamental international norms cannot be an official act of state, the doctrine does not apply. They will likely win on this argument.

Regarding the *forum non conveniens* defence, the plaintiffs would respond that the US court is the appropriate forum since (a) Israeli courts are biased, (b) the US Congress through the ATCA and TVPA intended to create a forum for foreign plaintiffs in US courts to vindicate the interests protected by those statutes, and (c) a large multinational corporation would not face a great burden by being required to defend the case in the US.

Regarding jurisdiction, plaintiffs will establish jurisdiction if they sue a corporation that (a) does continuous and systematic business in the jurisdiction where the US court is located, either directly or through an agent that works only for the company and is indispensable to its business, or (b) is the parent or subsidiary of the entity directly responsible for the harmful acts, and the parent and subsidiary are unified in interest and control (through shared day-to-day management, commingling of funds, and so on) so that the court should 'pierce the corporate veil' and consider them one entity. The plaintiffs would have an easier time with the agency argument; it is much harder to convince a court to pierce the corporate liability shield.

PUBLIC LAW CHALLENGES

Lawsuit to Force State to Revoke Corporate Charter or Licence

US corporations are established by a charter issued by state authorities, typically a state Attorney General (AG). Foreign companies are issued licences to do business by the same state authority. States have the legal right to revoke the licence or charter where the company has abused or misused its power, is a consistent violator of the law, is deemed incapable of reform, or has engaged in crimes considered to be a serious breach of the public trust. Consistently approving or condoning illegal action that results in widespread human rights abuses, including war crimes, is outside the power granted by a charter or licence and should be grounds for revocation. Private citizens may sue for an injunction forcing the AG to revoke the charter or licence of a company. However, these suits are difficult to win because the court would defer to the AG decision unless it was 'irrational'.

CRIMINAL CHALLENGES

Aiding and Abetting War Crimes

A corporation is considered a legal person under US law, and thus can be prosecuted for crimes that apply to a natural person. Because war crimes are criminal offences under US domestic law, and aiding and abetting is criminalised under US law, a corporation could be prosecuted in the US for aiding and abetting war crimes committed overseas. If such a prosecution were initiated against the military contractors, they would argue the court cannot exercise jurisdiction over actions and parties outside the US. US war crimes statutes approve the exercise of extraterritorial jurisdiction to prosecute grave breaches of international criminal law by and against US nationals. Thus, the US-based military contractors, and the foreign contractors that *harmed US nationals* will lose this argument as to *war crimes* prosecutions. However, extraterritorial jurisdiction would still be an issue in prosecutions of any of the military contractors for gross human rights abuses that are not war crimes, and in prosecutions of Israeli and other foreign companies that did not harm US nationals but only Palestinians.

The corporations can also argue they intended merely to profit, not to commit war crimes, and thus did not have the requisite criminal intent. Since no such prosecution has been pursued, there is no US legal precedent on this issue. A court might apply either the knowledge or purpose standard described above – that is, that the company officers (a) knowingly provided the IDF with assistance to commit war crimes or gross human rights abuses, or (b) did so for the specific purpose of facilitating the commission of the war crimes or abuses.

RICO Prosecution

The RICO statute allows both a civil claim and a criminal prosecution. The military contractors can be prosecuted for forming an illegal enterprise with the Israeli government to engage in a pattern of extortion and 'racketeering activity' including murder, robbery and physical violence. The issue of extraterritorial jurisdiction applies here as in the RICO civil claim discussed above.

POLITICAL PRESSURE

Foreign Assistance Act

The US Foreign Assistance Act authorises the president to provide military and economic aid to foreign governments, but in doing so must take into account whether such assistance would (a) contribute to an arms race, (b) increase the possibility of outbreak or escalation of conflict, or (c) prejudice the development of bilateral or multilateral arms control arrangements. Further, assistance may not be granted to any government that engages in a consistent pattern of gross human rights violations unless the president finds that extraordinary circumstances warrant such aid. Israel's aggressive wars against its neighbours and ongoing gross human rights abuses in Palestine violate these conditions, and activists could pressure the US government to enforce them by reducing or ceasing its annual aid appropriations to Israel.

Arms Export Control Act

Under the Arms Export Control Act, the US may sell weapons and other military assistance to friendly countries *solely* for (a) internal security, (b) legitimate self-defence, (c) preventing or hindering the proliferation of weapons of mass destruction, (d) participation of UN-approved collective security arrangements, and (e) in less developed countries, to protect economic and social development efforts. Activists could pressure the US government to investigate the use of the weapons it sells to Israel and, if the above conditions are found to have been violated, to cease such sales.

COMPANIES PROVIDING SERVICES TO AND MANUFACTURING IN SETTLEMENTS

Private Law Claims

With respect to companies that provide services to or manufacture in illegal Jewish settlements in the OPT the following private claims may be pursued.

ATCA (Apartheid, Crimes Against Humanity, Geneva Convention)

Palestinians can sue US or foreign companies *providing services* to settlements under the ATCA on the grounds that the companies are either directly committing acts or aiding and abetting Israeli government acts necessary to sustain a system of apartheid in the OPT. Because apartheid is a crime against humanity (under the Rome Statute), Palestinians can also base their ATCA claim on the grounds that the companies are directly committing, or aiding and abetting the commission of crimes against humanity. In addition, Palestinians can argue these companies are aiding and abetting the violation of Geneva Convention prohibitions on transfer by an occupier of its civilian population into occupied territory. As noted earlier, US courts are divided on the standard for aiding and abetting under ATCA, so the plaintiffs should sue in a jurisdiction that applies the lower knowledge standard by choosing a company doing business in that jurisdiction.

If US or foreign companies manufacturing in settlements offer any form of revenue or benefit to the settlement or the Israeli government generally, then Palestinians can sue these companies for all the above claims on the grounds that their revenues or assistance is necessary to sustain a system of apartheid.

RICO Civil Claim

US citizens, and Palestinians with jurisdiction through ATCA, may sue companies providing services to or manufacturing in settlements under RICO to recover property loss or damage, alleging that the companies have formed an illegal enterprise with each other and with the Israeli government/military and through that enterprise have engaged in a pattern of extortion (that is, theft) of Palestinian land and resources. As discussed above, plaintiffs must establish that RICO applies extraterritorially by showing that the companies' acts have an effect in the US, or that the company directed or planned its illegal acts in the US or offered financial or technical assistance from the US to commit the illegal acts in the OPT.

Traditional Torts

With respect to companies providing services to or manufacturing in settlements, Palestinians who reside in or are denied entry to the OPT and who have gained access to US courts through an ATCA claim can add claims for intentional or reckless infliction of emotional distress.

Shareholder Breach of Fiduciary Duty Claim

The same discussion applies as in the section under 'Companies Providing Arms and Repressive Infrastructure' above.

Defences

The defences and counter-arguments discussed in the section under 'Companies Providing Arms and Repressive Infrastructure' above apply equally here.

PUBLIC LAW CHALLENGES

Revocation of Charter or Licence

The same discussion regarding revocation of corporate charters or licences applies here. The plaintiffs would argue that the state should revoke a company's charter or licence because it is committing acts necessary to sustain a system of apartheid, a crime against humanity, and such crimes are a serious breach of the public trust.

CRIMINAL LAW CHALLENGES

RICO Prosecution

State authorities may prosecute companies providing services to or manufacturing in settlements under RICO for forming an illegal enterprise with each other and the IDF to engage in extortion (i.e.

theft) of land and resources. Plaintiffs must be able to establish that RICO applies extraterritorially as discussed above under the civil RICO lawsuit.

POLITICAL PRESSURE

Although the US government considers the Jewish settlements in the West Bank to be illegal, it still permits the import of goods produced in them. Activists could pressure the US government to prevent such imports.

Yasmine Gado is a US lawyer who writes on the subject of human rights in Palestine, and is a legal consultant for Badil, the resource centre for Palestinian residency and refugee rights.

TRANSCRIPT OF JURY Q&A: YASMINE GADO

John Dugard: Yasmine: referring to the doctrine of *forum non conveniens* again, you say that one could argue in a US court, that a US court was more appropriate, because I quote you, Israeli courts are biased. Now let's be realistic: if one looks at the jurisprudence of the United States, particularly in the case, such as the recent Dichter decision, isn't it very clear to say that US courts are, to put it kindly, highly sympathetic to the Israeli government, the Israeli position? And at the same time I think it's clear from what you have said in relation to recent interpretations of the Alien Tort [Claims] Act that there is a hostility towards claims against corporations, so if you add these two together: first of all the attempts on behalf of the courts to protect the corporations from the Alien Tort [Claims] Act, and secondly these decisions which do show a certain degree of sympathy for the Israeli position: isn't it unlikely that one is going to get a sympathetic hearing before a US court?

Yasmine Gado: Yeah, I agree. And I just do want to point out that when you mention hostility towards cases against corporations under the Alien Tort Claims Act, I think – and maybe Maria [LaHood] can back me up – that was a kind of surprise decision. This was a principle that had been assumed in the Alien Tort Claims Act against corporations, so it's not a uniform hostility, is I guess what I am saying – that's one thing. But yes I agree, there is bias in the US courts against cases by Palestinians. In fact, I think that every case that has been brought against an Israeli defendant has been unsuccessful.

*   *   *

The French Courts
William Bourdon

The objective of this paper is to assess whether it is possible to find companies having business relations with the state of Israel while knowing that the products sold would be used to commit offences under international humanitarian law or international constitutional law.

For the purposes of this paper, it has been assumed that a criminal offence being either a crime or a misdemeanour, could be applied to either the Israeli army or to Israeli companies acting in the Occupied Palestinian Territories (OPT).

It must be emphasised that it seems very difficult to find criminally liable – because of a difficulty to prove the requisite *mens rea* – companies supplying products to Israeli companies acting in the OPT. On the other hand, a civil liability seems more possible.

Regarding war crimes, it must be said that French law enacting the Geneva Convention has not yet been incorporated, per se, in France.

THE CRIMINAL LIABILITY OF BUSINESS ENTITIES UNDER FRENCH LAW

Criminal liability of legal persons constitutes one of the most important innovations introduced into French law by article 121-2 of the Criminal Code.

It must be emphasised that this principle does not, however, apply uniformly to all legal persons and that it does not apply to all crimes.

Thus, criminal liability may arise for:

- For-profit private legal persons (civil or commercial companies, economic interest groups),
- Not-for-profit private legal persons (associations, political parties or groups, unions, employee representative institutions) and

- Public legal persons, with the sole exception of the state (territorial collectivities, public institutions).

Groups not endowed with legal personality cannot be declared criminally liable. The legal personality requirement can be justified for reasons of efficacy and logic: it would be difficult to convict an entity that has neither legal identity nor physical existence.

This is the case for partnerships, undisclosed partnerships, and companies in the process of formation. Concerning undisclosed partnerships, a tort committed by a representative of one partner in the partnership engages the liability of all the companies in the venture and not that of the partner company stripped of its legal personality.[78]

The situation is the same for groups of companies, which cannot be convicted as such. French criminal law does not, in effect, recognise the concept of the group, by virtue of the principle of the autonomy of legal persons in relation to one another.

POSSIBLE CRIMINAL LIABILITY

Complicity under French criminal law

Repression of complicity presupposes the existence of a principal crime, according to the legal principle of 'assumption of criminality'.

In order to engage a person's accomplice liability, that person must have participated in the reprehensible act of the principal perpetrator; her participation must have taken one of the material forms and must have been intentional in character. The theory of assumed criminality requires that the participation of an accomplice must be linked to the principal punishable act, that is, the act designated a felony or misdemeanour by law. In so far as acts committed abroad are concerned, article 113-5 of the Code states that:

> French criminal law is applicable to any person who, on the territory of the French Republic, is guilty as an accomplice to a felony or misdemeanor committed abroad if the felony or misdemeanor is punishable both by French law and the foreign law, and if it was established by a final decision of the foreign court.

Conversely, crimes committed abroad as an accomplice that are linked to a principal crime punishable in France are, of course, punishable in France.[79]

While complicity, in order to be punishable, must be linked to a punishable principal act, it is not necessary that the perpetrator of the act is also effectively punished. It is possible that the perpetrator evades punishment for reasons either of fact or law, without changing the fate of the accomplice.

To be punishable as an accomplice presupposes material participation corresponding to one of the forms started in article 121-7 of the Criminal Code. Complicity also indisputably presupposes the accomplishment of a positive act and it has been concluded from that, that there can be no complicity by abstention.

An individual who assists in the commission of a crime as a neutral spectator will not be held criminally responsible as an accomplice, even if he could have opposed the realisation of the crime.

This principle, has, however, been criticised in theory. In fact, one who participates as a spectator in the commission of a crime is not necessarily a passive and indifferent witness. There are people whose presence imply moral support for the crime and constitute aid from the perpetrator's perspective; since she finds her criminal activity facilitated – in other words, people whose presence can be considered to have played a causal role in the realisation of the crime.[80]

It also follows from the terms of article 121-7 of the Criminal Code that the participation of accomplices must necessarily occur before or during the commission of the crime, and not afterwards. Nevertheless, such acts can be punishable under the heading of accomplice liability if they result from an agreement made before the realisation of the crime.

Article 121-7 of the Criminal Code outlines precisely three forms of material participation of an accomplice: aiding or abetting, provocation, and giving instructions. It is sufficient that one of these means exists to justify a conviction.[81]

In our particular case, it could be argued that companies did supply material means for the commission of the offence committed by the Israeli army, and that companies did supply these means, at least partially, on French territory.

Therefore, complicity by aiding or abetting could be considered.

Complicity includes not only a legal and material element, but also a moral element. The accomplice must have intended to participate in the crime committed by another person. This third condition is expressly formulated by the texts. Article 121-7 is in fact directed at 'the person who knowingly' makes himself an accomplice.

The criminal intent required for an accomplice is distinct, however, from that of the principal. It is none the less made up of two elements: awareness – of law and also of fact (that is, of the criminal character of the acts of the principal) – and the will to participate in the crime.

That said, it is not necessary that the intent of the accomplice conforms completely to that of the principal. The criminal chamber of the Court of Appeal in its judgment of 23 January 1997 indeed declared that

> ... the last paragraph of article 6 of the Statute of the Nuremberg International Military Tribunal does not require that an accomplice to crimes against humanity adhere to the ideological policy of hegemony of the principal perpetrators, nor that he belong to one of the organisations declared criminal by that Tribunal.

The requirement of aware and willing participation in a specific crime leads to two types of problems: that of the relation between the intent of the accomplice and the crime accomplished by the principal, and that of complicity in strict liability crimes. As to the first question, jurisprudence has traditionally decided that if the crime committed was, as to its elements, different from the crime that was planned, then the accomplice cannot be punished.

If the role of the accomplice seems so determinative that one can establish between the protagonists simultaneity of action and reciprocal assistance, the courts do not hesitate to make the person, who was only an accomplice, into a co-principal.[82]

Concerning legal persons, they can be prosecuted not only in the capacity of principal perpetrator of a crime, but also as an accomplice – article 121-2 defines the criminal liability of legal persons, indeed by reference back to articles 121-6 and 121-7, relative respectively to liability as a principal and accomplice.

However, in certain scenarios, and more particularly when crimes of omission or negligence are concerned, characterised by the absence of criminal intent or the material act of commission, the liability of the legal person could be triggered even when the criminal liability of the natural person could not have been established. Certain acts can be committed by collective organs of the legal person without it being possible to identify the role of their members and impute personal liability for the crime to a specific individual.

Therefore, in this case, it must be demonstrated that the companies were aware of the possible use of the material they sold. This particular issue should not cause too many difficulties given the wide publicity of the Israeli army's behaviour in the OPT.

William Bourdon is a lawyer based in Paris and president of the Sherpa Association, France.

TRANSCRIPT OF JURY Q&A: WILLIAM BOURDON

William Bourdon: [Concluding remarks] ... And of course, your tribunal knows that the criminal French code does not admit complicity by abstention, complicity by silence, complicity by neutrality. This cannot be considered as a relevant base for complicity, but let's convince – let's try to convince the tribunal of perhaps another legal avenue. What is in my understanding for the next future, a real relevant legal avenue. I invite your tribunal to bring together not only formally the Criminal Code, because I've sufficiently stressed the fact that it was not so easy to demonstrate the existence of the moral element, and all of you have understood that the moral element is not only the awareness, but the willing, the intention, but what should convince you to shift from the awareness to the willing or to the intention is, one: the fact that the violation of international law is unanimously, almost unanimously accepted – the fact that repeatedly, daily and daily, war crimes are committed in Israel. This is one: second[ly], the fact that the same companies that could be considered as complicit multiply commitments in favour of sustainable development and human rights, and this create[s] new obligations – you cannot say if you are a company: I commit myself in favour of human rights and refuse that this commitment may be considered as a reinforcement of your liability and of your responsibility. And three: I invite your tribunal to consider that the development of this recommendation of this special rapporteur for responsibility of transnationals, all the works done by United Nations, the fact that all these companies are more or less linked to global compacts is the beginning of the creation of customary international law appl[ic]able to transnationals – this is new, this is before our eyes, that there is this ... this new emergence of customary international law appl[ic]able to the companies, so I do consider that, more and more, because of the companies themselves, we will have the basis to prosecute them before a French judge. I thank the tribunal for its attention.

Cynthia McKinney: ... You've talked about the laws, the state laws and the international legal framework within which we are considering this subject matter today. My question is: is the legal framework sufficient for our mission in trying to find ways in which we can find ways to hold corporations accountable? Or do we need additional law? And if we need additional law, in what venue do we need it?

WB: Well this is a very burning issue – very burning, very crucial question. So I've tried to demonstrate that at the stage we are, the French law if you mix together – if you bring together the French law with the commitments of the company, if you watch the website of Veolia, if you watch the website of the bank which invest all over the world and also in the West Bank, you will see that the company commits themselves in favour of human rights. This did not exist ten years ago; this is absolutely new. And they cannot afford to say, we commit ourselves to human rights, but we don't want that anyone opens consequences of this commitment. And in my opinion as jurist, and I have tried already to plead this, and I want to give you an example, I have pleaded before the tribunal and court of appeal for various NGOs in the *Erica* case. [The] *Erica* case was this absolutely tremendous, awful pollution caused by the wreckage of the boat called *Erica* and I've said to the court, ten years ago: Total commits itself in favour of sustainable development so it means that this personal commitment of Total has created an obligation of vigilance, of cautiousness which doesn't come from the law, but comes from this commitment, so of course idealistically, idealistically, I hope that we will be able to be at the origin of an international, compelling system appl[ic]able to the transnational. It's too early to say if it will be possible. This framework for the moment does not exist, but the combination of the national law, of the emergence of the customary international law and the commitments of the companies are sufficient in my assessment to prosecute them.

Michael Mansfield QC: Thank you very much. Can I just pick up on ... I've just been provided with a response, that Veolia have sent to the Russell Tribunal on the very point you've just mentioned ...

[Mr Mansfield then read out part of the Veolia response. See Appendix 2 for the full text]

WB: Yeah, I comment on this paragraph [paragraph 2]: I'm not so sure that Veolia would not have succeed[ed]. It's possible that plaintiffs who have [inaudible] the French tribunal would have seen at the end their request rejected, but what is new is the fact that one of the consequences of this ethical commitment of companies has created an opinion tribunal – a worldwide, civil society tribunal court. And the reactivity of the company when they enter in a controversial matter make them renounce their investment before any judgment even if they are juridically the possibility to win, they prefer to renounce than to lose before the opinion tribunal.

2
Corporate Activities in and Around Israeli Settlements

The Settlement Industry and Corporate Involvement in the Occupation

Dalit Baum

'Who Profits From the Occupation' focuses on exposing corporate interests in the Israeli Occupation in order to provide accurate, reliable and well-documented information for corporate accountability campaigns. All of our information is public, derived from the companies' own publications, site visits and official documents. We have set up a database, <www.whoprofits.org>, listing hundreds of corporations and describing their specific involvement. Additionally, as an information centre, we provide ongoing information support to dozens of campaigns, both internationally and locally.

Early on in our research, we set out to analyse the main areas of corporate involvement in the Occupation. Our resulting three categories – 'Settlement Industry', 'Control of Population' and 'Exploitation' – have since become a useful tool to researchers and activists.

Israeli industrial zones within the Occupied Palestinian Territories (OPT) host hundreds of companies, ranging from small businesses serving local Israeli settlers to large factories that export their products worldwide. The main factories are located in the three main industrial zones of Barkan, Atarot and Mishor Adumim. About two dozen settlements, especially in the Jordan Valley and the Golan Heights, produce agricultural goods, such as fruits and flowers, and sell them in Israel and abroad.

Settlement production benefits from low rental rates, special tax incentives, lax enforcement of environmental and labour protection laws and other governmental support. For example, all industrial zones in the settlements enjoy a special tax status usually offered as a special incentive to develop areas in remote areas of Israel, but the main settlement industrial zones are all very close to Israel's urban centres, and this gives them a competitive advantage over other industrial areas near the centre. Environmental regulations are hardly enforced in these industrial zones and tend to attract highly polluting factories that would otherwise find it difficult to operate inside Israel.

Palestinians employed in these industrial zones work under severe restrictions of movement and organisation. All workers must obtain special permits and gain clearance from the Israeli General Security Service (*Shabak*) just to be able to enter these factories. And their dependency on these permits limits the workers' employment choices and makes organising almost impossible. Israeli labour laws have been extended to Palestinian workers in the settlements, but not in full. With hardly any governmental enforcement or protection (especially given that Palestinian workers are effectively prevented from demanding their rights), employment under occupation is always exploitative, resulting in routine violations of labour rights.

Settlement production constitutes just a small fraction of what we consider to be corporate involvement in settlements. The intense focus on settlement production may obscure the fact that settlement industries are few, the revenues from them are very limited, and for all but a handful of agricultural settlements, they do not contribute substantially to the settlements' economic sustainability. Consequently, under the heading 'the settlement industry', we include the entire economic sustenance of the settlements. In addition to settlements' agricultural and industrial production, we investigate real estate and construction in the settlements, infrastructure and the provision of all vital services and utilities to the settlements. Israeli and international corporations build roads and housing units, provide services such as public transportation, waste management, water, security and telecommunication, provide loans, and market goods. The settlements' continued existence depends on services provided by these companies.

This wider settlement industry includes most large Israeli retailers and service providers. These companies claim to employ a policy of 'nondiscrimination', meaning that they provide equal services inside the official borders of Israel and in the OPT – to the Jewish-Israeli settlers. Their intended services map does not include the Palestinian residents of the West Bank. In other words, their policy is not only a policy of systematic discrimination; it is a facet of the ethnic segregation between Palestinians and Jews in the occupied West Bank.

The settlement industry does not exhaust the different ways in which corporations benefit from Israeli control over occupied land; our mapping adds two more categories of corporate involvement. The second category studies corporations involved in Israeli control over the Palestinian population in the OPT. This includes the construction and operation of the separation wall and the checkpoints and, in general, the supply and operation of means of surveillance and control of Palestinian movement inside the OPT and between the OPT and the state of Israel. The growing global market of the homeland security industry has contributed significantly to the growth of the Israeli high-tech market. Often, the Israeli-controlled area is perceived as a testing ground or a laboratory for new innovations to be 'tested on Palestinians'. We have seen this used by sales representatives of Israeli homeland security products as a blunt marketing strategy.

The third category of involvement points to corporations that directly benefit from the systemic advantages of Israeli control over Palestinian land, people and markets. This category includes the companies that plunder natural resources such as gravel or water in the occupied area, use it as a dumping ground for Israeli waste, profit from the exploitation of Palestinian labour and benefit from access to the captive Palestinian consumer market.

For example, many Israeli food manufacturers and distributors benefit from selling low-grade products in the West Bank, while Palestinian competitors are stopped at Israeli military checkpoints. Similarly, telecommunication service providers exploit Israeli control of airwaves in the occupied land to illegally penetrate the Palestinian market.[1]

Dalit Baum PhD is project coordinator of 'Who Profits From the Occupation', a project of the Coalition of Women for Peace in Tel Aviv – < www.whoprofits.org>.

TRANSCRIPT OF JURY Q&A: DALIT BAUM

Mairead Maguire: Thank you very much Dalit for your excellent work and all yous are doing. I would like to ask if you would speak to the issue of, within the settlements themselves, the fact that more and more foreign nationals are working within that area, what is the actual workforce. I would like also if you would speak a wee bit more about the access to the settlements i.e. roads only for Israelis, and what that means to Palestinians in their everyday life. And also the fact that in the settlements in the West Bank the security that is put on to facilitate these illegal settlements on Palestinian land and what affect that has on the Palestinian families.

Dalit Baum: All Israeli settlements in the West Bank are special security zones (that's how they're termed) and that means there is no access to Palestinians unless they have a special permit – Palestinians of the West Bank, not Palestinians from Israel (but in some cases also Palestinians from Israel). And that means that many of the services provided in the settlements are actually inaccessible to Palestinians living nearby, including public transport in many cases. There are very, very cheap buses – I can take a bus in Tel Aviv that cost twice than going to a far-away settlement from Tel Aviv, because it's much cheaper over there than going to a settlement. As to your first question about workers: Palestinian workers are dependent on special security permits in order to work within the settlements. Currently there are about I think less than 30,000 Palestinians working the settlements – in the settlement industrial zones. I hope Hugh Lanning will discuss that in more detail. But because they so depended on the security permits, it makes it very, very hard for them to organise. Because it's very, very easy to pull out the security permit of anyone who tries to organise. Also we have heard about cases when the army has been used against workers trying to organise. It is just very, very easy to use that powers against people who maybe have some legal rights, but don't have any civil rights where they are.

Ronnie Kasrils: Thanks. Just a quick question from Mike Mansfield.

Michael Mansfield QC: I appreciate the difficulties you face and I'm not wishing to put you into any more difficulties with the Israeli authorities. However, you have a hands-on, and considerably detailed knowledge of what is going on on the ground, and what is interesting obviously from our point of view, and as I introduced today, we need to identify who is involved in the violations. The settlements themselves are a violation. Now, who is contributing – by which I mean: which companies are contributing? I give but one example: as I understand it, one of the communications companies that you've already mentioned, although not by name, Bezeq, has now got a very close alliance with British Telecom. Now is it possible, given your knowledge, to draw up (and I think you may have been able to do it in the past) for our benefit, a list of companies – not just British ones – a list of companies and corporations that are involved in violations within the settlements?

DB: Yes. In fact, this is what we have been doing for the last four years, so I'm very glad that you asked this question. Our website whoprofits.org is actually a database and it lists about 400 companies presently, according to their area of involvement, specifying their explicit involvement and also tracing their ownership, location, etc. We also serve as an information centre, so we receive queries from all around the world of different organisations and individuals that want to know more about the complicity of this or that company. In the case of Bezeq, this is a very, very simple example of one of the – it's the biggest Israeli communication company. Of course, it provides the basic landline telephone services in all the settlements. It's very easy, you just go on the telephone book and you can see it. They also provide internet services to all the settlements. These are very basic core services, that they 'do not discriminate' and therefore supply in all the settlements.

MM: Just a quick supplementary: the information on the database relating to the 400 companies – obviously if we are to rely upon a database of that kind … has there been any challenge to the information and its authenticity?

DB: This is a very important question, because we work within Israel so of course we are exposed to the Israeli legal system, and we really hope we will have a sympathetic judge, but we cannot count on it. So what we do is we never, never publish anything based on secondary sources. We have a full file of documentation and proofs for each and every company and each and every sentence we publish. We have received some threats of lawsuits in the past – it never came to anything. I think companies also realise that they have a lot to lose from challenging things that are obviously true. We don't know what will be next: we know that the new law will allow them to sue us just for giving out that information, even if it is true. So that would probably be a bigger problem for us to deal with. [The new Israeli law forbidding calls for boycott passed in the Knesset on 11 July 2011.]

RK: … this point about the difficulties of identification of products from the illegal settlements etc. is clearly a very important one in terms of worldwide campaigns, pressure, boycott, so this really is something that needs to be tracked through the websites and so on. But you say it's almost impossible to get to the root of this. Just briefly: in what percentage – because there is huge number of products that are well identified internationally.

DB: There isn't a huge number of products, because if you look at a company like SodaStream, they are very well identified, and even they have more production sites, we just know what things are being produced in their settlement factory, which is their biggest factory, their main factory. In fact, there is a very short list of products, and therefore just thinking about how to ban settlement trade is not enough, because the settlement production is actually tiny. It's not the main support of the settlements in their economy. Most settlers do not work in the settlement industrial zones. Their sustenance is actually based on the general Israeli economy. And this is I think what I have tried to show here ... the main point would be to try and look at companies that are involved in the Occupation, or profit from the Occupation in some significant way, and that in this case would include companies like Bezeq, companies like the cellular phone companies that network the entire West Bank with their antennas, it would include many big players in the Israeli market that makes this possible.

RK: Thanks very much, because that's extremely important. You're saying that the settlements economy and products are so enmeshed within the Israeli economy as a whole, that the question of a boycott, selective of the settlements, is something that's tricky. And clearly – I don't want to put words in anybody's mouth when I'm here as a juror, but I think that the conclusion here is obvious ... .

DB: [crosstalk] Yes.

RK: – from what you tell us. Want to thank you very much. I listened when you said that the view of the employer and the state in Israel is that Palestinian workers are accustomed to those [bad] conditions [working in settlements]. That's exactly what we used to hear in South Africa. The precise phraseology. Thank you very much.

*   *   *

Business Practices in Relation to Settlements and the Settlement Industry

Hugh Lanning

My evidence will concentrate specifically on business practices and conditions facing workers and is based on personal observation and meetings with settlement workers, their representatives, the PGFTU and Kav LaOved. I will also be drawing substantively from the recent 2010 ILO delegation report 'The Situation of Workers of the Occupied Arab Territories'.

I will preface with what should be obvious, but is the fundamental point – that the situation facing Palestinian workers in settlements cannot be seen in isolation from the issues facing Palestinians living under an illegal Israeli occupation. The only solution is a political one, which is obviously not resolved by simply looking at Palestinians' terms and conditions of work in settlements, but by ensuring that full Palestinian rights are finally achieved, including the right to self-determination.

TERMS OF REFERENCE

- Kav LaOved (Worker's Hotline) is an NGO committed to protecting the rights of disadvantaged workers employed in Israel and by Israelis in the Occupied Territories, including Palestinians, migrant workers, subcontracted workers and new immigrants.
- The Palestinian General Federation of Trade Unions (PGFTU), with its head offices based in Nablus, is the national trade union centre in the Palestinian Territories. It has an estimated membership of 290,000, and is affiliated with the International Trade Union Confederation.
- The International Labour Organization (ILO) is the tripartite UN agency that brings together governments, employers and workers of its member states in common action to promote decent work throughout the world.

For thousands of Palestinians, there is no other option to secure an income other than working in Israeli settlements in the West Bank, including East Jerusalem, despite their illegality under international law. They work knowing that settlements are built on their stolen land, and that settlements deplete natural resources, restrict access and movement, and cause territorial fragmentation that impedes Palestinian development. They are placed in an invidious position choosing between abject poverty and donor aid handouts, or working with Israeli occupiers. They are vulnerable to violations of labour rights and exploitation and acts of violence perpetrated by Israeli settlers. Palestinian construction workers work on constructing the apartheid wall or building settlements, which Israel is using to create 'facts on the ground' to entrench its occupation.

Figure 2.1   Thousands of Palestinian workers queue from 3 a.m. onwards to get to work in Jerusalem. It takes hours to pass the Israeli checkpoint – Bethlehem, 2008. Courtesy Anne Paq/Activestills.org.

There are many reasons why Palestinians elect to work on settlements: chronic unemployment in the West Bank, roadblocks and checkpoints making it untenable to attend work, and many Palestinians no longer have their own land or are able to work their own land due to the Occupation. Restrictive measures mean that legitimate Palestinian businesses cannot obtain necessary permits to develop businesses in Area C (under the Oslo Accords) where most of the settlements are located.

Faced with limited opportunities for decent work, Palestinians are faced with a real dichotomy, compounded by the fact that the average daily wage offered for settlement work is almost double the average wage for work in the public or private sector.

Average Palestinian daily wages in New Israeli shekels (NIS)
Equivalents in GBP as of 28 March 2011

Public sector – 88.80 NIS (£15.69)
Private sector – 79.60 NIS (£14.07)
Settlements – 156.40 NIS (£27.65)

Source: *Palestinian Central Bureau of Statistics Labour Force Surveys (2008–09)*

Businesses in settlements benefit from special subsidies and various tax benefits for businesses, designed to promote industry and commerce. As Shir Hever in 'The Settlements – the economic cost to Israel'[2] points out, it is impossible to obtain data since funds transfers to settlers are clandestine. The reasons for this are to avoid public outrage at favouritism that settlers enjoy, and that the special subsidies given to settlers encourage people to move and operate in the area, thus violating the Fourth Geneva Convention that forbids the transfer of civilian population to an occupied country. Subsidies are distributed into countless special one-time grants, ad hoc funds and special budgets that create a financial maze that can only be navigated with great difficulty.

Settlement businesses also use Palestinian workers as a reserve of cheap labour, where in times of economic difficulty workers can be easily sacked. In 1999, the United Nations Economic and Social Council criticised the practice of Israeli companies moving their facilities to the West Bank to escape the higher wages, health and environment standards applicable in Israel. And while western governments and the United States moved industry to countries like Pakistan, India and China to exact the highest amount of profit, Israeli businesses had an expendable reserve of cheap labour on their doorstep.

According to Kav LaOved, business practices of exploitation and abuse in Israeli settlements include:[3]

- Working with toxic and hazardous substances.
- Working in unsafe conditions with no health and safety training or induction.
- Evidence of child labour in agricultural enterprises.
- Paying under the national minimum wage, with women being paid less than men, and all Palestinians being paid less than Israeli workers or below the Israeli national minimum wage.
- No contracts or illegal registration, rendering the worker invisible – no formal proof of employment means no health

insurance or access to social security; if workers leave their job or are sacked, no references are required to be supplied.
- No compensation for industrial injury.
- Permits issued under a different name.
- Lack of health and safety inspectors.
- Falsification of attendance and hours worked, and pay slips issued with fewer working days than those actually worked so that it appears that the minimum wage is being paid.
- No medical aid provided to the injured party in industrial accidents.
- High incidence of bullying.
- Refusal to grant sick leave or holidays.
- Excessive working hours and insufficient breaks.

Palestinian workers can find themselves labouring in extremely dangerous conditions. One example is the Nitzanei Shalom ('Buds of Peace') industrial zone. As a recent article in *Palestine Monitor* points out:

> ... the land was expropriated by the Israeli army in the 80s to be developed as a site for dangerous chemical factories, illegal in Israel. Geshuri Industries is one such factory, producing pesticides, insecticides and fertilisers. It was originally located in the Israeli town of Kfar Saba, until a court declared it a health hazard, forcing it to close down in 1982. The owner avoided Israel's strict environmental laws by moving the factory to Nitzanei Shalom.

Palestinians have no power to oppose such developments. Dr Kifaya Abu-El Huda of Cairo University believes all the water in the western basin's wells is polluted. Air pollution causes respiratory diseases and eye infections in the area's residents. The *Palestine Monitor* article continues: '... the Geshuri factory operates for eleven months in the year when winds blow the fumes into the West Bank. It closes down for the period when the winds change and blow into Israel, to ensure the toxic fumes do not pollute the Israeli environment.'[4]

The Sol Or factory repairs gas bottles in Nitzanei Shalom, with Palestinians working there without the specialised masks needed for this highly dangerous task. According to Kav LaOved, 'Five workers have died here over the past decade from accidents in which they were burnt by chemicals. One worker now has cancer.'[5]

The involvement of Palestinian intermediaries – often referred to as middlemen – continues to adversely impact on the situation of Palestinian workers in Israeli settlements. Unregulated and uncontrolled, these middlemen require workers to pay high fees, while workers hired through them may not even be issued a labour contract. They often withhold workers' permits and take responsibility for paying them. The workers may not be aware of their employer's identity or of the amount paid by the employer to the middleman. In practice, there tends to be no clear separation between the fees paid by the enterprise to the middleman and the worker's wages.

The PGFTU are not allowed permits to enter the settlements, meaning workers are denied access to advice and information and de facto the right to organise. The PGFTU state that, for them, settlements 'are like a closed military zone'. It is therefore virtually impossible to provide workers with protection and representation which is in direct contravention of ILO conventions, to which Israel is a signatory.

According to international humanitarian law, the responsibility of assuming the welfare and safety of Palestinian workers in the settlements and industrial parks constructed along the borderline is incumbent upon the State of Israel. It must protect their human rights and among these the right to a safe and hygienic work environment. But as Hannah Zohar, Kav LaOved's director has stated, in reality 'It's like the wild west, no laws, no limits, no rights.'

According to Hani Ben-Israel at Kav LaOved, the reality at the moment regarding enforcement of labour laws and work safety laws is that there is no enforcement whatsoever. The employers do not deny this, saying 'We don't send inspectors to the settlement areas, we do nothing to force the employers to maintain work safety regulations'; whilst in the past the army claimed that it was coordinating with the Ministry of Industry, Trade and Employment, the ministry itself stated at the Knesset's Foreign Workers Committee that 'we have no coordination, we do nothing together' and that the situation at the moment is that it is a no-man's land.

An example of industrial action taken by workers highlights the injustice they suffer. In May 2009, women working for the Royalife Factory in the Barkan industrial zone were sick of 'low pay, dangerous conditions and bullying treatment', first complained to the factory management and then went on strike, supported by Kav LaOved. They were fired, reinstated under a court order and then fired again. They said, 'We were paid only $1.50–$2.00 an hour [6–8 shekels]. Men are paid 12 shekels.' The Israeli minimum wage is 20 shekels per hour – three times that being paid to the striking women.

Their working conditions were horrific; Umm Raed, one of the workers, said:

> We get no vacations, no sick pay, not even pay slips … There is no air conditioning or heating in the factory, so it's hot in summer and very cold in winter … the managers are always screaming and shouting at us, trying to pressure us to work harder … There are often accidents … There is no protection from the machines and no proper safety equipment.

The workers in that particular factory also reported working from 6.30 am till 5.00 pm, sometimes for seven days a week to fulfil orders.[6]

In fact, agricultural business and industrial parks on settlements are away from the eye of the law and many companies go unpunished for their profitable exploitation of Palestinian workers. In addition, goods are often illegally marked 'Made in Israel', meaning that they benefit from the EU preferential rate of import duty not applicable to settlement produce. As the international boycott, disinvestment and sanctions campaign against Israel's violations gains momentum, the exploitation of Palestinian labour by Israeli companies operating on occupied Palestinian land is coming under scrutiny.

In recent years, the number of Palestinians working in settlements who have obtained permits has risen, to an estimated 25,000 in 2009. According to estimates by Palestinian trade unions and Kav LaOved, there may be an additional 10,000 Palestinian workers without permits in the settlements. Work in the settlements involves mainly work in agriculture, industrial undertakings, construction, and employment by Israeli municipal authorities. Women tend to be engaged predominantly in agriculture or industry.

The 1995 Interim Agreement on the West Bank and Gaza (aka Oslo II) excludes Area C, where settlements are situated, from the legislative authority of the Palestinian institutions and assigns full security and administrative jurisdiction there to Israel. The Palestinian Labour Law of 2000 therefore does not apply to work in the Israeli settlements, nor is the Palestinian Authority in a position to take any action to protect workers employed in the settlements.

The Israeli High Court of Justice decided in a 2007 case that Israeli labour law, including the Minimum Wages Law, is applicable to labour contracts between Palestinian workers and Israeli employers for work carried out in Israeli settlements. The ruling, however, appears to allow the application of Jordanian law, if agreed between the parties.

Once a settlement enterprise decides to hire a Palestinian worker, always through a middleman, the worker must apply for a work permit and magnetic identity card to access the settlement; these are granted subject to detailed security checks. The permit (which they are charged for) binds the worker to the enterprise and is subject to renewal every three months; the worker is only allowed to be on the settlement during the hours indicated on the permit. This practice is unregulated, uncontrolled and open to corruption.

The dependency of Palestinian workers is exacerbated by the fact that their permits and security clearances binding them to the employer can be withdrawn at any stage, and by the apparent absence of labour inspection. This dependency leads many Palestinian workers to accept any terms and conditions to avoid losing their jobs. Workers without permits are even more vulnerable and are at the greatest risk of abuse.

While there are workplaces that treat their workers fairly and correctly, Palestinian workers employed in Israeli settlements in the OPT remain vulnerable to violations of labour rights and exploitation. The abundant evidence in this regard suggests that such practices are widespread. This problem can hardly be addressed in isolation because its root causes lie in the Occupation and the settlement policy it entails, including the establishment of a complex legal system primarily aiming to serve the needs and interests of Israeli citizens and enterprises present in the West Bank. Palestinian workers are left with no other option than to litigate in Israeli courts, which is costly and will remain, for most of them, unfeasible. And, as we have seen, successful litigation often results in sacking and blacklisting.

The Palestinian Authority regards the employment of Palestinian workers in Israeli settlements as unacceptable. Apart from the illegality of the settlements under international law and the risks of labour rights violations and exploitation, employment in settlements, while providing some income, is perceived as detrimental to the Palestinian economy and an impediment to the ongoing building of a Palestinian state. The Palestinian Minister of Labour stated that his ministry had stopped facilitating employment in Israeli settlements, while it continued its facilitating role with respect to work in Israel.

On 26 April 2010, President Abbas signed a decree banning trade in Israeli settlement-made goods in the occupied Palestinian territory. In this connection, the judgment made by the European Court of Justice in February 2010, that products manufactured in Israeli settlements cannot be imported to Europe under the preferential conditions provided for under the Euro-Mediterranean Association Agreement between Israel and the European Community, is noteworthy.[7]

The bleak economic, social and humanitarian situation throughout Palestine creates an environment in which, according to the ILO:

> … workers' rights and human dignity are jeopardised. The public sector has reached the end of its absorptive capacity, while the private sector is incapable of creating jobs at a level sufficient to absorb the growing and increasingly young Palestinian labour force in a situation where economic growth continues to be constrained. In the absence of other opportunities, many Palestinians are bound to seek work in the informal economy, often at the price of precarious working conditions and poor labour protection. High rates of poverty indeed suggest that decent work for all Palestinian women and men remains a distant goal.

Palestinian men and women are struggling to secure for their families the most basic means of livelihood, dealing with injustice and humiliation every day. With the increased attacks by the Israeli government on Palestinians, international trade union solidarity has dramatically increased, as witnessed by the motion passed at the 2010 Trades Union Congress in Britain, which represents over 6 million workers.[8]

Condemning the continuing Israeli Occupation, its siege on Gaza and its attack on the *Mavi Marmara*, the motion passed at the TUC continued:

> Congress believes that the effective annexation of massive swathes of land by Israel in defiance of international law, using walls and checkpoints and destroying Palestinian homes in the process, is a deliberate strategy to undermine the viability of the West Bank and thereby the potential for an independent Palestinian state. Congress calls on the UK Government and the EU to take much stronger political steps to ensure Israel abides by UN resolutions. Congress instructs the General Council to work closely with the Palestine Solidarity Campaign to actively encourage affiliates,

employers and pension funds to disinvest from, and boycott the goods of, companies who profit from illegal settlements, the Occupation and the construction of the Wall ... Congress agrees to join unions around the world for maximum coordination internationally for active solidarity.

This motion, and similar motions and actions carried out across the union movement internationally, clearly recognise that only an end to occupation and a free Palestine will deliver meaningful rights to Palestinian workers.

Hugh Lanning is Deputy General Secretary of the Public and Commercial Services union and Chair of the Palestine Solidarity Campaign.

TRANSCRIPT OF JURY Q&A: HUGH LANNING

Ronnie Kasrils: Thanks very much indeed. I've got an immediate question: In view of Dr Dalit Baum's input about the difficulty of simply boycotting settlement products and consequently the point you're making about how to identify the companies concerned linked to those difficult-to-identify products, it really is a question of the wider boycott of Israel per se, and of course the whole question of the settlements is clearly key to Israel's government and its policies. How would the TUC view this type of challenge ... would you care to say?

Hugh Lanning: Yes I would, I mean we're actually talking with them about it at the moment in both hats [that is, in both his PSC and PCS capacities], as it happens. It is clear and I think it's the view that we've come to ... it is clear that you cannot just concentrate on settlement goods and you cannot purely identify, if you like, simply those firms. But what we're trying to do with the TUC is a bit like – and you'll recall it in the South African campaign – is identify the biggest complicit firms, the ones that you can target most. Because you can spread your fire very thinly across an awful lot, but what we want to try and identify is those companies which really play a major part in the economy like we did with Barclays in terms of South Africa, that we can demonstrate are complicit, that we have evidence about, and try and come up with a shortlist of both companies and products that we can easily explain to people in this country and try and make a difference and have an impact, be it on BT, be it on Caterpillar through disinvestment, or Veolia, or through direct products in the supermarkets. And one thing that we have agreed in terms of practice: with the British supermarkets, we will be writing to them all, saying 'prove yourself innocent in terms of your supply chain', rather than 'we will try and prove you guilty.' We know that these are the big – Carmel-Agrexco and so on – these are the big firms with which you trade, we believe they are complicit, you should not be working with them. So it's gonna be … the basis of proving innocence will be with the supermarkets if they don't want to face the consequences of the boycott action.

RK: Thanks so much. Mairead?

Mairead Maguire: Thank you very much for your report and thank you very much to all the great work that you do, the Palestinian solidarity group and the trade unions and so forth. We are seeing the multi-corporations [*sic*: multi-national] and corporations really with little rules that they have to respond to. We do call for ethical investment but I think that a convention, a treaty, whereby corporations are held accountable – like we have the treaty to protect children and so forth: are the trade unions working in this field of pushing for having a treaty whereby multi-corporations and corporations are actually made accountable and there are rules and regulations under which they apply?

HL: There's been for quite a long time a sort of a policy around ethical trade and there [are] trade unions working with corporations to try and do that. The issue though in relation to Palestine and Israel is that, if you like, most of the Israeli companies that are players aren't part of that process – maybe some of the corporations and companies in this country with which they deal. And also I think, you know, to be honest, this is a policy that has only become the trade union policy over the last few years. There was a lot of opposition within the British trade union movement to adopting this sort of policy for a long time. So we're still looking for all the right tactics and all the right approaches to follow it through. And I think our starting point is – building on the work that's been done through Who Profits – is to give to ordinary people in this country clear evidence of which are the complicit firms and which are the ones that we want to target. And we've been using a phrase about 'let's try and jump together' – we want everyone to try and focus on the same companies and the same organisations so that you can have maximum impact. And we think that would be the best approach rather than a more scattered approach which has tended to be the case in the past.

Anthony Gifford QC: ... I wanted to ask you more specifically – I didn't want to ask Dr Baum to avoid getting her into trouble, but I can ask you ...

HL: You didn't mind me getting into trouble then? [laughs]

AG: No! You say in your written evidence, which we are going to receive, that you identify the companies that you're referring to. But tell us: who are top of the list? British companies that you would be recommending a boycott?

HL: You will get me into trouble in a sense. We've just recently done a campaign, started and signed, around BT and their involvement and that's one direct. We are putting a challenge to all of the big British supermarkets that they should either come clean or they will become targets. We are identifying major companies like Carmel-Agrexco, Veolia, Caterpillar and so on, who are on the regular list. What we haven't yet identified and agreed is this public shortlist of the ones that we want to be the targets. We hope to do that early in the new year [that is, January 2011] when we get a response from the supermarkets and others to the challenge that we're putting to them. We can give you the list of the, if you like, culprits in general terms but we do think it's important to try and focus on those who are most involved and the ones that we can do the most to target. And the other thing that we're working on which relates to this is that we're trying to work with the workers inside the companies and the organisations that they should apply pressure as well for them to withdraw from Israel. So watch this space and there shortly will be the list, hopefully before you finish your deliberations.

RK: We're going to watch that space! We've got time for just one quick question.

Cynthia McKinney: I'm amazed that the actions that you just described are being done by unions inside the UK. Well that's amazing to me because in the Unites States our unions are complicit because they actually purchase Israeli bonds. So I guess you have an entirely different point of view.

HL: It is the case – I mean, if you go back ten years, we'd have been amazed that the British trade union movement was adopting this position. I mean, partly it has been a target within those who support Palestine that given the historic role British trade unions played on South Africa, to try and get them in to that same sort of position on Palestine and that has gradually come about. We're starting to try and spread the pool internationally but we are meeting the sort of resistance that you describe. And recently at the ITUC, a motion from COSATU (the South African trade union) to raise this issue, got ... 'clobbered' I think would be the best way to describe it – got heavily defeated. So there is an awful lot of work to do in the wider trade union movement, in the international trade union movement, to adopt the same view. But the British trade union movement traditionally has been one of the – it is one of the oldest and still one of the stronger ones, and hopefully we're going to use that to spring-board into trade unions elsewhere.

*   *   *

The Reality of Israeli Settlements in Palestine
Fayez al-Taneeb

Editors' note: The British authorities did not issue a travel visa to this Palestinian speaker, so his presentation was given via pre-recorded video. The following is a transcript of the English translation.

My name is Fayez al-Taneeb from the region of Tulkarem and I am a farmer. I'm also a member of the coordination of popular committees in Palestine. I was from 2000 to 2003 coordinator for the union of Palestinian farmers and in the '80s I was a secretary-general of a trade union in Palestine.

In 1985, we were surprised to see Israeli bulldozers working in the region next to us and we didn't know what was the reason. But after a period we understood that what was happening was the construction of an Israeli plant. And when we asked why this plant is being built here the response we had is that this is a chemical plant that was in an Israeli village and the Israeli farmers had complained about this to the courts – to the Israeli courts – and the Israeli courts had decided to expel that plant and that plant decided to come to the Palestinian region and to build this chemical plant there. And we have the documents proving that the Israeli courts expelled this plant from Israel.

Three–four years after the construction and the functioning of this plant, it was clear that there were crimes happening due to this plant, in different aspects. The first aspect was the use of liquids going into the lands and heading towards our farms. And in these lands, we were unable to plant on them anywhere and they were considered as dead lands. In addition, there was chemical dust coming out of this plant and they were wind-driven towards the region of Tulkarem, the city of Tulkarem. Over 70,000 people live in Tulkarem and this plant is metres away from the first houses of this region. And the owners of this chemical plant began dealing with the farmers and the population as if they were settlers, as if they were part of the settlement activity in the region, and began harassing the farmers in the different aspects of their daily lives. And they began expropriating land, agricultural land, and to expand their chemical plants on our lands. And today we have in this area eleven chemical plants polluting our lands.

After a while, we went to the Israeli courts, tried to stop these activities and the pollution we were enduring. We went to the Israeli courts but the Israeli courts said they needed evidence of what we were saying. And when we took samples of these poisons that were being spread on our land, the Israeli laboratories refused to provide us with the results of the examination that was done.

Then we used demonstrations, popular peaceful demonstrations, but that didn't give any result. And then we began welcoming people coming from the international solidarity [groups] to provide them with the facts.

When they [the Israeli authorities] felt that we were active and heading towards shutting off the plant, they began using a different policy completely. And this policy began by closing the roadways towards our farms. They cut off the pipes that provided our lands with water. They destroyed the plastic that was protecting what we were planting on our land. And these policies continued until 2002, the end of 2002, when it was made clear to us that the Israeli Occupation intended to build a wall on our land in Tulkarem. And we had 15 days to appeal this decision and we went to the courts but they refused our appeal; we went to the Israeli High Court of Justice, but unfortunately the decision was made to build the wall on our land – that took 60 per cent of my farm.

And this wall continued its route from the north in Tulkarem to the south towards Qalqiliya and the construction began on the 5th of April 2002 and this led to the suffering of the Palestinians in all the aspects of their daily lives.

This wall was at the beginning made of electronic fence, and there's two roads on each side for Israeli jeeps. But there's also another kind of wall, which is the cement wall which is from 6–12 metres high depending on the areas. Secondly, we have a photo [displayed on screen] that shows the reality of the situation on the ground. The fertile Palestinian lands – and 40 days later we see the same land, the same region, after the entry of Israeli bulldozers that were building the route of the wall – and you see how much destruction these bulldozers had left behind for the Palestinian people and for Palestinian farmers.

Add to that the houses that have been demolished by the Israeli authorities, either partly or completely, and in one of these photos you can see a house that has been destroyed – half of it has been destroyed and the other half is where the family lives now. And the wall is 3 metres away from this house, or what's left of this house, and when the family opens the windows of this house they feel as if they were in a prison.

Adding to that you see a photo [on screen] showing the destruction and the death being spread by this wall. We see somebody killed for protesting against the demolition of his house; as well as attacking people who are resisting peacefully again the building of this wall – as we can see for protesters in [villages such as] Bil'in, in Na'lin.

The big problem is that this wall has effects on every aspect of our lives. In many regions, in many areas, Israel said – or pretended – that it's easy for farmers to have access to their land through doors that were built within the wall that the Israelis established. But these doors have a very particular system of functioning depending on the area.

For example, in the image you see [on screen] there is a particular system for us to access our lands and go back to our house. These doors are open only for half an hour in the morning and the farmers can then have access to their lands and they exert all their activities during the day, and they can harvest their lands. And then they have to have them on their hands and take them in boxes and put them next to this door, all day long, waiting for the moment where the Israeli jeep will come back in the evening to open (for half an hour) the doors again.

So this is the system being put in place by the Israelis and this led to cases of death, of suffering, of many farmers. During this period of this year, October or November, we have tens of thousands of farmers that go to their land to harvest the olives – and you know that the Palestinian people has millions of olive trees – and these farmers go there and stay there all day long. But with all of this activity, sometimes some of them fall from the trees, they can be sick or have problems or be wounded, for any reason they [may] need to return back to their homes – but they are not able to do that. They can only do it in the evening when the Israeli jeep allows them through opening the doors to go back to their homes and to their farms again.

We see in this system of walls, we believe this system is worse than the apartheid system in South Africa. This wall that will isolate 48 per cent of the land of the West Bank. We have the feeling that we're left into prison cells, cantons, bantustans. If we look into the image now [on-screen image comparing maps of Palestine with South Africa], what is remaining from the historical Palestine is 12 per cent and what was left for the black South Africans during the apartheid system was 13 per cent. The West Bank is divided into three cantons, isolated from each other, in South Africa we had 14 bantustans or cantons, and you can see in the images: the humiliation we endure in 600 checkpoints, as we could witness in South Africa when blacks were trying to go from one bantustan to another. The image below shows that we have the same practices. We see the martyrdom of our children when there are Israeli air strikes or attacks as we had in Gaza in 2004, and you have the same image of the death of children on their land in South Africa.

This system of walls makes us bear a heavy suffering and if you add to that the settlements within the West Bank, you have a very big suffering in the Palestinian lands and in the season of harvest, the settlers have been extremely violent. They uproot the olive trees; they wait for the Palestinians farmers, to steal what we have harvested; and sometimes they even prevent us from having access to our own farms, and sometimes we are obliged not to go to our farms and that is why the solidarity of international people is very important for us.

The issue of chemical plants is the biggest model we can give to the apartheid system we are describing. Especially because when we headed to the Israeli courts with the Israeli farmers, the response of the court was to say 'these chemical plants are in the West Bank, they are not in Israel.' And when the Israeli farmers went to the owners of the chemical plant directly, the owner of the plant said he was sorry for any damage resulting from the activity of the plant.

The reality is that in Palestine, the wind throughout the year goes towards the east but for forty days the wind goes towards the west – towards Israel. And the owner of the chemical plant said to the Israeli farmers, 'during the 40 days when the wind goes towards Israel, we will stop the activity of the chemical plant, to avoid polluting the winds. But throughout the year when the winds go towards the Palestinian territory, then the activity continues.' And this shows the mentality of apartheid, of discrimination, that we find in the Israeli authorities.

My farm is between the apartheid wall and the chemical plants and we have the feeling that they complete each other, that they are complementary in the same system; each side helping the other side to put pressure on us and to increase our suffering in order to expel us from our lands.

[On screen note: Recorded in Brussels on 15 November 2010]

Fayez al-Taneeb is coordinator of the Palestinian Farmers Union and part of Stop the Wall, Palestine.

*   *   *

The Situation in the Jordan Valley
Wael Natheef

The attack of Israeli settlers against Jerusalem is of increased recent concern. This has been represented by the acquisition of houses and the expulsion of Palestinian inhabitants from their homes, new racist laws (for example, the Jewish state laws), and the general Israeli policy of 'Judaising' Jerusalem.

The West Bank is 5.65 square km, with a population of about 2.4 million. The number of workers in the Palestinian territories is 755,900, and unemployment is at 28.6 per cent. There are 565,200 workers in the West Bank, among them 110,500 women while 190,000 working in the Gaza Strip – 23.200 of them women.

Unemployment in the West Bank is 21.1 per cent or 151,000; in the Gaza Strip, the figure is 44.3 per cent: 151,900 unemployed.

Due to economic and social reasons, 41,000 children, aged 7–17, are workers. Research shows that the highest percentage of unemployment is among young people aged 19–29, at 31 per cent. The total number of graduates in 2007 and 2008 was 25,275.

The 2010 statistics indicated that one person out of five suffers from poverty: 15.5 per cent in the West Bank and 33.2 per cent in the Gaza Strip. Research shows that 7.5 per cent of people in the West Bank and 20 per cent in Gaza suffer from extreme poverty. Poverty rates are higher in larger families.

COLONIES IN THE WEST BANK

There are 440 Israeli colonies in the West Bank; this number includes settlements, outposts and external outposts. The number of settlers in the West Bank (including occupied East Jerusalem) is about 500,000. Five hundred kilometres of the separation wall has already been constructed; 99 per cent of the wall is constructed on the lands of the West Bank, which was occupied in 1967. When the wall is completed, it will be 810 km long.

In parallel with this, there are 565 checkpoints: 65 controlled by soldiers full time, and 22 part time, as well as 410 barricades and trenches and 80 gates in the wall that are only open part-time. There are also about 300 flying checkpoints.

The West Bank has suffered from attacks by settlers – operating under the protection of the Israeli army – including the following:

- Destruction of olive groves in villages in the Nablus and Ramallah areas
- Pollution of olive trees at Deir al-Hatab village with sewage water generated by the Elon Moreh settlement in the Nablus region
- Burning the holy Quran in Hosan and Nablus mosques
- Burning of the school library in al-Sawiah girls' school
- Attacking olive pickers in Bureen village by settlers from Bracha
- Attacking peaceful marches organised by Palestinians and supporters.

THE PALESTINIAN RIFT VALLEY

The Palestinian rift valley is located on the eastern side of the West Bank and extends from the Jericho region north to the Tubas region, and is 68.5 km long. From the coast of the Dead Sea in the east, to the western slopes of Tubas and Jericho in the west, the valley is 24 km in width. The Jordan River valley occupies 840 square km, 14.9 per cent of the total West Bank. This includes the regions of Jericho, which is inhabited by 42,320 people in 14 local communities, and of Tubas, which is inhabited by 50,260 in 21 local communities. Due to the fertility of its soil, ample supply of groundwater and good weather, the Jordan Valley is regarded as the main source of agricultural products in the West Bank; this area is also rich with livestock. All these factors offer good incomes in local and international markets.

There are 400,000 dunams of arable lands in this area, 50,000 of which is cultivated (one dunam is 1,000 square metres). Ten springs produce 32.5 million cubic metres water generation annually. There are 140 drilling wells, but there are 87 operated wells, with 13 million cubic metres annual water generation. The Israeli settlements use 80 per cent of the available water.

THE SETTLEMENT OUTPOSTS

Betweenn 1996 and 2009, settlers constructed 32 outposts in the eastern separation area, where the outposts are regarded as branches of the core settlements. Usually, a settlement begins with mobile caravans.

Since 1967, Israel has constructed 133 military bases to protect settlements. These occupy 33.2 square kilometres. We can conclude that settlements, outposts and military bases added more hindrance to Palestinian society, making a real threat to the Palestinians' way of life.

CLOSURE POLICY

The closure policy and the military checkpoints in the Jordan River Rift Valley are complementary to the racial isolation policy in the eastern area in order to clamp down on citizens and forcing them to leave to acquire their lands. Israel has done the following:

- Established 35 military roadblocks on main entrances that link the Rift Valley with the rest of the West Bank, as well as setting up roadblocks on entrances linking Palestinian communities.
- Dug a series of trenches from the north of the valley down to the middle.
- Isolated thousands of agricultural dunams and prevented farmers from reaching their lands.

- Prevented livestock farmers from using their agricultural lands and pastures.
- Destroyed homes.
- Uprooted trees.
- Restricted the movement of farmers in the region through checkpoints.
- Dumped industrial wastes (from Vered Yeriho settlement) that pollute soil and groundwater.
- Opened the Ar al-Jiftlik dumping site, where 200 tons of solid waste are buried there daily, leading to soil and underground water pollution.
- For 'security reasons', banned the use of some fertilisers.

LABOUR CONDITIONS IN ISRAEL

Palestinian workers in Israel face difficult circumstances, and are exploited; they are often deceived by Israeli employers, and many are forced to sleep rough.

There are several settlement industrial zones: Mishor Adumim near Jericho, one near Tulkarem and Ma'ale Afrayam near Nablus.

Palestinian workers in both Israel and the settlements receive low salaries, tough work conditions and a lack of safety and tools. The settlement industrial zones have a negative effect on the Palestinian environment through disposal of industrial waste on Palestinian lands.

Conditions of Palestinian Workers in the Industrial Zones

There are 24 Israeli settlements in the Jordan River Rift Valley, and two of them are industrial. In Mishor Adumim industrial zone, there are 8,000 workers from the West Bank and 800–1,000 from Jericho, 300 of whom are women. There are 155 factories for plastic, food, chemical, and mining industries. Workers are paid 10 NIS per hour and they work eight hours per day. There are also a hundred workers in Dead Sea tourism.

Conditions of Palestinian Workers in the Agricultural Settlements

Altogether, there are 7,000 Palestinians working in agriculture settlements in the Jordan River Rift Valley, 4,000 from Jericho and 3,000 workers from the Tubas region; 35 per cent are women, and 5 per cent are children under 17. The number increases during the date and grape-picking season (from July to October).

Most agricultural labourers work without any documentation, earning between 60–70 NIS daily for 7–8 working hours. They climb palm trees or work in greenhouses, often without any safety equipment. The Israeli minimum wage law is not applied. Some settlements have installed fingerprint machines to check workers at the entrance of settlements.

Israeli Export Company Agrexco

There are many Israeli companies working on marketing of Rift Valley settlement products, such as vegetables, roses, herbs, grapes and dates. The Israeli export company Agrexco exports these products. The main transport hub and refrigeration facility is in al-Jiftlik. From there, products are transferred to be exported by plane or ship. In the summer of 2010, Agrexco started using a new export label: 'Israel, West Bank settlement'. There is a blackout on the activities of Agrexco and its way of working in the Jordan Valley.

Wael Natheef is general secretary of the Jericho branch of the Palestinian General Federation of Trade Unions, Palestine.

*   *   *

Veolia Environnement SA
Adri Nieuwhof

In Barcelona, the Russell Tribunal on Palestine found states of the European Union in violation of international law by tolerating illegal European commercial operations in the Occupied Palestinian Territories (OPT), including the Jordan Valley Tovlan landfill site and the East Jerusalem Light Rail construction. French multinational company Veolia Environnement SA plays a key role in the Jerusalem Light Rail, in the Tovlan landfill site and in bus services to settlements.

One way of holding Veolia to account in Europe is for public bodies to lawfully exclude Veolia from bidding for public contracts, or reject bids because of the company's commercial operations in the OPT. Article 45 of EU Directive 2004/18/EC of the European Parliament and of the Council of 31 March 2004 on the coordination of procedures for the award of public works contracts contains the power to exclude 'economic operators' on the grounds of the 'personal situation of the candidate or tenderer'. Specifically, Article

45 (2)(d) allows this where the individual or organisation 'has been guilty of grave professional misconduct proven by any means which the contracting authorities can demonstrate'. All 27 member states will therefore have local laws which enable them to exclude Veolia on this basis.

THE JERUSALEM LIGHT RAIL PROJECT

The Jerusalem Light Rail project will connect West Jerusalem with a number of illegal Israeli settlements in and around occupied (and illegally annexed) East Jerusalem. The Light Rail is designed as part of the 'Jerusalem Transportation Master Plan' sponsored by the Israeli government and the Jerusalem municipality of March 1996.[9]

In 2002, the City Pass consortium, consisting of Alstom, Veolia Transport, Bank Hapoalim, Bank Leumi and two other Israeli companies, won a tender of the Israeli government for the building, maintenance and running of the Jerusalem Light Rail, as well as for the manufacture of tramway cars and signals. When City Pass and Veolia Transport signed a contract in 2005, Veolia obtained a 5 per cent share in the City Pass consortium and the right to operate the service. As an operator, Veolia will be responsible for the day-to-day operational functions of the system, including customer service, service planning, ticketing and fare collections, and track control. On the occasion of the signing of the contract, then Prime Minister Ariel Sharon said the Light Rail would 'sustain Jerusalem for eternity as the capital of the Jewish people, the united capital of the State of Israel'.[10]

Although Veolia tried to abandon the project in 2009, it will play a key role in the tramway project. In 2009, Veolia tried to sell 49 per cent of its contract with the City Pass consortium to the Israeli transport company Dan Bus, but the deal did not materialise. In October 2010, Veolia reached in principle a new agreement with Israeli transport company Egged on the sale of 80 per cent of its shares in the contract with City Pass. The shares will be gradually transferred to Egged over a five-year period from the first day of the Light Rail's operation. Egged will also pay increasing percentages of the sale as the Light Rail becomes increasingly profitable.

The first line of the tramway was due to open in the spring of 2011 and will link the illegal settlements of Pizgat Ze'ev and French Hill with West Jerusalem. A station at Ammunition Hill will operate as a feeder station for traffic from Ma'ale Adumim, a large Israeli settlement in the West Bank, and Israeli settlements in the Jordan Valley. It is intended that the system will be extended to link the illegal settlements of Neve Yaacov and Gilo to West Jerusalem. The tramway will reinforce the permanence of those illegal settlements and contribute to the expansion of new settlements.

All the settlements to be served by the tramway are on the Israeli side of the wall which has been built to separate the settlements from the West Bank and the Palestinian-populated areas of East Jerusalem. The tramway therefore reinforces the process of incorporation by Israel of the settlements and the sections of the OPT between the wall and the Green Line into Israel.

The construction of the tramway involves the confiscation of Palestinian land and extensive damage to the roadway on which the tracks have been laid. For example, in Shu'fat, the station is built on 2,000 sq. m of land belonging to resident Mahmoud al-Mashni. More of his land will be confiscated for the parking lot next to the station.

The Palestine Liberation Organization (PLO) objected to the tramway and Veolia's involvement in the project. On 11 July 2001, the PLO stated in a press release that the project 'harms the Palestinian population and its rights to self-determination'.[11] In 2007, the PLO and the Association France Palestine Solidarité (AFPS) took Veolia to court in France, calling for nullification of Veolia's contract with the City Pass consortium. In November 2009, Dr Rafiq Husseini, director-general of the office of the president of the Palestinian Authority, called on Arab states to cease doing business with the companies involved in the tramway.[12]

In a letter to the Russell Tribunal on Palestine, Veolia claims it has 'sought at all times to obey International Law'. However, Veolia Transport wrote me a letter in response to my criticism. The company stated that they would seek 'independent legal opinions in order to increase our understanding of the situation'. Veolia contracted with Ove Bring, Professor Emeritus of International Law of Stockholm University and the Swedish National Defence College, for advice. Professor Bring informed Veolia that due to Israel's illegal occupation, the presumption is that the Light Rail project was also illegal.[13]

VEOLIA BUS SERVICES TO SETTLEMENTS

In addition to Veolia's involvement in the Jerusalem Light Rail, Connex, another wholly owned subsidiary of Veolia Transport, operates two bus route (routes 109 and 110), connecting Israeli communities in Israel to illegal Israeli settlements in the West Bank, including Beit Horon and Givat Ze'ev. Just like the Light Rail, the bus routes reinforce the process of incorporation of the settlements. Furthermore, Connex operates the services on a discriminatory basis: they are Israeli-only services. Palestinians who reside in the West Bank are not allowed to use the routes.[14]

Figure 2.2   Connex, an Israeli subsidiary of Veolia, operates bus routes to illegal West Bank settlements. Palestinians are barred from using them. Courtesy Anne Paq/ Activestills.org.

Discrimination Against Palestinians

Veolia's activities in the OPT are directly discriminatory in that they offer services exclusively to Israelis and not to Palestinians living under Israeli occupation. The two bus routes mentioned above are directly discriminatory because they are Israeli-only services. The tramway will be indirectly discriminatory in that it does not take into account the possible needs of the Palestinian people, because it was designed to serve mainly the Israeli settlers. Statements by City Pass consortium spokesperson Ammon Elian reveals that the project will entrench the status quo situation of segregation. In April 2009, he told Belgian researcher Karolien van Dyck, 'If Palestinians would want to make use of the light rail, both groups

will not meet on the train, because of their different life patterns.'
According to Elian, the existence of the network of buses used
by Palestinians made integration of Palestinian residents in the
tramline 'redundant'.[15]

Palestinians will not be able to access and use the tramline because
the prices will be significantly higher than local bus routes. The fare
will be the Israeli shekel equivalent of about $1.37, which most
Israelis in the settlements can afford. By contrast, the bus fare on the
service used by Palestinians is equivalent to about 82 cents. Almost
all Palestinians are likely to remain on the bus service and ignore
the tram. In any event, virtually all the stops planned on the route
are to illegally colonised 'Israeli areas' (going east and west), with
the exception of one stop at the Palestinian suburb of Shu'fat, and
as such will be of no value to Palestinians. Why would a Palestinian
in Shu'fat get on the tram there when it goes only to Jewish areas
east and west?

The discriminatory policies of City Pass consortium (in which
Veolia Transport participates) appeared in a survey among
residents of Jerusalem. City Pass asked residents whether they
were comfortable with the tramline including stops in Palestinian
neighbourhoods of occupied East Jerusalem, and whether they
were bothered by both Jews and Arabs entering freely 'without
undergoing a security check'. Even Israeli officials described the
questions as 'racist'.[16]

In addition, Veolia's recruitment policies for the Light Rail
are another example of discrimination against Palestinians. An
advertisement for new staff was broadcast on Israeli television in
August 2010; it cited the completion of Israeli military service duty,
and knowledge of Hebrew and English as job requirements. These
criteria effectively mean that Palestinian job seekers are excluded,
because Palestinian Israelis are rarely allowed to serve in the Israeli
army. Furthermore, Arabic (an official language in Israel) is not
included as a requirement.[17] This discriminatory employment
policy is illegal, also under Israeli laws. Veolia was criticised, and
denounced the televised advertisement immediately, but it remained
for some time on Veolia's website in Hebrew.

In some countries, these race discrimination issues may be
another basis for Veolia to be excluded from contracts, quite
apart from the 'grave misconduct' provisions. Lawyers need to
give consideration to this.

THE TOVLAN LANDFILL IN THE PALESTINIAN JORDAN VALLEY

Tovlan landfill site is located beside the Jordan River in the OPT. Onyx, a subsidiary of Veolia Waste Management, is contracted to operate the site. The Tovlan site was established in 1999 and serves at least five illegal Israeli settlements. Veolia Waste Management stated that the site also serves the Palestinian town of Nablus. However, in reality, Palestinians' use of the site is highly restricted due to the number of Israeli check points which need to be crossed in order to access the site, and the high fees charged to dump waste at the site. Although Veolia claimed that Tovlan landfill was no longer in use, the company's trucks have been observed picking up waste from the settlements of Tomer and Massua in the Jordan Valley.[18,19]

GRAVE MISCONDUCT

Veolia has signed the UN Global Compact, thus committing itself to support and respect the protection of international human rights and to ensure that the company is not complicit in human rights abuses. However, by building and maintaining the Jerusalem Light Rail, by operating Israeli-only bus routes in the OPT, and by operating the Tovlan landfill in the OPT, Veolia is facilitating Israel's breaches of the Fourth Geneva Convention, including grave breaches, and is complicit in its perpetuation of those breaches. In other words, Veolia is aiding and abetting on-going war crimes. It is also facilitating, exacerbating, aiding and abetting Israel's breach of the Hague Regulations. Furthermore, it is discriminating on the grounds of race and/or religion in the provision of its services. As such, there can be no doubt that Veolia is guilty of 'grave misconduct' in relation to its activities in Israel and the OPT.

European states, and by extension their public bodies, are required under article 1 of the Fourth Geneva Convention to 'respect and ensure respect for the present Convention in all circumstances' and under article 146(3) IVGC to take all measures necessary for the suppression of all (non-grave) breaches of that Convention. Moreover, all public bodies have the responsibility to protect against human rights abuses by transnational corporations and to formulate policies which ensure transnational corporations respect human rights.[20] Therefore corporations implicated in human rights abuses and violations of international humanitarian law should not be rewarded with public contracts in Europe.

Adri Nieuwhof is an independent consultant and human rights advocate from the Netherlands.

TRANSCRIPT OF JURY Q&A: ADRI NIEUWHOF

Anthony Gifford QC: ... the tribunal has written to this and other companies and institutions who may be criticised, and when they write, their letters must be given due recognition [Veolia's letter is in Appendix 2]. There was one other sentence that I wanted to ask you about, in the second-last paragraph, after talking about the changes making the project ever more complex and polemical. They say this: 'at the same time Veolia has been approached by a transport company and has decided to initiate the divestiture ... ' (it means 'getting out of it') '... the divestiture of its interests in the project, subject to fulfilling its contractual obligations'. I'm glad it's back on screen so you can see the full subtlety of that sentence. But I would like to know whether you feel that this is the beginning of at least a partial victory? Or whether it is just going to mean that the project is taken over by somebody else?

Adri Nieuwhof: I would say that Veolia tries to sell-off its shares in City Pass consortium, and its contracts. Because it has become a burden to them. You know the actions in Europe [that is, successful boycott and divestment campaigns] ... They have lost contracts, their image is damaged. So I can imagine they want to get out of it. There was a deal in principle last year with [Israeli public transport company] Dan Bus and it didn't go through. And this time it is with Egged, another Israeli company. I don't think any European company wishes to take over Veolia's shares because they know what would happen. That's, at least, what we made clear. And with Egged the deal is that they will take over the 5 per cent ownership on the consortium and the shares into the contract to run and operate the Light Rail but over a period of five years. And, if I am correct ... when the Light Rail in these five years becomes more profitable they will receive more money for the shares. So they are in it for five years, at least.

Michael Mansfield QC: ... Just on that paragraph Tony's been asking you about: do we have any idea who the transport company is? Because I am very suspicious of companies who have subsidiaries and they have a veil and in fact it may not be an independent transport company – it may be part of their group. Do you know anything about that?

AN: It's Egged and it is separate ... .

MM: It's separate?

AN: Yea, it's not linked to Veolia, no. And it is not a cover up.

MM: Right. In the first paragraph it ends with this sentence: 'We have always made it very clear that unless there was to be equal access by all, we would withdraw from the project.' Now, that's quite plainly not happened ...

AN: Yes.

MM: They must have known that it was not happening, so where is there any public statement by this company that that was a precondition for their involvement?

AN: I haven't read it, but they came up with this argument when the pressure increased. They said: we adhere to our principles of non-discrimination and they will be implemented also in the Jerusalem Light Rail. But I don't know if it was a precondition on the contract. I would say that it was not. Because I think Veolia didn't realise ... It's quite amazing for such a big company, but they did not realise what type of project they were entering in. And one could argue that the French government maybe pushed them quite a bit to take on these contracts.

*   *   *

THE ACTIONS OF CEMENT ROADSTONE HOLDINGS (CRH) IN ISRAEL/PALESTINE
John Dorman

Ladies and gentlemen of the tribunal jury, good afternoon. My name is John Dorman. I am a human rights activist based in Dublin. I am the divestment officer of the Ireland-Palestine Solidarity Campaign.[21]

Today, I am here to speak about an Irish construction materials company called CRH plc. It is my intention to draw several issues to the attention of this tribunal jury. It is my submission that CRH plc are in breach of the international guidelines on corporate responsibility. Furthermore, I intend to convince the jury that they are guilty of complicity with Israel's breaches of international law. In that regard, I will discuss the following issues.

First, I will outline the nature of CRH's involvement with the settlement industry and construction of the illegal separation wall in the Occupied Palestinian Territories. I will identify why CRH activities are complicit with Israel's breaches of international law. Secondly, I will discuss two important internationally accepted frameworks on corporate responsibility. I will identify how CRH have failed the corporate responsibilities set out in these guidelines. Finally, I will outline the nature of CRH's own Code of Business Conduct.[22] I will identify their failure to comply with their own guidelines on ethics, responsible business strategy and the respect for human rights.

To begin, I will give the jury a brief background to CRH plc itself. CRH is an international diversified building materials group with operations in 35 countries worldwide. CRH are Ireland's largest company quoted on the stock exchange. In 2009, the company recorded sales of over €17 billion and recorded profits of €598 million net.[23]

In 2001, CRH purchased 25 per cent of the Israeli company Mashav Initiative and Development Ltd. The Clal Group own the remaining 75 per cent. Mashav wholly own Nesher Israel Cement Enterprises Ltd. Nesher are Israel's sole cement producer,[24] supplying 75–90 per cent of all cement sold in Israel and the Occupied Palestinian Territories.

The use of Nesher cement has been well documented[25] across many construction sites in the West Bank settlements, their infrastructure and in the construction of the Jerusalem Light Rail in illegally annexed East Jerusalem. In 2004, CRH admitted to Amnesty International that 'in all probability'[26] their subsidiary's cement was being used in the construction of the wall.

Furthermore, the Mashav Group, through its subsidiary Nesher, has several other subsidiaries extensively involved in a broad range of construction activities.[27] Nesher own 50 per cent of Ta'avura, who wholly own Tastit Construction Machinery. Tastit are the sole importers of Liebherr excavators and cranes, which have been documented destroying Palestinian farms and olive groves to enable the construction of the illegal separation wall.[28]

Figure 2.3   Nesher cement being used to build an illegal Israeli settlement in the West Bank. Courtesy Anne Kennedy, Project Clean Hands.

These activities facilitate the continued ethnic cleansing of Palestinians from their land and the expansion of Israel's colonial project in Occupied Palestine.

The construction of the settlements and their infrastructure is contrary to several Articles of the Fourth Geneva Convention. These constitute breaches of international humanitarian law. The International Court of Justice reaffirmed this in the 2004 advisory opinion on the legality of the separation wall and the settlements.[29]

The impact of the separation wall,[30] the settlements and their infrastructure on the Palestinian people are contrary to basic rights enshrined in the Universal Declaration of Human Rights[31] and subsequently breach many provisions of international human rights law.[32]

Some of these breaches of international law by Israel constitute war crimes and crimes against humanity. CRH, through their part-ownership of Mashav are complicit with these violations of international law.

In 2006, the Divestment Task Force of the New England Conference of the United Methodist Church wrote to CRH expressing their concerns that the company's activities 'support in a significant way the Israeli occupation of Palestinian territories'.[33] CRH's response was that they had no control over the end-use of their products and that they could not discriminate who they sold their product to. This did not satisfy the task force's ethical criteria and the Church subsequently placed CRH on their divestment list.

In March 2010, the Ireland-Palestine Solidarity Campaign wrote to the chief executive and board of directors of CRH requesting that CRH support and respect the protection of internationally proclaimed human rights within the company's sphere of influence.

This letter illustrated the nature of the human rights abuses which are occurring in the Occupied Palestinian Territories and the nature of CRH's complicity with these abuses. It also put the company on notice of that complicity and invited them to divest from Mashav.

In response, CRH claimed that they were aware of their responsibilities to respect human rights but washed their hands of any responsibility for their subsidiaries' activities. It is our submission that CRH are fully aware of their complicity and continue to ignore and evade responsibility for it.

They continue to ignore the requests of human rights and church organisations to divest from Mashav. At this stage, it seems that the only way of encouraging CRH to divest from Mashav is by raising public awareness of CRH's illegal activities and to encourage state, church, financial and other investors to divest from CRH.

As a result, the IPSC have instigated a global CRH divestment campaign. We welcome the decisions by both the United Methodist Church and the Dutch ethical bank ASN to divest CRH from their pension funds.

INTERNATIONAL NORMS ON CORPORATE RESPONSIBILITY

I now refer to the two key international frameworks on corporate responsibility. I will focus primarily on the United Nations 'Protect, Respect and Remedy' Framework for Business and Human Rights[34] and make reference to the OECD Guidelines for Multinational Enterprises.[35]

In 2005, the Secretary General of the United Nations appointed Professor John Ruggie of Harvard University as his special representative to clarify the roles and responsibilities of states, corporations and other social actors in business and human rights spheres.

In June 2008, Ruggie presented his report outlining a framework for business and human rights to the United Nations Human Rights

Council. He identifies three key principles which outline the duties and responsibilities which must be addressed in order to maintain and ensure compliance with national and international laws.

The first of these principles is the 'State's duty to protect against human rights abuses committed by third parties, including business'. This highlights that states have a primary role in preventing and addressing corporate-related human rights abuses.

The second principle is the 'corporate responsibility to respect human rights which require business to act with due diligence to avoid infringing the rights of others'. The company's responsibility to respect human rights 'applies across its business activities and through its relationship with third parties connected with those activities'. This implies that there is a direct corporate responsibility to comply with national and international law in respecting human rights.

In order to discharge this responsibility, the company must engage in due diligence to 'prevent and address adverse human rights impacts'. Due diligence consists of positive action by the company to ensure that their business conduct does not contribute to human rights abuses. Companies should assess the risk of human rights abuses in countries where they operate on an individual basis and tailor their policies accordingly. They should assess what contribution their operations, whether as producers, service providers, or employers, may make to human rights abuses.

Complicity amounts to an indirect breach of human rights by the company through their action, inaction, or association with the acts of third parties. Due diligence is required to prevent complicity.

Ruggie's third principle is that companies must implement effective grievance mechanisms and access to remedies. The corporate responsibility to respect human rights requires a mechanism for the remedy of the breach of those rights. The responsibility lies with both the company and the state to ensure that an effective grievance procedure, whether judicial or non-judicial, exists.

The second framework is 'The OECD Guidelines for Multinational Enterprises'.

The guidelines are recommendations by governments covering all major areas of business ethics, including corporate steps to obey the law, observe internationally recognised standards and respond to other societal expectations.

Two of the key policies state 'that enterprises should respect the human rights of those affected by their activities consistent with the host government's international obligations and commitments', and that they should 'Encourage, where practicable, business partners, including suppliers and sub-contractors, to apply principles of corporate conduct compatible with the Guidelines'.[36]

It is my submission that CRH have failed and neglected to comply with the UN framework and the OECD guidelines. They are guilty of failure to implement business practices which respect international law in accordance with the due diligence process.

CRH have been put on full notice of their complicity with these human rights abuses. They have full knowledge of the nature of these abuses and have failed to take positive action to prevent complicity. CRH have failed, and continue to fail, in their corporate responsibility to protect against human rights abuses in their business dealings. Their action and inaction makes a direct contribution to the perpetration of human rights abuses against the Palestinian people.

CRH AND THEIR CODE OF BUSINESS CONDUCT

That brings me to my third and final submission in relation to CRH's own 'Code of Business Conduct.[37] This code of conduct claims to ensure that 'CRH has in place clear guidelines on business conduct and ethical behaviour'.

However, it is my submission that in fact CRH's code of business conduct fails to address these issues in relation to their investment in the Mashav Group. In line with John Ruggie's recommendations, CRH have a responsibility to assess the particular risks associated with operations in particular parts of the world. CRH's code of business conduct fails to do so.

The code maintains that CRH 'supports the United Nations Universal Declaration of Human Rights in so far it is applicable to our companies', and that 'The Group respects the protection of human rights within our areas of influence.' However, the code does not address the risk of breaches of human rights through investments such as their part-ownership of the Israeli company, Mashav Limited.

While CRH profits from their subsidiary's activities in the West Bank, they continue to maintain that they are a company who protect human rights. Clearly, this is not the case.

It is submitted that CRH's failure to address these issues amounts to a breach of their guidelines and ethical code. CRH cannot continue to promote themselves as an ethically sound organization unless these issues are addressed.

Meanwhile their complicity continues. I call on the tribunal to urge the Irish government to hold to account CRH for their complicity with Israel's illegal actions. I call on the tribunal to take action against CRH's unethical business conduct and irresponsible investment. I call on this tribunal to take action against CRH's complicity, where they have failed to take action themselves. I call on the tribunal to make findings of guilt in relation to CRH's complicity with Israel's violations of international law in the Occupied Palestinian Territories.

Finally, I call upon the tribunal to support the call for CRH to divest from the Israeli company Mashav Initiative and Development Ltd. Thank you for allowing me the opportunity to highlight the shameful complicity of this Irish company with Israel's violations of international law.

John Dorman is divestment officer for the Ireland-Palestine Solidarity Campaign.

TRANSCRIPT OF JURY Q&A: JOHN DORMAN

Anthony Gifford QC: We wrote – the foundation wrote to CRS [*sic*: CRH], as it did to all companies, inviting their participation. As you've heard, Veolia have replied in writing. CRS – I will be corrected if I'm wrong – we've received nothing. We invite CRS if they are listening over the internet to these proceedings to submit anything they wish to say in comment or in response to what John Dorman has said to this tribunal before it completes its deliberations. On the same theme, I just wanted to ask John whether he had – he or his organisation had any response from CRS to the letter they wrote in March of this year or indeed whether he is aware of any other statement by CRS in response to these charges that are made against them.

John Dorman: Yes they did respond, and they responded in much the same manner as they responded to the United Methodist Church, saying that they can't discriminate against any group who they sell their cement to. That's the essence of their answer. And then they would also make reference to Ruggie, I think in part because we made reference to Ruggie, and were very selective in the response to that. But we would still put it back in their court that they have an obligation in terms of due diligence: they know what's happening there, they know where the cement is going, they know that they're making profits, and they shouldn't be there.

Michael Mansfield QC: ... I think you said that there are two directors of this Irish company that are also on the board of one of the Israeli companies, and in fact I think the company you named – unless I misheard you – was Mashav. Or are they also directors of another subsidiary Nesher?

JD: My understanding is that they have two directors on the board of Nesher because Mashav is a holding group, so then they are entitled – they have a 25 per cent stake so they're entitled to have two board directors.

MM: Right: so the question of, first of all, knowledge is not just a general question of they will have read it in a newspaper. They are actually sitting on the board of one of the companies that is in fact manufacturing the cement.

JD: That's correct.

MM: So either they do actually know or should know, so there's no question about that. Is that right?

JD: That's correct.

MM: Now, second question: do we know who those two directors are?

JD: We do.

MM: And could you kindly name them please?

JD: [laughs] I'm sorry I don't have the names to hand, but I do know who they are and I can supply you with that information [he later named them as: John Madden and Máirtín MacAodha].

MM: Would you be kind enough to let us know who they are. If they're watching, they'll know who they are, and ... we would be very grateful for any response from them. But just going on from the question of knowledge, it also can be readily inferred if they're sitting actually on the board of the company taking these decisions, that they have a management and control role.

JD: Absolutely.

MM: Right. Now I want to just pursue it a little further. Have there been in Ireland any challenges to this situation either at the level of the Irish government or the company itself? Legal challenges.

JD: No there haven't. And some members of the Irish parliament, the Dáil, have raised questions about CRH and their activities in Israel and the Occupied Palestinian Territories. And interestingly enough the response that comes back from the minister is ... it's like he is taking a press release from CRH itself.

MM: Well in that context, and I hope everyone here will forgive me for a moment, one of the most – you've mentioned it in passing, that is the ICJ, or World Court, decision on the wall in 2004. Now that was a dramatic watershed decision that not only held that there were severe breaches of human rights law and international humanitarian law, an overwhelming judgement 13-to-1. There is a particular paragraph that I'm going to cite so the company if they are listening can go back and have a look at it themselves. It's paragraph 159 of their judgment, and it brings in the Irish government as well as the company itself, and the guidelines you've mentioned ...

> Given the character and the importance of the rights and obligations involved, the Court is of the view that all States are under an obligation not to recognize the illegal situation resulting from the construction of the wall in the Occupied Palestinian Territory, including in and around East Jerusalem. They are also under an obligation not to render aid or assistance in maintaining the situation created by such construction. It is also for all States, while respecting the United Nations Charter and international law, to see to it that any impediment, resulting from the construction of the wall, to the exercise by the Palestinian people of its right to self-determination is brought to an end.

It goes on. Now, those are fairly clear terms are they not?

JD: They are, yeah.

MM: Right. Now, the first thing at one level is: has there been any approach to the ICC or any other international organisation or tribunal, to be precise, to in fact see if this can be carried through in the case of the Irish government?

JD: Not that I'm aware of.

MM: Right, so we could be in a position to petition the ICC to have a look at this. Since, in fact, it's the ICJ who are passing judgment on this. The second thing is of course that the Irish government under this have a very clear obligation, and they plainly haven't fulfilled it, so the second level is we could petition the Irish government to get on with it straight away. No question about that: that's their obligation.

JD: Yes.

MM: And of course they – if they are listening to this internet broadcast, or any part of them are listening to this or get to hear of it, they could take action in the way the Dutch government did in an entirely separate case. In other words, tomorrow morning they could raid the offices of this company and confiscate their computers. Is that right?

JD: Yeah. And I'd certainly encourage it. [Audience laughs.]

3
Trade and Labelling of Israeli Settlement Goods

Production and Trade of Settlement Produce: Unlawful Exploitation of Natural Resources in the Occupied Palestinian Territories

Salma Karmi-Ayyoub

INTRODUCTION

The production and trade in settlement produce raises many different legal issues under international, EU and domestic law. Products that are manufactured inside settlements in the West Bank (from raw materials that originate outside of the OPT) raise different legal issues to those involving the extraction of resources from the West Bank. Private and state actors are involved in the trade, and differing legal standards and norms are applied to each.

I will focus on individual/corporate responsibility for the production and trade in settlement goods and will address: (i) whether the production and trade of settlement goods that involves the extraction of natural resources from the West Bank amounts to the war crime of pillage; and (ii) whether those responsible for the trade in settlement goods could be considered to be 'aiding and abetting' the transfer of parts of Israel's civilian population to the West Bank.

The legal framework is international humanitarian law, in particular the Fourth Geneva Convention of 1949 and the Hague Regulations of 1907, which regulate the behaviour of the Occupying Power, Israel, in the OPT and protect property against unlawful appropriation (see the ICJ's 'Wall Opinion' for applicability of the Fourth Geneva Convention and the Hague Regulations to the Occupied Palestinian Territory).

THE PROHIBITION AGAINST PILLAGE

Article 33 of the Fourth Geneva Convention and Articles 28 and 47 of the Hague Regulations prohibit pillage. Pillage is defined as the appropriation of private or public property (in the context of an armed conflict or occupation) without lawful basis or legal justification (*The Prosecutor* v *Milan Martic*, Trial Judgment, ICTY, para. 102).

The elements of the crime of pillage are: (1) the appropriation of property by the perpetrator (2) without the consent of the owner (3) without justification under the Hague Regulations (4) in the context of and associated with an armed conflict.[1]

'Appropriation' includes the direct appropriation of property (for example, the taking/extraction of resources). Appropriation can also be indirect, through the receipt or purchase of unlawfully appropriated property by others (see, for instance, the Nuremberg cases of *Wili Buch*, *IG Farben*, *Krupp*, *Roechling*).

The property must be appropriated without the consent of the owner. Ownership of the property must therefore be determined. Natural resources are often owned by the state. The customary international law concept of permanent sovereignty over resources (for example, see the ICJ case *DRC* v *Uganda*) might also be relevant in cases in which peoples and/or states have an unrealised right to self-determination over the territory of the resources. The lack of the consent of the owner of the property must be established. Consent achieved through coercion is not consent.

In cases of state-owned immovable property (which natural resources often are considered to be),[2] the requirement is to establish that the resource was extracted in breach of the rules of usufruct, rather that without the consent of the owner (see below).

The appropriation must be committed in the context of and in association with an armed conflict (or occupation). This has been interpreted to mean 'closely related' to an armed conflict, meaning where the armed conflict plays a substantial role in the ability to commit the crime, the decision to commit the crime, the manner in which the crime is committed, or the purpose for which the crime is committed (*Prosecutor* v *Kunarac et al.*, Appeal Judgment, ICTY).

The mental element needed for pillage will depend on the jurisdiction that prosecutes the offence. As a general rule, the perpetrator would have to have acted with intent and knowledge, that is, the perpetrator would have to mean to appropriate the property in the knowledge that the owner does not consent to the appropriation (or in cases involving usufruct, in the knowledge that the rules of usufruct have been breached). In some jurisdictions, the lesser mental element of subjective recklessness/indirect intent – in which the perpetrator appropriates the property perceiving the risk that the owner does not consent/aware the owner probably does not consent – may well also suffice (*Martic Trial Judgment*). In addition, the perpetrator must be aware of the factual circumstances establishing the existence of an armed conflict or occupation.

THE RULE OF USUFRUCT

Natural resources of an occupied territory are usually regarded as state-owned immovable property. The Occupying Power is only allowed to act as the administrator and usufructuary of such property (Article 55, Hague Regulations).

Traditionally, this meant that an occupant was able to exploit and consume the fruit from an occupied orchard on condition that the value of the trees and land was preserved. Changes to the character and nature of the property are prohibited. There have been contradictory applications of the rules of usufruct to the exploitation of natural resources in occupied territory. Generally speaking the position is that if an Occupying Power is to exploit natural resources, the proceeds must be applied to the expenses of the occupation, meaning the needs of the local population (*DRC* v *Uganda*, ICJ, 2005). The proceeds must not be applied to finance the general war effort or to enrich the civilian economy of the Occupying Power (for example, the *Bataafsche Petroleum* case).

SELF-DETERMINATION

The principle of self-determination in economic matters, which includes the right to dispose freely of natural resources, also informs the ability of an Occupying Power to exploit the natural resources of occupied territory. It suggests that the exploitation must not be carried out in a way that divests the people of the occupied territory of the effective exercise of their right to self-determination (see, for example, Article 16 of the Charter of Economic Rights and Duties of States of 1974). The concept is particularly important in the case of Israel's prolonged occupation of the OPT, in which the exploitation of natural resources is creating permanent changes to the territory and preventing the Palestinian people from using and benefiting from their natural resources.

CRIMINAL RESPONSIBILITY OF CORPORATIONS FOR PILLAGE

It is generally accepted that private persons, including corporate officers, can commit war crimes. Under international law, companies themselves cannot currently be prosecuted for the commission of crimes. In certain domestic legal systems (for example, Holland and the UK), it is possible to prosecute companies for crimes, but it will still be necessary to establish that certain persons within the companies committed certain acts. The way in which individual criminal responsibility is attributed for the commission of war crimes is often a major challenge in prosecutions, due to the complex nature of the crimes, and the fact that the actors may be remote from the physical commission of the crimes. The prosecution of corporate officers can be further complicated by the complex structure of companies and the difficulty in determining the roles and responsibilities of different persons within the company. Several different modes of criminal responsibility exist, which might be relevant in prosecuting corporate officers for the pillage of natural resources, such as joint criminal enterprise, co-perpetration and 'aiding and abetting'.

APPLICATION OF THE CRIME OF PILLAGE: AHAVA

Ahava Dead Sea Laboratories is a privately owned company based in the Israeli settlement of Mitzpe Shalem, in the occupied West Bank. Its cosmetics contain minerals and mud extracted from the occupied section of the Dead Sea.[3] It exports these products to western markets and has several distributors in other countries, including the UK. Thirty-seven per cent of the company's shares are held by the West Bank settlement of Kibbutz Mitzpe Shalem, and 7.5 per cent by the West Bank settlement of Kibbutz Kalia. The Ahava factory also employs persons from these settlements (and on the website of Mitzpe Shalem, Ahava is listed as one of the employment opportunities for residents of the settlement).[4] Is Ahava, or its corporate officers, liable for the war crime of pillage?

Do Ahava's activities fulfil the actus reus of pillage?

Appropriation

Ahava[5] in Israel is involved in the extraction of minerals from occupied territory. Ahava's subsidiaries/distributors in other countries might also be considered directly liable for this extraction by way of their involvement in a joint criminal enterprise, or for indirect appropriation by receiving the appropriated minerals. Much depends on the corporate structure, the details of how the company operates and the contributions made by different persons to the enterprise.

In the context of armed conflict (including occupation)

The company is extracting resources from territory that is under military occupation. There is the necessary nexus with the armed conflict in that the occupation is providing the opportunity for the resource extraction. The fact that Ahava is based in an Israeli settlement is also indicative of the nexus with the armed conflict.

Ownership of resources and breach of usufruct

This is a factually complicated matter. Under the laws in place before Israel's occupation (Ottoman, British Mandate and Jordanian law), the minerals of the Dead Sea would probably be determined to be pubic property, belonging to the state (that is, state-owned immovable property), or at least not in private ownership.[6] The fact that the proceeds of the resource extraction by Ahava is not used for the benefit of the local (Palestinian) population breaches the rules of usufruct.

Do Ahava's representatives fulfil the mental element of pillage?

Intention and knowledge of the factual circumstances

Ahava's employees in Israel, especially its senior management, would appear to be responsible for the purposeful extraction of Dead Sea minerals, in the knowledge that the minerals come from occupied territory and that the proceeds of the extraction are not applied for the benefit of the local Palestinian population. Senior representatives of Ahava abroad are likely also to have this knowledge, especially given the public campaign against Ahava's activities.

CONCLUSIONS

The elements of the offence of pillage might therefore be capable of being made out against Ahava in Israel and against those involved in the supply chain of its products.

A similar reasoning could be applied to other Israeli companies involved in the exploitation of natural resources in the occupied West Bank, such as the companies that are involved in quarrying, water extraction, and in the production of agricultural goods such as dates, flowers, and herbs.

Does the trade in settlement produce 'aid and abet' transfer of the Israeli civilian population into the occupied West Bank? In order to address this question, the elements of the war crime of the 'transfer of the civilian population' have to be ascertained.

Elements of the crime of transfer of the civilian population

The transfer directly or indirectly by the Occupying Power of parts of its civilian population into occupied territory is prohibited by the Fourth Geneva Convention and is criminalised in Additional Protocol I to the Geneva Conventions. It also appears as a crime in the Rome Statute of the International Criminal Court.

In order for the crime to have been committed, there must be a 'transfer' of substantial numbers of Israeli nationals ('part of' the Israeli civilian population) by persons acting on behalf of the Occupying Power (Israel), or by persons supported/encouraged by the Occupying Power, so that the transfer is directly or indirectly 'by' the Occupying Power. The transfer must occur in the context of and associated with an armed conflict.

'Transfer' is not defined in the Fourth Geneva Convention. According to the ordinary meaning of the word, 'transfer' would seem only to mean the conveyance of persons to occupied territory. If 'transfer' is read, however, within the context of the prohibition against the Occupying Power making permanent changes to occupied territory/the colonisation of occupied territory, it might also include many of the activities associated with the establishment and maintenance of civilian settlements, such as the planning of settlements, the construction of settlements, the installation of settlement infrastructure and the provision of essential services to settlements.

Secondary participation in the crime of transfer of the civilian population

It is recognised that there are secondary modes of liability for the commission of war crimes that is, persons can be convicted for encouraging or assisting the commission of war crimes by others.

In order to be liable for 'aiding and abetting' a crime, an individual must have intended to assist the commission of the crime, with knowledge of the circumstances constituting the offence being assisted. Under international law, there is also a requirement that the assistance has a 'substantial effect' on the commission of the crime. There may be a similar requirement in domestic legal systems.

Therefore, someone criminally liable for assisting in the transfer of the civilian population would have to intentionally provide assistance to the movement of settlers into occupied territory, or (possibly) the establishment and maintenance of settlements, and in so doing, make a substantial contribution to the transfer.

Application of the law to Ahava's activities

The revenue obtained from Ahava's production and trade in Dead Sea products appears to provide some economic support to two residential settlements in the occupied West Bank (Mitzpe Shalem and Kalia), both of which own shares in the company. Ahava also seems to provide employment to the residents of Mitzpe Shalem.

Ahava's activities might therefore constitute assistance in the economic viability of the settlements. If this economic assistance were having a substantial effect on the ability of the residents of the settlement to continue to reside there, or was encouraging other Israeli nationals to move to the settlements, it is possible that Ahava's commercial activities could be said to be aiding and abetting the transfer of Israel's civilian population to the occupied West Bank.

More legal and factual research needs to be undertaken, particularly in respect of the nature of the crime of transfer of the civilian population and the requirements of aiding and abetting, before the issue can be more confidently addressed.

Salma Karmi-Ayyoub is a barrister in England and Wales and a legal researcher for renowned Palestinian human rights group al-Haq.

TRANSCRIPT: SALMA KARMI-AYYOUB INTRODUCTION

Editor's note: Salma Karmi-Ayyoub gave the following introduction to her spoken presentation, in relation to a question that a previous witness had been unable to answer.

SK: I'm meant to be addressing you on the issue of settlement produce but just before I do, because the previous witness [John Dorman] was asked about the Dutch company that there has been action against, I was hoping to just use half a minute to be able to tell you a little bit about the case, because it resulted from a criminal complaint that was lodged by al-Haq in conjunction with a Dutch lawyer against the company. The company is called Riwal;

it's a Dutch private rental company and has been supplying mobile cranes and aerial platforms for the construction of the wall in the West Bank.

And, in summary, there was some public campaign against the company when it was discovered that it was renting its equipment for the wall, back in 2006. And the Dutch government approached the company and asked them about their activities. Initially, they tried to deny their involvement by saying that the company in charge of the supply was in fact an Israeli company. That was discovered to be incorrect and it became apparent that that was a Dutch company which was involved in the supply.

Then the company was approached again and said that it had stopped supplying its cranes, but a year later, it was found that its equipment was still being used for the construction of the wall. And eventually, as I've said, a criminal complaint was lodged with the public prosecutor in Holland, alleging that the company is complicit in war crimes which result from the construction of the wall, in particular, the unlawful destruction of land, the crime of apartheid and persecution of the Palestinian population. And as a result, the prosecutor in Holland has opened an investigation which resulted in the raid of the company's offices a few weeks ago, in Holland. So that's where we've got to with that.

TRANSCRIPT OF JURY Q&A: SALMA KARMI-AYYOUB

Anthony Gifford QC: I like the way that some of these old conventions call things by their proper name without any euphemisms. The word 'pillage' – I mean, when we listened to the speaker who couldn't get here from Palestine talking about what happened to his farm [Fayez al-Taneeb] – that was pillage. And it's good that the law can sometimes call things by its proper name. Salma, my only question really, and you began to touch on it: as a lawyer and an activist, would you agree that the way forward on issues like Ahava lies in a combination of sound legal research and popular action and pressure?

SK: Yes, absolutely, I think sound legal research which leads potentially to litigation against these companies, can very well supplement campaigns which are conducted against them and which may not always be effective and making them stop their activities. And at the same time, those campaigns can supplement cases which could be brought. Because we derive a lot of information about the companies' activities from the act of these campaigns which force them to make responses or to address those who complain against them.

Cynthia McKinney: ... As a lawyer, a human rights lawyer ... Universal jurisdiction is becoming less universal. Where are the best places to bring such cases?

SK: It is true that universal jurisdiction is, unfortunately, becoming less universal, as you've put it, because of the actions of governments in changing their laws. I think, unfortunately, those who've brought those cases have become the victims of their own success. In a sense that it's a fact that the cases got as far as they did, which caused tremendous pressure and meant or enabled the government to change laws to restrict their application. And that's why I personally am interested in instances in which you have companies or individuals who are domiciled or residents of countries outside of Israel and Palestine, and in which jurisdiction can be asserted not on the basis of universal jurisdiction but some other link, such as usually through the defendant being resident or domiciled. So I gave the example of Ahava having this distributorship or subsidiary in the United Kingdom, which is a UK company, domiciled here, and would potentially be able to afford us that foothold in terms of jurisdiction.

I think that's something that needs to be thought about more by those who are interested in bringing cases in order that we don't continue, I suppose, to perhaps weaken what's becoming a more and more fragile mechanism with universal jurisdiction.

*   *   *

Agrexco Agricultural Export Ltd
Christophe Perrin

THE CONTEXTUAL BACKGROUND TO AGREXCO'S ACTIVITIES

Although the share of agriculture in Israel's overall economy is very small, accounting for only 3 per cent of GDP, agricultural activity has played and continues to play a key role in the Palestine colonisation enterprise. The symbolic status of 'working the land' is universal. Working the land amounts to appropriation of the land.

This state of affairs is particularly evident in the Jordan Valley, the most fertile region of the Palestinian territory occupied in 1967; under the Oslo agreement, the Jordan Valley was placed in Area C, which is fully controlled by the Israeli army. The farming settlements on the banks of the Jordan cover 50 per cent of Area C and 28.5 per cent of the total area of the West Bank. Nine thousand settlers, inhabiting 39 illegal settlements, consume the equivalent of 75 per cent of the annual water consumption of the entire Palestinian population of the West Bank.[7] In Area C, the Israeli army exercises unlimited power over the local population, callously imposing colonial order with the manifest aim of compelling the indigenous Palestinians to take flight: house demolitions, destruction of wells, a ban on the drilling of new wells, and harassment of the Bedouin, whose conditions of survival are particularly difficult.[8] Dispossessed of their land, the majority of Palestinian farmers have no choice but to work for the settlers. The wages earned by Palestinian labourers amount to less than half the legal minimum wage in Israel, and they have no health coverage.[9]

THE AGREXCO COMPANY

Agrexco has been the leading Israeli exporter of agricultural produce since 1956. It has made inroads into markets all over the world, especially in Europe. The company is 50 per cent state-owned. A further 25 per cent is owned by producers' organisations and 25 per cent by Tnuva (the leading Israeli milk producer). Agrexco exports about 450,000 tons of fresh agricultural produce each year, principally to Europe, and has a turnover of about €650 million.[10]

COLONIAL EXPLOITATION IN THE PALESTINIAN TERRITORIES

According to data from the Tel Aviv Central Bureau of Statistics for 2007, settlement output (which is largely export-oriented) accounts for 3 per cent of Israeli agricultural production.[11]

In January 2006, seven activists appeared before the Uxbridge Magistrates Court, charged with having participated in a blockade of the Agrexco warehouse in Middlesex. During the proceedings, the manager of Agrexco UK, Amos Orr, stated that 70 per cent of settlement produce was exported by his company.[12] Producing a report on transactions between Agrexco and its suppliers (which included the settlements of Tomer, Kibbutz Kalia, Mekhora, Hamra,

Mehola and Argaman), Mr Orr admitted that settlement produce accounted for 5 per cent of the total volume of Agrexco exports.[13]

In March 2010, reacting to the campaign launched by the *Coalition contre Agrexco*, which objected to its establishment in the port of Sète, the Agrexco management sent a letter to all the company's French customers stating: 'We are an apolitical trading company ... 99.4 per cent of our articles come from farmers living within the State of Israel. The remaining 0.4 per cent come from producers located in Judea and Samaria [that is, the occupied West Bank].'[14]

These figures are basically of no great importance. When it comes to war crimes, the offences of perpetration, involvement, or complicity are not measured in percentage terms. Only the facts matter. So what are the facts?

First, as we have just seen, the Agrexco company publicly acknowledges its involvement in the economic exploitation of the Occupied Palestinian Territories. This confession is doubtless attributable to what may be termed 'habitual reliance' on the impunity granted by western powers and international bodies to public and private Israeli actors.

Secondly, investigations conducted on the ground by Palestinian and Israeli organisations – or mere eyewitness accounts – confirm that Agrexco has physical facilities in virtually all Jordan Valley settlements, where agricultural produce can be preserved and packaged.[15] The company also has offices in the vicinity of the settlement Regional Council of Arvot HaYarden.

FRAUDULENT PRACTICES

Israeli exports to Europe have been fully exempt from customs duties since 2005 under the Euro-Mediterranean Agreement.[16] A recent ruling by the Court of Justice of the European Communities (*Brita* Judgment)[17] reaffirms that goods produced outside the frontiers established in 1949 do not qualify for preferential treatment under the agreements. Israel is required under the agreements to certify the origin of produce. However, it is common knowledge that massive fraud occurs under the EU/Israel agreement, since Israel exports products bearing Israeli certificates from the OPT. The state of Israel disputes their characterisation under international law as Occupied Palestinian Territories and treats the settlements as an integral part of its territory. Agrexco's practices in this regard have been documented by Palestinian or international NGOs. In July

2009, a team of *Coalition contre Agrexco* investigators equipped with a camera and guided by Palestinian farmers gained access to Agrexco's packaging centre in the Gilgal settlement. It found and filmed evidence of fraud: the aromatic herbs produced by the settlement, mixed with the produce of Palestinian farmers, was packed in crates labelled 'Made in Israel'.

These fraudulent practices have been publicly condemned, for instance, in January 2010 by both Phyllis Starkey in the UK House of Commons[18] and Nicole Kiil-Nielsen in the European Parliament.[19]

IMPUNITY

In the introductory part of the *Brita* Judgment, the European Court of Justice, endorsing the findings of Advocate-General Yves Bot, concluded that Israeli certificate of origin practices are untrustworthy.

Pursuant to European case law, the importing state may itself check the authenticity and accuracy of the certificate[20] where doubts exist regarding the origin of the goods,[21] or where there has been a transgression on the part of the exporting state.[22] It is customary in the European Union for a CJEC ruling to be followed speedily by remedial measures on the part of EU states. In the case of the *Brita* Judgment, however, no such action has been taken. Not a single European government has ordered its customs authorities to check the validity of the certificates of origin accompanying goods marketed by Agrexco or by any other Israeli company.

In the face of such persistent impunity, notwithstanding the CJEC legal ruling, European civil society must take steps to compel states to respect the rules that they have themselves established. It was with this end in view that French member organisations of the *Coalition contre Agrexco* decided to take the place of the French authorities and initiate proceedings against the Agrexco company before the competent civil court.[23] The proceedings will first seek to establish that the produce marketed by Agrexco is fraudulent under European law. A second set of proceedings will then be instituted to demonstrate the unlawful (criminal) nature of the produce involved: it is unconscionable to market the product of a war crime.

Christophe Perrin is a member of the French social organization CIMADE and part of the Coalition Against Agrexco, France.

*   *   *

Ahava Dead Sea Products In Israel/Palestine

Nancy Kricorian and Rae Abileah

Editor's note: In May 2011, Code Pink released new evidence that Ahava is involved in the crime of pillage, in the form of confirmation from the Israeli occupation authorities that a mining permit for mud on the shores of the Dead Sea in the occupied West Bank had in fact been issued to Ahava in 2004. See 'Document from Israeli Civil Administration proving that Ahava sources mud from Occupied Shores of Dead Sea', Code Pink, May 2011 <www. codepink4peace.org>.

Ahava Dead Sea Laboratories[24] is a privately held Israeli cosmetics company that manufactures products using minerals and mud from the Dead Sea. Its products generate nearly $150 million in annual sales in 30 countries.[25] The company's main factory and visitors' centre are located in the Israeli settlement of Mitzpe Shalem in the occupied West Bank. (All Israeli settlements in the West Bank are illegal under international law.[26]) Thirty-seven per cent of the company shares are held by the settlement of Kibbutz Mitzpe Shalem, 34 per cent by Hamashbir Holdings (the investment fund

Figure 3.1   Ahava's main factory and visitors' centre are located in the Israeli settlement of Mitzpe Shalem in the occupied West Bank. Courtesy Rae Abileah, Code Pink.

of B. Gaon Holdings and the Livnat family), 18.5 per cent are held by Shamrock Holdings (the investment fund of the Roy E. Disney family), and 7.5 per cent by the West Bank settlement of Kibbutz Kalia.[27]

The settlements of Mitzpe Shalem and Kalia are cooperatives owned by the settlers living in them, and together they own 44 per cent of Ahava. Both of these settlements are deep inside Palestinian territory. Mitzpe Shalem is about 9 km from the Green Line and Kalia is 30 km from the Green Line. Ahava's profits are therefore subsidising these illegal settlements and their residents. According to mapping done by Adalah (the Legal Centre for Arab Minority Rights in Israel), formerly there were a few Palestinian communities on the lands on which these two settlements are located: Nabi Musa where Kalia is now situated and 'Arab al-Ta'amira near Mitzpe Shalem.[28]

Ahava labels its goods as 'products of Israel' when in fact they are made in the occupied West Bank. According to international law, including the relevant UN Security Council Resolutions and even according to findings of Israel's own Supreme Court,[29] the West Bank cannot be considered to be part of the state of Israel. The UN Security Council,[30] the UN General Assembly,[31] the United States,[32] the EU,[33] the International Court of Justice,[34] and the International Committee of the Red Cross[35] refer to it as Israeli-occupied Palestinian territory. Misleading labelling makes it difficult for consumers to identify the actual source of the products they are purchasing. Consequently, this labelling is under investigation in the Netherlands[36] and the UK,[37] and activists in France have filed suit against French cosmetics chain Sephora for carrying these products because of Ahava's illegal practices.[38]

A journalist who was researching an article about the boycott campaign against Ahava received no reply from the company's spokesperson to his queries about the company's illegal practices, but an Israeli government spokesman offered this answer: 'The Palestinians did nothing with this land when they had it ... And the Palestinians still have access to the Dead Sea. If they wanted to, they could set up a factory themselves.'[39]

This response was at best disingenuous, as it has been well documented that Palestinian access to the Dead Sea for even a day at the beach is highly restricted by the Israeli Defense Forces and their extensive system of roadblocks throughout the occupied West Bank.[40] Additionally, the entire occupied area on the shores of the Dead Sea is classified as 'Area C'. That means that in order to build there the Palestinians need permission from the Israeli Civil Administration. As reports from human rights and other organizations show, the Civil Administration does not allow any Palestinian construction in Area C. This is true for much smaller projects such as building toilet facilities for a school inside a Palestinian village, let alone building an entire factory.[41] So his statement is a blunt lie.

In conclusion, we find that the company Ahava Dead Sea Laboratories, because of the location of its factory and visitors' centre on occupied land, its subsidies to two illegal settlements and their residents that are co-owners of the enterprise, and its fraudulent labelling practices, is clearly an Israeli profiteer in occupied Palestinian territory.

Nancy Kricorian is campaign manager of Code Pink Women for Peace, USA, and Rae Abileah is national organiser for Code Pink.

TRANSCRIPT OF JURY Q&A: NANCY KRICORIAN AND RAE ABILEAH

John Dugard: I am very interested that in your evidence you have focused attention on the fact that Ahava is clearly situated in a settlement. And that is beyond dispute.

Nancy Kricorian: Yes.

JD: What does seem to be in dispute is the question of whether mud is collected from the occupied territory or from the part of the Dead Sea that falls within Israel's jurisdiction. I've heard Ahava justify its actions on the ground that it does not use products from occupied territory. Which is a way simply of distracting attention from the fact that it is clearly based in a settlement. Do you have any ideas on the subject of the extraction of mud from the Dead Sea? Is there any clear evidence on the subject?

NK: You know, we have, as we said, worked very closely with Dalit and Merav from Who Profits, who provided us with a lot of the information that we have. And there have been reports, that they are actually excavating mud from the shores of the Dead Sea near Kalia. Because we have no documentary evidence of this, we have no absolute proof of it. We have decided, we don't use that because we don't have documentary proof. So if we could somehow sneak there with cameras – but apparently the place where they excavate is right next to a military base. So there's really no way to get access to see who is it who is digging, when they are doing it and, you know, if the company is actually doing it. If we could get documentary – we believe that it is the case, but we have no documentary proof.

Rae Abileah: I can just add that I was at the factory a year ago, the summer of 2009, and also was unable to obtain that proof on the ground, so that's why we don't speak to pillage in our report. [But see editor's note above.]

JD: But it's really unnecessary to make a conclusive finding on that issue, when it is so absolutely clear that Ahava as an enterprise is situated within a settlement.

NK: And the other part – not only that it's located within the settlement but that the profits from the company are directly going back in to subsidise the settlers who live in these two settlements.

JD: And has this become an issue in the US as a result of Shamrock Holdings?

NK: You know, a boycott campaign is strategic and we have sort of been doing things one piece at a time. We started out by getting Oxfam to suspend Kristin Davis, who is an American actress who was a spokeswoman for Ahava while she was being an Oxfam goodwill ambassador. Since Oxfam has come out against settlement products, we thought this was a contradiction to have someone who shills for settlement products, you know, being an Oxfam goodwill ambassador, so through our pressure campaign, Oxfam suspended her from publicity work for the duration of her contract with Ahava. So that was our first – and you know, Shamrock is on our list. It's just harder to get at. When we tried contact – we know people at Shamrock and we were talking to them. The former CEO of Shamrock was a guy who was more in line with the thinking of the Ahava CEO than with, you know, international law. So, we didn't feel like we have much leverage there but he has since retired, about five months ago, and so Shamrock is on our list but we haven't yet come out with quite the leverage point to go after them.

RA: And I'll just add for the record that after the Oxfam incident, Kristin Davis did not renew her advertising contract with Ahava, so she is no longer their spokeswoman.

JD: I think that what is interesting about Ahava is that its products are perhaps the most visible products of Israeli settlements. In the sense that in so many shopping centres, malls, one finds persons selling Ahava products. Has there been any attempt to draw attention to this in shopping centres in the United States?

NK: Well, you know, as the campaign manager, when people ask me … I constantly get people saying: they're selling it at Sears, they're selling it at Nordstrom, they're selling it in the mall! And it really is literally like playing a game of Wack-a-Mole – like you hit it and it pops up some place else. So we don't have the capacity to take it all on. Another thing we've been focusing on is the sales at Nordstrom, which is an American retail chain that has a socially responsible business code that they abide by and we actually have one of our boycott supporters who lives on the West Coast near the store, have a conversation with Blake Nordstrom, the CEO of Nordstrom about the contradiction between their social responsibility code and the fact that they were carrying these products and he said: 'I have to talk to my lawyer.' So he got his lawyer to talk to Ahava's lawyer. And they came back and said: 'No they absolutely follow the American labelling law, to the tee.' The thing is that the American labelling law is so lax, especially around cosmetics, you know, but then she said to him: 'Just because it's legal doesn't mean it's right.'

RA: Also in response to your question about has there been any action in stores: this campaign has inspired much grassroots advocacy people doing very creative protests, at stores all around the world actually which helps to put public pressure and get media attention that may ultimately push for legal findings or other actions as the former speaker did discuss.

*   *   *

Trade and Labelling of Settlement Goods
Phon Van Den Biesen

It is estimated that up to one-third of Israeli exports 'are either fully or partially made in the occupied territories'.[42] An unknown, but presumably very substantial part of these products are sold under labels stating 'Product of Israel' or using similar language.

An important impetus for using this type of labels is to be found in the Association Agreement between the European Union and Israel.[43] This treaty provides both the parties with a preferential treatment (no customs duties) as to their goods being imported into the other party's territory. In practice, it turned out to be extremely difficult, if not impossible, for European customs authorities to verify the true origins of goods being imported into the EU. This led the EU and Israel to agree on an additional 'technical arrangement', which includes the obligation for Israeli customs authorities to include postal codes on written declarations accompanying goods that are exported from Israel. This arrangement took effect from 1 February 2005.

The need for such an additional agreement was confirmed by the European Court of Justice when it found that products originating from the OPT 'do not fall within the territorial scope of ... [the EU-Israel Association] agreement and do not therefore qualify for preferential treatment under that agreement'.[44]

So, in principle, these issues seem to be settled. However, there exists a great amount of confusion about the effects of the technical arrangement, since the document holding the technical arrangement, including the list of postal codes presumably referring to the settlements, is exempted from the public access of documents regulation of the EU. At the same time, there is reason to believe that neither Israeli manufacturers nor Israeli customs authorities are living by the rules of this technical arrangement. After Israel had made the arrangement with the EU, it established a special fund to reimburse manufacturers for the loss of the benefit of importing their products duty-free into the EU. Apparently, this special fund is hardly used at all which seems to provide for a strong indication that in practice the arrangement is not respected.[45]

In any event, in Europe as well as in the United States, a great number of products are offered to the public, which are labelled as 'Product of Israel'.

In a series of findings, the British Advertising Standards Agency (ASA) Council has reported that advertisements promoting holidays in 'Israel' are misleading if the texts of these materials as well as the maps displayed in fact include the OPT as part of Israeli territory.[46] Recently, the Dutch sister organisation of ASA reached the same conclusion in a combined complaint against a series of Israeli Ministry of Tourism publications.[47] Both the ASA and the Dutch RCC apply regulations which are in conformity with European

Union law.[48] The findings of these specialised agencies provide for a strong basis for litigation against this type of misleading advertising on the basis of regular tort law before national jurisdictions, while legal actions at the EU level seem to be worth additional study as well.

Phon Van Den Biesen is a lawyer specialising in civil litigation issues on war and peace and international and European law from the Netherlands.

*   *   *

Sodastream

Geneviève Coudrais

The Israeli company Soda-Club was founded in 1991 by a British citizen called Peter Wiseburgh, who had been Israel's exclusive distributor for the SodaStream tap water carbonation fountain until 1998, when Soda-Club bought the British company Sodastream.

The Soda-Club company then built two factories in Israel, one in Ashkelon for the production of syrups, and the other in Mishor Adumim for the manufacturing of the soda fountain. Yet Mishor Adumim, at the heart of the Ma'ale Adumim colony, is the second largest Israeli industrial area in the West Bank. The existence of this settlement is beyond any doubt since it is mentioned in some of the Soda-Club company's own documents, as well as on its website.

The company currently boasts about its leadership in the home carbonation of drinks as it can be found in more than 30 countries. Its products are available in more than 35,000 retail outlets, supplying six million homes. The Jewish National Fund signed a partnership agreement with this company in 2007.

The company is one of the EU's approved exporters, but problems surged on the first semester of 2002, when the Brita company, which imports SodaStream products into Germany, claimed preferential tariff treatment under the EC-Israel agreement, informing the German customs that the goods came from Israel. The refusal of the German customs authorities resulted in a referral to the European Court of Justice on the applicability of the preferential treatment at stake. On 25 February 2010, the Court of Justice ruled that products originating in the West Bank were outside the territorial scope of the EC-Israel Association Agreement's section 83 and should therefore not be granted the preferential tariff regime involved. The German customs authorities could therefore refuse to apply the preferential tariff regime to goods originating in the West Bank.

In 2008, following the investigations of a Swedish journalist who incidentally called for the boycott of the product, the local chairman of the company questioned the minister of foreign affairs, who answered him that doing business with colony-based companies was considered inappropriate by the Swedish government. The chairman of the company then announced that all goods destined to Scandinavia would from then on be shipped from factories other than Mishor Adumim. No evidence of this has been produced ever since. In the event of a similar case in another country, the transfer of the facility to another place would cost €25 million.

That very same year, the company chose to tap the French market. We're planning to act at three levels: the intrinsic illegality of the product, the breach in community law and the fraud on the origin of the product, which is deceptive for the consumer. The France-Palestine Solidarity Association has many a time referred the matter to the ministries of Economy, of Budget, of Customs Authorities, of Foreign Affairs, as well as to the Secretary of State for trade – all to no avail.

The association also referred to the French customs authorities, and was recently informed of the fact that the French customs authorities had indeed inquired into this product, and ordered an appraisal on the OPM importer company about the inapplicability of preferential origin. This breach has been notified to the OPM company.

For the violation of our consumer regulations, which are mentioned in section 6 of 'Directive 2005/29/EC of the European parliament and of the Council of 11 May 2005 concerning unfair business-to-consumer commercial practices', our association as well as its local groups alerted the competent French *Direction Générale de Protection des Populations* as to the breach in the rights of the consumers who were misled by the origin of the 'Made in Israel'-labelled product. The *Direction Générale de Protection des Populations* expects to be informed on the certificate of origin by the French customs authorities, which should not take long.

During our boycott campaign on retail outlets, which led to a significant number of product withdrawals, the manager of one of these outlets, who had asked the import company for further information after our initiative, provided us with a copy of a certificate of origin he received from SodaStream that did mention the product was made in 'Mishor Adumim's industrial area, Ma'aleh Adumim – Israel'.

Genevieve Coudrais is a retired lawyer and member of Association France-Palestine solidarité.

4
The Financial Services Sector

The Israeli Financial Sector and the Occupation
Merav Amir

Israeli banks provide the financial infrastructure for all activities of companies, governmental agencies and individuals in the continuing occupation of Palestine and the Syrian Golan Heights. The services provided by the banks support and sustain these activities. Additionally, it is evident that the banks are well aware of the types and whereabouts of the activity that is being carried out with their financial assistance. Our research has identified six categories of involvement of Israeli banks in the Occupation.[1] There is solid evidence of the involvement of most of the major Israeli commercial banks in the following categories:

MORTGAGE LOANS FOR HOME BUYERS IN SETTLEMENTS

Israeli banks provide mortgages to individuals who wish to buy or build housing units in West Bank settlements. The purchased property is used as collateral for the return of the loan, as is standard with mortgage loans. Thus, the bank that provided the loan is a stakeholder in a real estate property in a settlement and, in cases of foreclosure, the bank may end up fully owning that property.

SPECIAL LOANS FOR BUILDING PROJECTS IN SETTLEMENTS

Israeli banks provide loans for various construction firms for the explicit purpose of constructing housing projects in Israeli West Bank settlements. These are loans provided under terms that are regulated through 'accompaniment agreements' ('*Heskemay Livuy*'), certain aspects of which are regulated under the Sale (Apartments) (Assurance of Investments of Purchasers of Apartments) Law – 1974. The relevant articles in the Sale Law ensure home buyers that a bank vouches for the construction project, backs the construction company and protects the buyers' investments by providing the

Figure 4.1   Advertisement for a project called Yair Heights in the West Bank settlement of Ma'ale Adumim, 2004. At the bottom it says: 'Bank accompaniment and mortgages: Bank Tefahot'. Courtesy Dror Etkes.

purchasers with a bank guarantee. In some cases, the accompanying bank also holds the real estate property as collateral until all of the housing units in the project are sold to buyers. Home buyers' payments for the properties are then deposited in a dedicated bank account in the accompanying bank, and the bank monitors the financial status as well as the development of the project.

FINANCIAL SERVICES TO LOCAL AUTHORITIES OF SETTLEMENTS

Regional councils, local councils and municipalities of Israeli settlements in the occupied West Bank and the Golan Heights depend on the financial services provided by Israeli banks. Most importantly, Israeli banks provide loans to the local authorities of settlements, which are used for the development of infrastructure, the construction of public buildings and the provision of municipal services to the residents of these settlements. Additional services to these local authorities include managing bank accounts, the provision of fund management services and the transfer of funds from the government and other sources to local authorities for the construction of schools, community centres and the like.

OPERATING BRANCHES IN ISRAELI SETTLEMENTS

Most Israeli banks have several branches in Israeli settlements. Through these branches the banks provide financial services to settlers and to commercial companies in settlements. The bank branches are part of the service infrastructure that enables the continued development of the settlements.

PROVIDING FINANCIAL SERVICES TO BUSINESSES IN SETTLEMENTS

Israeli banks provide financial services to businesses in the settlements, including businesses whose entire commercial activity is related to the Occupation. For instance, Israeli banks provide loans and offer bank accounts to factories located in the industrial zones of settlements or whose main area of activity is the construction of settlements or infrastructure projects for the use of Israelis in the occupied area. The property of these businesses in the occupied area is, many times, used as collateral for such loans.

THE PALESTINIAN MONETARY MARKET AS A CAPTURED MARKET

Restricted by the agreements which were signed between the Palestinians and the Israelis as part of the Oslo process, the Palestinian monetary market cannot operate a currency of its own. Palestinian banks are therefore dependent on other banks for the provision of financial services. The Israeli shekel dominates most of this market because of the subordination of the Palestinian market to that of Israel. Palestinian banks must rely on Israeli banks, which serve as correspondence banks, for the transfer of funds and shekel-clearing services. According to official Palestinian sources, the Israeli banks which provide these services demand high cash collaterals, of more than a billion shekels in total, which are deposited by the Palestinian banks into the Israeli banks. Additionally, the Israeli banks charge high commissions for these services and impose limitations on the transfer of money, both of which increase the costs of such operations and the risks involved for the Palestinian banks. It should be noted that the Israeli banks are only willing to work with some Palestinian banks; the Israeli banks refuse to include the newer banks in these agreements. Consequently, this restriction hinders the ability of the Palestinian monetary market to grow and develop. Additionally, as of the end of 2008, Israeli banks have severed their contractual connections with the Palestinian banks in Gaza and stopped providing any and all services to them. This has had a significant impact on the financial market in Gaza, bringing it to the brink of total collapse.

These six categories clearly portray the scope and extent to which banks in Israel are implicated in the financing of Occupation-related commercial activity. The evidence we have collected clearly shows that Israeli banks not only provide these services and enable these activities, but are also fully aware of the type of activities for which they provide financial support. In addition, Israeli banks reap financial benefits for Israeli financial institutions from the subordination of the Palestinian financial market as a captured market.

From a more general perspective, it can be stated that any and all aspects of Israeli control over the OPT have a financial foundation and that none of these financial activities by individuals, organisations, governmental institutions and commercial companies could take place without the active support of banks. Israeli banks are principle beneficiaries of financial activity in the illegal Israeli settlements in the OPT and in Israeli control over the Palestinian financial market.

Merav Amir is research coordinator for 'Who Profits from the Occupation', Israel.

TRANSCRIPT OF JURY Q&A: MERAV AMIR

Michael Mansfield QC: You mentioned five major groups, banking groups, that are involved – this was the start of your evidence, and that all major European banks were investing in those groups. I ask this question because of what has happened in the United Kingdom, and the recent bail-out and the ownership of banks basically by the public here, and by the government. So are the five major banks in the United Kingdom all involved in the five major banking groups in Israel?

Merav Amir: I can't say that because we didn't research the British banking system. So I don't know what their portfolio of investments are. But from looking at other major financial institutions – all of them that are invested in Israeli companies – some are not invested in Israel at all, but any that are invested in the Israeli economy, usually are invested in these five banking groups.

*   *   *

The Financing of Israeli Settlements in the Occupied Territories by the Belgian-French Financial Group Dexia

Mario Franssen

Editor's note: In May 2011, it was reported in the Israeli press that Dexia would sell its stake in Dexia Israel by the end of the summer – 'even at a loss'. The news was announced at a shareholders' meeting at which campaigners argued against Dexia's involvement in the illegal West Bank settlements. See 'Dexia Israel to be sold "even at a loss"', 15 May 2011 <www.globes.co.il>.

My statement concerns the proof linking Belgian-French banking group Dexia to the construction of the Israeli settlements in the Occupied Palestinian Territories (OPT). I have opted for a chronological build-up of the different elements relevant to this case. This is important to show how Dexia is and was fully aware of what it is doing and has been aware of it from the beginning.

The alliance between Dexia and Israel starts at the end of the twentieth century. The ambitious banking group wanted to become the number one banker in the world for 'Public and Wholesale Banking, providing local public finance operators with comprehensive banking and financial solutions'. Dexia started to invest in banks which are active in markets all over the world, including Israel, where they bought the bank Otzar Hashilton Hamekomi.

Since 1 January 2001, during the second intifada, Dexia consolidated its operations in Israel. Presently Dexia holds two-thirds of the bank's share capital, voting rights and rights for appointing directors. It is clear that for almost ten years, Dexia has been in absolute control of this Israeli bank – which they renamed Dexia Israel.

During these ten years, Dexia didn't do anything to prevent their subsidiary in Israel from investing in the settlements. In April 2001, the first letter was sent to the board of Dexia to warn them about their possible involvement in the financing of the settlements in the OPT.

The documents we found (and also introduced as proof to the court) date from 2003 and cover the period until 2009. Dexia never contested them, and I also want to stress here the origins of these documents. In 2007, some settlements introduced a complaint against Dexia Israel to the financial committee of the Israeli parliament, the Knesset. The settlements accused Dexia Israel of discriminating against them. According to the settlements, Dexia Israel refused to give them loans because they were situated behind the Green Line.

This committee called David Kapah – the CEO of Dexia Israel – to come and defend himself against these accusations. Kapah did this with brio. First of all, he stated that Dexia is a bank and the basis on which they consider loans are purely economic. Secondly, he stated that Dexia Israel, between 2005 and 2007, gave loans to ten different settlements, so they don't discriminate at all. The loans cover a 12-year period. Together with another loan to the settlement Ma'ale Efrayim in 2003, the total sum of these loans is up to €5.5 million. The report of this meeting was, and still is, available on the Knesset website.

The importance of Jerusalem forces me to go into this case a little more. In June 2008, Dexia Israel gave an €8 million loan to Jerusalem (which, according to Israel, also includes East Jerusalem). When we confronted Dexia about this loan during the General Assembly of Dexia, the president of Dexia, Jean-Luc Dehaene (who is a former Belgian prime minister and current member of the European Parliament) even stated that East Jerusalem doesn't exist! He is copying the viewpoint of Israel.

In their defence (and no, I'm not taking the defence of Dexia here, I hope somebody from Dexia will do that in the last session of the day), Dexia gives several arguments against stopping the financing. I'll run briefly through some of them and will give some counter-arguments.

Dexia says the financing was a problem of the previous board of directors. Since June 2008, when new president of the board Dehaene, and new CEO Pierre Mariani (he is a close associate of President Sarkozy) took control, Dexia changed its policy.

But this is contrary to the proof we introduced to the court. In 2008 and 2009, Dexia Israel played a key role as 'middleman' between settlements who needed loans, and investors who wanted to invest through buying these loans. These are the so-called 'mortgage loans'. According to the Israeli registry of loans, we are talking about loans to 12 settlements. The total amount of these loans is over €34 million in a two-year period.

Secondly, there is a whole range of services that Dexia is giving to the settlements. Mifal Hapais (the Israeli national lottery) is financing the settlements. It has an exclusive contact with Dexia Israel so every shekel going to the settlements from Mifal Hapais is also going through a Dexia account. Since June 2008, we are talking about 43 different settlements. Unfortunately, we don't know the budgets that are involved.

Yes (Dexia says) we gave loans, but they are being phased out. Once again, Dexia is not telling the truth. They don't consider loans to Jerusalem or mortgage loans to be problematic. When they give figures about their loans 'before and after 2008', they don't mention either. And don't forget that most loans are for a 12-year period or more. This means they will continue this financing until at least 2017.

The third argument is the following. Dexia Israel says it doesn't discriminate because they also finance Arab villages. To be honest, we don't really care who they are financing in Israel as long as they don't support the Occupation. Next to that, this argument makes us very suspicious. It seems Dexia is keeping records of loans on an ethnic basis. We wonder what the reason for this is.

As if all this is not yet enough, in February 2003, Dexia joined the United Nations Global Compact. This means Dexia says in its own ethical code that they should support and respect the protection of internationally proclaimed human rights, and make sure that they are not complicit in human rights abuses. I'll leave it up to the jury to judge if Dexia is in accordance with this.

I also want to draw your attention here to the first session of the Russell Tribunal in Barcelona. Although Dexia is seen as a private company, the Belgian and French states are important actors. The biggest shareholder in Dexia, with 17.6 per cent, is the *Caisse des dépôts et consignations* which is linked to the French government. The Belgian *Holding Communal* (which represents Dexia shares controlled by the Belgian municipalities and provinces) holds 14.8 per cent. The Belgian and French governments each hold 5.7 per cent and the three Belgian regions together also hold 5.7 per cent. All these shares add up to 49.5 per cent of the total shares of the Dexia Group. This shows once more the relevance of the Barcelona session of the Russell Tribunal.

To conclude, I will give you a list of the settlements financed by, through, or with the aid of the Belgian-French Dexia group through their subsidiary Dexia Israel. Several of them have received support more than once: Ma'ale Efrayim, Alfei Menasheh, Elkana, Ariel, Beit Aryeh, Giva'at Ze'ev, Kedumim, the region of the Jordan Valley, the Har Hebron region, Samaria, Jerusalem, Gush Etzion regional council, Beitar Illit, Shomron regional council, Emanuel, Oranit, Golan Heights regional council, Mate Benyamin, Itamar, Alon Shvut, Elazar, Eshkolot, Beit El, Beitar Illit, Bney Yehuda,

Geva Binyamin, Dolev, Bik'at Hayarden, Har Hadar, Hagay, Hinanit, Hashmonaim, Yakir, some settlement neighbourhoods in East Jerusalem, Kohav Hashahar, Kfar Adumim, Mevo Horon, Modi'in Illit, Ma'ale Adumim, Neveh Daniel, Nofim, Nili, Ofra, Etz Efraim, Atniel, Peduel, Kalia, Katzrin, Kiryat Arba, Karney Shomron and Shilo.

Mario Franssen is coordinator of the Belgian solidarity movement INTAL and spokesperson for the Dexia Campaign, Belgium.

*   *   *

PFZW – The Case of a Pension Fund Complicit in International Law Violations
Saskia Müller

Editor's note: Müller stated at the beginning of her presentation that the paper she had submitted to the tribunal (reproduced below) was now outdated, because of then very recent changes: 'after presenting it to the jury of the tribunal, I have found out that the investments I have worked with, that I thought PFZW was still holding, have changed earlier this year.' See the full video of Müller's presentation on the Russell Tribunal website, the Q&A below and PFZW's response in Appendix 2 for more details.[2]

INTRODUCTION TO THE CASE STUDY

PFZW is the second biggest pension fund in the Netherlands, securing the pensions of 2 million people, with total assets amounting to over €80 billion.

PFZW has investments in 27 companies either contributing to Israel's violations of international law, or profiting from Israel's 42-year long belligerent occupation of Palestinian territories. There are four ways in which these companies are involved: they have a factory or branch in a settlement area(s); they supply a settlement(s) or their inhabitants; they supply Israel with services or materials in support of the Occupation; or they use non-renewable Palestinian resources or land.

There is a strong legal basis to hold PFZW responsible for their material support to violations of international law through their investments in the companies mentioned above. The International

Court of Justice in its Advisory Opinion on the legal consequences of the construction of a wall in the OPT (2004), stated that Israel's Occupation, including construction of the wall, construction of the settlements and the associated regime that supports it, are illegal.

As an occupying power, Israel has legal obligations that it breaches in many different ways, namely (1) international humanitarian law, according to the Hague and Geneva Conventions; (2) the human rights of Palestinians according to various human rights treaties; and (3) the Palestinian people's right to self-determination, according to the UN Charter.

These three categories of violations of international humanitarian law by Israel were acknowledged and elaborated by the Russell Tribunal in Barcelona earlier this year.

Violations of international humanitarian law by Israel include: confiscating land not for military purposes, transferring its own civilian population to the OPT, and substantially altering the nature of the OPT.

Violations of international human rights law by Israel include: destroying Palestinian homes and property; severe movement restrictions to Palestinians, and arbitrary arrests, detention without trial and torture of people non-violently resisting.

Israel infringes the right to self-determination of the Palestinian people by maintaining control over the Palestinian territories in the West Bank, Gaza Strip and East Jerusalem through its belligerent occupation.

International humanitarian law, international human rights law and the right to self-determination of the peoples have an indisputable legal basis in the United Nations Charter, in Resolution 2625 of the UN General Assembly, in the International Covenants on economic and social and cultural rights (ICESCR) and civil and political rights (ICCPR) and the Convention on the Elimination of Racial Discrimination, amongst other treaties.

According to the Advisory Opinion of the International Court of Justice, all states are under an obligation not to recognise the illegal situation in Palestine and are not to render aid or assistance in maintaining the situation. All states should see to it that any impediment to the exercise of Palestinian self-determination (for example, by the construction of the wall) is put to an end. States party to the Fourth Geneva Convention (including the Netherlands) relative to the protection of civilian persons in time of war, must ensure compliance by Israel with international humanitarian law as embodied in that convention.

Based on the Dutch *Wet Internationale Misdrijven* (law on international crimes), Dutch companies are also subject to various sources of international criminal law, including international humanitarian law. On this basis, the Dutch public prosecutor is now investigating the business activities of Riwal, a Dutch company suspected of rendering services and goods supporting the Occupation, and particularly the construction of the wall, which is the first step in a possible prosecution of the company.

In addition to binding obligations in international law, international organisations and initiatives underpin the obligations of private companies in international law, including: the OECD with its Guidelines for Multinational Enterprises, the UN Global Compact, and the UN Principles for Responsible Investments.

The International Commission of Jurists[3] and John Ruggie,[4] take these obligations as a starting point for their work.

HOLDING PFZW ACCOUNTABLE: THE EXAMPLE OF VEOLIA

Through its subsidiary Connex Israel, Veolia is one of the companies in the City Pass consortium, contracted to operate the Jerusalem Light Rail Project, which is under construction. The Light Rail Project is designed to connect the western part of the city of Jerusalem with the illegally constructed settlements in East Jerusalem. The construction of the light rail renders the forced displacement of many Palestinian families a permanent 'fact on the ground', severely restricting the movement of Palestinians and discriminating against non-Jews – all for the exclusive benefit of the illegal settlements.

Through its subsidiary Veolia Environmental Services Israel (which has bought TMM Integrated Recycling Services), Veolia owns and operates the Tovlan landfill in the occupied Jordan Valley, using captured Palestinian land and natural resources for the needs of Israeli settlements.

The subsidiary Connex also operates regular bus services to illegal settlements in the West Bank, including Beit Horon and Givat Ze'ev along road 443, which is a road for the exclusive use of illegal settlers, and referred to by many human rights advocates as an 'apartheid road'.

MATERIAL SUPPORT TO SERIOUS VIOLATIONS OF INTERNATIONAL LAW

By investing in the Veolia Corporation, PFZW provides direct, material support to serious violations of international law, including international humanitarian law and human rights, for at least three aforementioned activities that substantially alter the nature of the OPT in a way that does not benefit the local (occupied) population[5] and discriminates against non-Jews.[6]

CONCLUSION

According to both Dutch and international law, and a moral imperative enshrined in various documents, PFZW, as well as other pension funds and investors in a similar situation, is obliged to divest in all 27 companies contained in its investment portfolio, including Veolia, that violate international law, as described above.

Saskia Müller is an independent researcher on the involvement of Dutch pension funds in the Israeli occupation from the Netherlands.

TRANSCRIPT OF JURY Q&A: SASKIA MÜLLER

Editor's note: In this question-and-answer session, Michael Mansfield read out extracts of the six-page response that PFZW sent to the tribunal and noted that the full document would be made available for anyone to read. You can find it in Appendix 2.

Saskia Müller: As I said, PFZW has withdrawn from many Israeli companies, but they have reinvested in some Israeli companies – at least in two, and the third one is not certain, and I had to check it all in one week. One of these companies is, as I said, Super-Sol [aka *Shufersal* – an Israeli supermarket chain with branches in the settlements] that's a company which we know they profit from the Occupation, that's something that I was sort of surprised about. I thought, well, when you withdraw from all these Israeli companies, do it in a proper way. Don't reinvest in Super-Sol again. Stay out of it. But they haven't.

Anthony Gifford QC: ... I just wanted to draw attention to and ask your view about section seven of PFZW's letter, which seemed to me particularly interesting ... The companies with which they are engaging are those that contribute in different ways to sustaining the Occupation. What they mean by engagement is to ask the companies to provide information on their polices, and the final outcome may or may not be the decision to include the company from its investments.

SM: Yeah. Well I think an engagement procedure is better than not talking to these companies and not trying to influence them. On the other hand, I know that since quite some time they have been in such a procedure with Veolia, a company we discussed earlier yesterday. To my opinion, that's quite long. I mean, we know quite a lot of things about Veolia that are not right. When you are of the view – and I am – that companies investing in companies that profit from the Occupation are in fact breaching international law, I think you shouldn't ...

AG: So what you're saying is the information, in your view, is already there for all to see. And you don't need to find out any more?

SM: I think so. Yes.

Ronnie Kasrils: ... Have you had interaction with the pension fund and are they responsive?

SM: I have talked to them last Thursday when I knew of his letter and I discussed it with one of their spokespeople. Yes. It was a very nice, good contact. We didn't fight!

*   *   *

War-Profiteering and SWIFT Sanctions: a Civil Society Imperative
Terry Crawford-Browne

THE GOLDSTONE REPORT AND THE GAZA CONVOY

The United Nations Human Rights Council (UNHRC) appointed South African Judge Richard Goldstone to investigate allegations of war crimes perpetrated by both the Israeli Defence Force and by Hamas during the December 2008/January 2009 bombardment of Gaza. The essential findings of the Goldstone Report have been confirmed by Amnesty International and Human Rights Watch, in particular that Israeli actions in Operation Cast Lead were disproportionate, and thus constituted a war crime.

Operation Cast Lead killed about 1,400 Palestinians in Gaza, and destroyed about 3,350 homes, hospitals, ambulances, mosques, schools, a flour factory and sewage treatment facilities. A UN warehouse was gutted by fire set off by a white phosphorous bomb. The Goldstone Report recommended that both Israel and Hamas in Gaza must immediately conduct credible, independent investigations into the alleged grave violations of human rights and humanitarian law.

Complementing the Goldstone Report, there is a huge body of literature by Amnesty International, Human Rights Watch and the International Crisis Group confirming human rights abuses of Palestinian civilians.

Despite violations of the 'rules of war', Operation Cast Lead failed in its primary objective of regime change in Gaza – to remove Hamas from power even though it had won a 'free and fair' election in Palestine in January 2006.

The attack on the Gaza Flotilla in May 2010 again confirmed that the present Israeli government is a menace that repeatedly and wilfully defies its obligations to the international community. Israel's real aim is not peaceful coexistence with its Palestinian neighbours, but military domination.

The UN General Assembly in November 2009 endorsed the Goldstone Report by a vote of 114 to 18, with 44 states abstaining. The Report was also endorsed by the European Parliament in March 2010. The matter however, remains stymied because of opposition by the United States government, and its abuse of veto powers at the UN Security Council to protect Israel from the consequences of war crimes.

In fact, the United States under the Obama administration is increasing rather than decreasing its supplies of armaments to Israel, further escalating the risks of war in the Middle East. Israel is equipped with an estimated 200–300 nuclear weapons plus other advanced military technology, thus any military confrontation is out of the question.

Given the complicity of the governments of the United States and the European Union in supporting Israeli war crimes, a non-violent strategy by international civil society is imperative.

The parallels with UN decisions and resolutions regarding apartheid South Africa during the 1970s and 1980s are striking. Israel complains that the UN Human Rights Council is biased against Israel, just as apartheid South Africa complained about the UN. Israel declares that the UNHRC has no credibility amongst countries regarded as 'democratic'. Yet it was the United States and British governments that until 1990 repeatedly flouted UN decisions such as the 1977 arms embargo, and undermined sanctions initiatives by civil society to end apartheid in South Africa.

KAIROS PALESTINE

The Kairos Palestine document 'A Moment Of Truth' – presented in December 2009, and adopted by the World Council of Churches – draws heavily on the 1985 South African Kairos document, which made a significant contribution towards the relatively peaceful triumph over apartheid.

Kairos Palestine demands that all peoples, political leaders and decision makers put pressure on Israel and take non-violent, legal measures to oblige the Israeli government to end the Occupation and its disregard for international law. In particular, it calls for economic sanctions and boycotts.

The international banking sanctions campaign against South African banks stemmed from the South African Kairos document. It was orchestrated by church and other leaders of civil society institutions – not governments – and proved to be the single most effective strategy against apartheid.

The campaign was premised on the realisation that because the US dollar is the settlement currency of the foreign exchange system, any significant economy would collapse without access to the New York bank payments system.

WAR PROFITEERING

Corruption and abuses of human rights are invariably interconnected. This is illustrated by Zimbabwe and Burma, just as Israel's military occupation of Palestine since 1967 has also corrupted almost every aspect of Israeli society. Religious, military, diplomatic and economic ethics are filtered and perverted through the issue of 'national security'. There are major vested interests that profit from the Occupation and thus strive to perpetuate it.

Israel is in violation of provisions of the Geneva Conventions that forbid annexation and settlement of territory, and targeting of civilians. The International Court of Justice, in an advisory opinion in 2004, held that the 750-km 'apartheid wall' is illegal and should be dismantled. An estimated 500,000 Israeli settlers now live illegally in occupied areas of East Jerusalem and the West Bank.

Who Profits, a website maintained by the Women's Coalition For Peace, documents the hundreds of international and Israeli companies that illegally profiteer from the Occupation – from construction of the wall and settlements, to agricultural produce grown on confiscated Palestinian land.

In October 2010, Who Profits released a report entitled 'Financing The Israel Occupation: The Direct Involvement of Israeli Banks in Illegal Israeli Settlement Activity and Control over the Palestinian Banking Market'.[7] The report finds that all Israeli banks are crucially involved in the financing of construction in the settlements, in financing the sale of property in the settlements, as well as in providing financial services to corporations illegally operating in the settlements.

Banking is the lifeblood of any economy, and the banking industry is an essential element in Israel's illegal occupation of the Palestinian territories. Most importantly, war profiteering requires access to the international payments transfer system. The Organisation for Economic Cooperation and Development (OECD) in December 2009 noted that whilst the Israeli government has dedicated considerable efforts to fighting domestic corruption, there is a lack of commitment to tackling international corruption.

SWIFT

With computerisation, the international bank payments system has advanced dramatically since the 1980s. Although access to New York banks remains pivotal, interbank transfer instructions are now conducted through the Society for Worldwide Interbank Financial Telecommunication (SWIFT), which is domiciled in Belgium and thus outside US jurisdiction. SWIFT links 8,740 financial institutions in 209 countries.

Without SWIFT, Israel's access to the international financial system would be very severely circumscribed. Without payment for import or exports and given its exceptionally heavy dependence upon trade, the Israeli economy would rapidly collapse. Money laundering is increasingly considered as a major international security threat, as illustrated by the United States subpoena after 9/11 of SWIFT data to track terrorist financing.

SWIFT complied with the US subpoena, but was severely criticised in Europe for violating European privacy protocols. That compliance still remains a contentious matter, with the European Parliament in February 2010 having rejected a European Union–SWIFT agreement with the US government. The international financial system is exceedingly sensitive to allegations of money laundering but also to any association with human rights abuses.

If international civil society is serious about the Israeli–Palestinian conflict and in ending the Occupation, then suspension of SWIFT transactions for international payments to and from Israeli banks offers an instrument to bring about a peaceful and non-violent resolution to the conflict.

Rather than the poor and politically voiceless, this strategy would impact rapidly upon the political and financial elites who have the clout to effect political change. Such a suspension would not affect domestic banking transactions within Israel and Palestine. It is economic warfare using weapons of non-violence, and makes redundant the use of armaments in conflict situations. It is a strategy that can be reversed as soon as its measurable political objectives have been achieved, without inflicting long-term structural economic damage.

Although owned by banks, SWIFT falls under the control of the Belgian central bank. Belgium applies 'universal jurisdiction' on human rights abuses. Although this commitment was watered down some years ago under Israeli pressure, SWIFT is domiciled in Belgium and thus falls under the jurisdiction of Belgian courts. SWIFT, rightly, will take action against Israeli banks only if ordered to do so by a Belgian court, and only in very exceptional circumstances. Such exceptional circumstances are now well documented.

Each bank has an eight-letter SWIFT code that identifies both the bank and its country of domicile. IL are the fifth and sixth letters in SWIFT codes that identify Israel. For instance:

- Israel Discount Bank   IDBLILIT
- Bank Hapoalim   POALILIT
- Bank Ha Leumi   LUMIILIT
- Bank of Israel   ISRAILIJ
- Mizrahi Tefahot Bank   MIZBILIT
- Jerusalem Bank   JERSILIT
- Union Bank of Israel   UNBKILIT

SWIFT is outside American jurisdiction, and also beyond the reach of Israeli military retaliation. In response to the Kairos Palestine document, this memo recommends that the Russell Tribunal should recommend and lead a SWIFT sanctions campaign against Israeli banks. What is required is an urgent application in a Belgian court ordering SWIFT to reprogram its computers to suspend all transactions to and from Israeli banks until:

- The Israeli government agrees to end its occupation of the West Bank including East Jerusalem, and that it will dismantle the 'apartheid wall'.
- The Israeli government recognises the fundamental rights of Arab-Palestinians to full equality in Israel/Palestine.
- The Israeli government acknowledges the right of return of Palestinian refugees.

Terry Crawford-Browne is a retired banker, who advised the South African Council of Churches on the banking sanctions campaign against apartheid South Africa.

TRANSCRIPT: TERRY CRAWFORD-BROWNE INTRODUCTION

Terry Crawford-Browne: Thank you, members of jury, for giving me the opportunity to testify before you. I am a former international banker with Nedbank, a major South African group in Cape Town, and in the mid-1980s my position was regional treasury manager for the Western Cape, meaning that I was responsible for international banking, including foreign exchange operations in the Cape Town area.

I was also, in 1984, appointed by Archbishop Philip Russell, who preceded Archbishop Tutu, to be one of four Anglican representatives to the Western Province Council of Churches. So, if you will, I was a conservative white banker by day and a revolutionary by night. It was rather a schizophrenic situation, hence I am now wearing this jacket representing the World Council of Churches. I am, at the moment, spending three months in Palestine monitoring checkpoints in Bethlehem and I spent three months in Jerusalem last year doing a similar assignment for the World Council of Churches. In the mid-1980s, Nedbank was the preferred vehicle for the South African government to evade sanctions. We specialised in international trade and we were very much involved in fraudulent letters of credit, phoney documentation, etc. ... .

5
The Security Industry and the War Industry

The Israeli Arms Trade and the Apparatus of Repression
John Hilary

Israel is one of the most heavily militarised countries in the world. Over the past decade, it has consistently devoted 7–9 per cent of its GDP to military expenditure. In 2009, Israel devoted $13.5 billion to military expenditure, including $2.5 billion supplied by the US to Israel as military aid.[1] Israel is also the only nation in the Middle East to possess its own nuclear arsenal.

Israel's arms industry plays an important part in the country's economy, with sales in excess of $6 billion in 2009. Companies such as Elbit Systems, Rafael Advanced Defense Systems, Israel Military Industries and Israel Aerospace Industries have become global players through the development of high-technology equipment for use by the Israeli military and other armed forces. In 2008, Israel was the seventh largest arms exporter in the world.

Other nations have benefited directly from weapons technology used in Israeli operations against Palestinian and Lebanese civilians, such as the unmanned aerial vehicles (UAVs) developed by Elbit Systems. Countries that have procured UAVs from Elbit include Australia, Canada, Croatia, France, Georgia, Mexico, Singapore, Sweden, the UK and US. Elbit's own promotional material boasts that its Skylark UAVs were used to great effect by the Israeli military in its 2006 war against Lebanon, while Elbit's Hermes 450 UAVs were widely employed in Gaza during Operation Cast Lead.[2] The British Army has awarded Elbit Systems and its partner company Thales UK a contract worth over $1 billion for the development of the Watchkeeper, the next generation of UAVs. The British company UAV Engines Limited, a wholly owned Elbit subsidiary, will produce the plane's engines.

The high-tech surveillance equipment which Israel has developed in the militarised context of the Occupied Palestinian Territories (OPT) is now being used in diverse ways by other states. Israeli intelligence company Verint has supplied video surveillance technology for use on the London Underground, while Elbit Systems formed part of the consortium that was awarded a $2 billion contract to secure the US's border with Mexico against immigrants. Elbit's experience in developing 'peripheral defence' technology in Israel was widely noted to be in its favour.

In addition to military hardware, Israel also boasts one of the most developed private military and security industries, selling militarised security services to companies and governments as well as training military and police forces the world over. In May 2007, War on Want sent an indicative list of 35 Israeli private military and security companies to the United Nations Working Group on the Use of Mercenaries for its research into the growing privatisation of armed conflict.

Western companies profit not only from sharing in Israeli military technology and contracts, but also from supplying Israel with weaponry for its own use. Between 2003 and 2008, EU member states' governments approved licences worth over €1 billion in arms sales to Israel. The largest European exporters to Israel are to be found in France (which accounted for over half of the total value of sales licensed during this period), Germany, Britain, Belgium, Poland, Romania and the Czech Republic. Finland has become the second largest supplier of missile technology to Israel after the US, with companies such as Insta DefSec and Patria engaged in profitable relationships with Israeli counterparts Rafael and Elbit Systems.[3]

European companies also profit from arms exports to third countries which are destined for final delivery to Israel. British arms giant BAE Systems provides holographic display components for F-16 fighters sold to Israel by US company Lockheed Martin, while display components manufactured by British firm Brimar are used in the Israeli Air Force's AH-64 Apache helicopters. The UK government has conceded that components licensed for export from Britain were 'almost certainly' used by the Israeli armed forces in Gaza during Operation Cast Lead.

Yet it is US companies that profit most from military relations with Israel. Firms such as Lockheed Martin, Boeing and Raytheon have signed multi-billion dollar deals with the Israeli military to provide fighter jets, helicopters and missiles, all of which have been used against civilian targets. The US construction equipment firm Caterpillar has supplied the Israeli army with militarised D9 bulldozers which have been used extensively in Palestinian house demolitions and urban warfare support. The former UN Special Rapporteur on the Right to Food, Jean Ziegler, complained to Caterpillar's CEO of the company's possible complicity in human rights violations as a result of supplying bulldozers to the Israeli military 'in the certain knowledge' that they would be used against civilian targets.[4]

Corporate complicity in Israel's violation of international humanitarian and human rights law has been noted by the international community more broadly.[5] The Church of England withdrew its investments from Caterpillar in December 2008 following a vote to divest on ethical grounds. The Norwegian government's pension fund announced its divestment from Elbit Systems in September 2009 as a result of the company's involvement in the construction of Israel's illegal apartheid wall, and Denmark's Danske Bank followed suit in early 2010.

John Hilary is executive director of the charity War on Want.

TRANSCRIPT OF JURY Q&A: JOHN HILARY

Mairead Maguire: How can we, as the Russell Tribunal, how can people, bring more pressure on the Israeli government and corporations who are complicit in war crimes in doing this? How can we help and bring a new consciousness that we all have to do something to end this occupation?

John Hilary: I'm happy to say madam chair that there is a very ready answer to that question, and I think that the [2005] boycott, divestment, sanctions call has precisely homed in on this empowerment of people to see where their money is being used and where it is being used to commit crimes. But the good news is, it is one of the areas where we have already seen significant movement. The General Synod of the Church of England, for example, voted two years ago to withdraw all of its investments from Caterpillar, and all of those investments have now been withdrawn. As we know, the Norwegian government pension fund announced its divestment from Elbit, the Danish bank followed suit, the Dutch pensions companies followed suit. There has been direct action taken against Raytheon and EDO in this country alone, where juries have acquitted all of those responsible for hundreds of thousands of pounds worth of criminal damage because they recognised that they were acting in the higher good. So I feel we are already on the way to making a great difference here, and that by giving more people the material to know what is behind the call for boycott, divestment and sanctions, that will actually take the movement to its next stage.

* * *

Caterpillar's Involvement in the Occupied Palestinian Territories
Maria LaHood

Since 1967, Israel has destroyed nearly 25,000 Palestinian structures in the Occupied Palestinian Territory (OPT).[6] Since 1967, Caterpillar, Inc. has been supplying to Israel the bulldozers that have been used in such demolitions. The Caterpillar D9 bulldozer is over 4 metres tall and 8 metres wide, weighs more than 60 tons with its armoured plating, and can raze houses within minutes. Human rights organisations began to condemn these home demolitions at least as early as 1989, and beginning in 2001, Caterpillar was specifically notified that it was aiding and abetting violations of international law by providing Israel with the bulldozers used to destroy homes. Caterpillar has continued to sell D9 bulldozers to Israel knowing they would be used to unlawfully demolish homes in the OPT. In addition to forcibly displacing more than 50,000 Palestinians, home demolitions have also resulted in injuries and deaths.

Between September 2000 and November 2004, Israel destroyed approximately 4,170 Palestinian homes in the OPT.[7] In 2002, the Israel Defense Forces (IDF) launched attacks on Nablus and Jenin. On 5 April 2002, the al-Sho'bi family home in the old city of Nablus in the West Bank was destroyed by a Caterpillar bulldozer, without warning, in an IDF attack in the middle of the night. Samir and his pregnant wife Nabila, and their three young children, Anas, Azzam and Abdallah, as well as Samir's father Umar, and his sisters Fatima and Abir were all killed while in their home.

On 9 April 2002, the Fayed family home was bulldozed in an IDF incursion into the Jenin Refugee Camp in the West Bank, in which at least 140 buildings, most of them homes, were completely destroyed, more than 200 were severely damaged, and 4,000 people were made homeless. Jamal Fayed, who was paralysed, was unable to get out of the house. Jamal's mother and sister alerted the bulldozer driver and tried to stop him, but he demolished the home, killing Jamal.

Over 2,500 of the home demolitions between September 2000 and 2004 were in Gaza, 1,600 of which were in Rafah, a 4 km-long strip of land on the southern border of Gaza. On 3 September 2002, a bulldozer demolished the Abu Hussein family's home in the al-Salam neighbourhood of Rafah, about 150 metres from where Israel was constructing the wall and a 'buffer zone' around it. The destruction began without warning at approximately 5.00 a.m., physically injuring six family members inside, and shocking and traumatising the whole family.

About six months later, and about 200 metres away, Rachel Corrie, a 23-year-old American human rights activist and college student, was in Rafah with the International Solidarity Movement. On 16 March 2003, Rachel stood in front of the home of the Nasrallah family, where Rachel had previously stayed, to protect it from demolition by a Caterpillar D9 bulldozer while the family was inside. The IDF soldier operating the bulldozer ran her over, killing her.

In a July 2004 incursion into Khan Yunis Refugee Camp in Gaza, the IDF demolished over seventy homes. Just after midnight, a bulldozer approached Mr and Mrs Khalafallah's home, where they lived with their five children, two daughters-in-law, and four grandchildren. Ibrahim Khalafallah was in his 70s, and was sick and unable to move or hear. When the bulldozer hit the house, Ibrahim's wife and daughter tried to get the bulldozer driver to stop, but he continued, destroying their home and killing Mr Khalafallah.

In 2005, the Center for Constitutional Rights and co-counsel brought a case against Caterpillar on behalf of these families in United States District Court. The case asserted international law claims that Caterpillar aided and abetted Israel's war crimes, including collective punishment, the destruction of property not justified by military necessity, and attacks against civilians (including articles 27, 32, 33, 53, and 147 of the Fourth Geneva Convention). These home demolitions constituted war crimes, and were carried out without warning and in some cases despite pleas that family members were still inside. Rachel Corrie was killed by a Caterpillar D9 bulldozer while she tried to protect a home from demolition with the family inside. Caterpillar has continued to provide D9 bulldozers to Israel knowing they had been and would be used to unlawfully demolish homes in the OPT, and it was foreseeable that civilians would be harmed in the process. Caterpillar aided and abetted war crimes by knowingly providing substantial assistance for their commission by the IDF.

The case was dismissed by the District Court and the dismissal was affirmed on appeal. In the Appellate Court, the US government submitted a brief asserting that it paid for the bulldozers at issue and arguing that the case would interfere with foreign policy because it made a determination to extend Foreign Military Financing (FMF) aid to Israel and 'to encourage equipment manufacturers like Caterpillar to sell its goods to foreign states receiving such FMF funds'. The Appellate Court did not rule on the merits of the case, but found that it did not have jurisdiction to decide the case because adjudication would intrude upon the US Executive's foreign policy decisions. The families sought rehearing, arguing that the court should not have looked beyond the record of the case, that the record did not support the court's findings, and that the issues before the court were legal, not policy determinations, and should be decided by the court. The Appellate Court denied rehearing in 2009, thereby ending the case against Caterpillar.

Maria LaHood is senior staff attorney at the Center for Constitutional Rights in New York city.

TRANSCRIPT OF JURY Q&A: MARIA LAHOOD

Ronnie Kasrils: I just want to go back to the question of the armaments industry in America or Israel, that is in partnership with Caterpillar. You made reference to the additional equipment, and are you aware of which armaments or security company Caterpillar is in partnership with, or is Caterpillar producing its own additional security equipment?

Maria LaHood: I think they are in partnership with other countries as well, and they have distributors.

RK: Can you name those?

ML: I cannot name those. I mean there's, you know, as far as the armoured plating there's actually an Israeli company, IMI [Israel Military Industries], that does some of the – that we understand does some of the ... add some of the armoured plating. But as far as other countries, I don't know. I've heard to some European countries but we don't have certain evidence.

[John Hilary is briefly recalled by the jury]

John Hilary: Yes it is indeed, as has been heard, it is certainly within Israel itself. Israel Aerospace Industries is also involved, I believe, in the militarisation of the Caterpillar D9 bulldozer. We also have companies here in the UK, who are subsidiaries of Caterpillar, who are involved in producing that. I will certainly happily give the tribunal jury a copy of the Caterpillar report we have, which also goes to the question asked by Professor Dugard. We have a nice picture of the D9 bulldozer with its hook, specifically added, which is – as you say – designed to be able to rip up water infrastructure and things like this. So maybe if I could leave these two copies with the tribunal jury [passes them to the jury].

*   *   *

US Government Complicity in the Supply of Caterpillar Bulldozers to Israel

Josh Ruebner

Since 1949, the United States has provided Israel a total of slightly more than $109 billion in military and economic aid, according to the Congressional Research Service.[8] In August 2007, the United States and Israel signed a Memorandum of Understanding (MOU) for the United States to provide Israel with $30 billion in additional military aid during financial years 2009–18, an annual average increase of 25 per cent above levels prior to the MOU.[9] Israel is the largest recipient of US foreign aid.

Each year, the president submits a budget request to Congress, which includes a proposed appropriation of military aid to Israel through a programme formally titled Foreign Military Financing (FMF). The House and Senate Appropriations Subcommittees on State, Foreign Operations, and Related Programs have jurisdiction over this portion of the US federal budget and have the authority to amend, approve, or deny the president's budget request. Once these subcommittees pass their budget, which includes FMF for Israel, both the entire Appropriations Committees and the full chambers of the House and Senate also have the opportunity to amend, approve, or vote against the budget. After a reconciled budget passes both the House and Senate, the president can either sign into law or veto the budget.

Once Congress appropriates FMF to Israel through this budget process, both the Department of State and the Department of

Defense separately administer different programmes to contract for and transfer US weapons to recipients of US military aid. The three major US governmental programmes that convey military aid to their recipients are: Direct Commercial Sales (DCS) – administered by the Department of State, and Foreign Military Sales (FMS) and Excess Defense Articles (EDA) – administered by the Department of Defense.

In *Corrie et. al.* v *Caterpillar Inc.*, a lawsuit filed in US federal court seeking redress against Caterpillar for the deaths of US citizen Rachel Corrie and other Palestinians killed by Israel with Caterpillar products, the corporation's General Manager, Defense and Federal Products, declared that

> ... the Defense Security Cooperation Agency ('DCSA') [an agency within the Department of Defense] gave approval for funding by the United States government under the foreign military financing ('FMF') program and found that the proposed procurement by the State of Israel was consistent with the Arms Export Control Act ('AECA') and the applicable FMF agreements.[10]

Except for large contracts, Department of State and Department of Defense public reporting on amounts, categories and corporate origin of arms transfers is opaque. Based on publicly available records, the total quantity and value of Caterpillar bulldozers transferred from the United States to Israel as part of its military aid package is not known, since neither department has an explicit category for bulldozers. The bulldozers may be categorised under 'other commercial vehicles' in the FMS programme, which amounted to $87.9 million in the financial years 2000–09.[11] This figure would appear to be in line with a document submitted by Caterpillar, cited above, in the *Corrie v Caterpillar* lawsuit, which revealed the approval by DCSA of $32.6 million in FMF for Israel's purchase of 50 Caterpillar D9R bulldozers in 2001.

Despite Caterpillar providing documentary evidence that the US government has certified that the provision of bulldozers to Israel is 'consistent' with the AECA, doubts remain about the legality of US arms transfer to Israel in general, and of Caterpillar bulldozers in particular. All US arms transfers and military aid – without exception – are subject to laws that are intended to prevent these weapons from being misused to commit human rights abuses.

The AECA (P.L. 80-829) stipulates that foreign countries either purchasing US weapons or receiving them as military aid must use them only for 'internal security' and 'legitimate self-defense'. The Foreign Assistance Act (P.L. 97-195), which regulates all US military and economic aid programmes, provides that 'No assistance may be provided … to the government of any country which engages in a consistent pattern of gross violations of internationally recognized human rights.' It also prohibits military aid to 'any unit of the security forces of a foreign country if the Secretary of State has credible evidence that such unit has committed gross violations of human rights'.

Israel's misuse of US weapons in general, and Caterpillar bulldozers in particular, would appear to place it in violation of all of these US laws. According to the Israeli human rights organisation B'Tselem – The Israeli Information Center for Human Rights in the Occupied Territories, since 29 September 2000, Israel has killed more than 3,000 Palestinian non-combatants (civilians and civil police who took no part in hostilities when killed) in the occupied Gaza Strip, West Bank and East Jerusalem. Of these fatalities, Israel killed 21 innocent Palestinian civilians, including 7 children, through house demolitions.[12] Most of these fatalities likely resulted from Israel employing Caterpillar bulldozers to demolish these Palestinian houses. Among those innocent Palestinian civilians killed by Israel are:

- Eight members of the al-Sho'bi family in Nablus, who were crushed to death when the Israeli military destroyed their home in April 2002 and did not give them enough time to flee the premises.
- Jamal Fayad, a paralysed man whose relatives informed Israeli soldiers that he was inside the house about to be demolished and unable to leave, who was crushed to death in April 2002.
- Ibrahim Khalafallah, a man in his seventies who was unable to move without assistance, who was crushed to death in his home in June 2004.
- These Palestinian fatalities are exclusive of the case of US citizen Rachel Corrie, who was killed on 16 March 2003 by the Israeli military with a Caterpillar D9 bulldozer as she nonviolently protected a Palestinian home in Rafah, Gaza Strip from being demolished.

In addition to Israel's violation of the most basic and fundamental human right to life, it also misuses Caterpillar bulldozers to commit other grave violations of human rights and international law, including the wanton destruction of personal property, the uprooting of olive trees, and the construction of illegal Israeli settlements and the apartheid wall, ruled to be illegal by the International Court of Justice in July 2004.[13]

Israel's use of Caterpillar bulldozers to violate human rights and international law in the course of a foreign military occupation cannot be considered to be for 'internal security' or 'legitimate self-defense'. According to the US laws cited above, Israel should be sanctioned and ineligible to receive US military aid as a consequence of its systematic human rights abuses of Palestinians. Unfortunately, the US government does not apply its own laws on an impartial basis; their implementation is subject to political calculations.

However, these calculations may be beginning to shift in a positive direction. On 25 October 2010, Israel's Channel 2 news programme reported that Caterpillar, most likely with US government pressure, has suspended the delivery of tens of D9 bulldozers – valued at $50 million – to the Israeli military. On 5 November, the US Campaign to End the Israeli Occupation delivered to the Department of State an open letter signed by 150 organisations and a petition signed by more than 11,000 individuals, calling on the Obama administration to make this temporary suspension permanent and to end bulldozer deliveries to the Israeli military.

International civil society in general, and US citizens in particular, must engage in this type of activism to demand that the United States hold Israel accountable for its misuse of US weapons, including Caterpillar bulldozers. Without such a change in US policy, the main conduit of arms transfers to Israel will only continue to increase and thereby vitiate any prospect of a just and lasting Israeli-Palestinian peace.

Josh Ruebner is national advocacy director of the US Campaign to End the Israeli Occupation.

*   *   *

G4S and the Occupation

Merav Amir and Dalit Baum

Editor's note: In March 2011, several months after the following presentation, G4S announced its intention to stop providing some equipment to West Bank settlements. The Marker (a financial supplement to Israeli daily Ha'aretz) said this came 'in the wake of public pressure in Denmark following a report from the Coalition of Women for Peace, which runs the "Who Profits?" project ... G4S said it intends to terminate contracts with security facilities in the [Occupied Palestinian] territories as soon as possible. The company stated, however, that it recognizes its contractual obligations toward its customers and will take these into account.'[14]

In 2002, the Danish security company Group4Falck bought one of Israel's biggest providers of security services: Hashmira. In 2004, Group4Falck merged with the British Securicor company and established Group4Securicor (G4S), which is now one of the largest companies providing security services internationally. G4S holds 90 per cent of the shares of its Israeli subsidiary, G4S Israel. Our research has found that G4S Israel is involved in the Israeli Occupation in four main ways:

- in providing security equipment and services to incarceration facilities holding Palestinian political prisoners inside Israel and in the occupied West Bank,
- in providing equipment and maintenance services to Israeli military checkpoints in the West Bank,
- in providing security systems for the Israeli police headquarters in the West Bank, and
- in providing security services to businesses in settlements.

INCARCERATION FACILITIES FOR PALESTINIAN POLITICAL PRISONERS

According to the company's own publications, G4S Israel has provided a perimeter defence system for the walls of Ofer Prison and installed a central command room in the facility, from which the entire facility can be monitored. The Ofer compound includes a prison, an army camp and a military court. This Israeli prison is specifically dedicated for Palestinian political prisoners. Despite being in the West Bank, the compound is located in what Israel defines as the 'Seam Zone'. Thus, access by West Bank Palestinians to this facility is highly restricted, both for family members of detainees and for their lawyers, and it is dependent on receiving a special access permit. The fact that the court is located in this facility severely limits the possibility of the public, and in particular the Palestinian public from the West Bank, from attending court sessions.

Figure 5.1   Outside Israel's Ofer military prison, East Jerusalem. Oren Ziv/Activestills.org.

Additionally, the company reports that it has provided the entire security system for the Ketziot Prison and a central command room in the Megido Prison. These prisons are defined as prisons for 'security prisoners', which, in fact, means that they hold Palestinian political prisoners. In violation of international law, these prisoners are held in facilities inside Israel and not in the OPT. Palestinians are defined as 'security' prisoners not only when found guilty of committing militant acts, but also when they are associated with any felony of a political character, such as belonging to an unauthorised political organisation, participating in demonstrations and the like. Prisoners in these prisons are deprived of many of the basic rights that other prisoners enjoy, such as access to a telephone, heavy limitations on reading materials, on receiving and sending letters and on visitation rights of family members. Political prisoners are also more likely to undergo torture. In particular, in these two prisons, prisoners are only entitled to one visit per month by immediate family members.

It is also important to note that these are the three prisons in which Palestinian administrative detainees are held. Currently, there are more than two hundred such prisoners in these prisons. Administrative detainees are held without being charged with any crime or violation, and they are imprisoned for months and even years without a release or court date. The incarceration of administrative detainees is in violation of any covenant of international human rights law.

G4S has also provided security systems for the Kishon ('al-Jalameh') and the Jerusalem ('Russian Compound') detention and interrogation facilities. These facilities are used for the interrogation and incarceration of Palestinian political prisoners. The operation of these facilities is not only in contradiction to many aspects of international law, but there is also evidence indicating that Palestinian prisoners undergo torture and abuse in these detention facilities.

SERVICES TO ISRAELI MILITARY CHECKPOINTS IN THE WEST BANK

G4S Israel has supplied luggage scanning equipment and full body scanners to several military checkpoints in the West Bank, including the Qalandia, Bethlehem and Irtah (Sha'ar Efraim) checkpoints. Additionally, the company provided full body scanners to the Erez checkpoint in Gaza.

All of these West Bank checkpoints are built as part of the separation wall, whose route was declared illegal by the International Court of Justice in its Advisory Opinion of 9 July 2004. The Qalandia and Bethlehem checkpoints are also part of the Israeli system of control that sustains its annexation of East Jerusalem, since they prevent Palestinian residents of the West Bank from entering the city. The Erez checkpoint serves as part of the Israeli closure policy over the Gaza Strip. The Barcelona session of the Russell Tribunal on Palestine defined the closure of the borders of the Gaza Strip as an act that may be characterised as apartheid; the annexation of East Jerusalem was found to be one of the grave breaches of international law against the Palestinian people.

ISRAELI POLICE HEADQUARTERS IN THE WEST BANK

G4S Israel has provided security equipment for the Israeli police headquarters in the West Bank, which is located in the E-1 area, next to the settlement of Ma'ale Adumim. The E-1 construction project was aimed at ensuring the contiguity of Israeli settlements between the settlement neighbourhoods of East Jerusalem and Ma'ale Adumim, cutting off the south of the West Bank (Bethlehem and Hebron) from the central and northern areas (Ramallah, Nablus and Jenin) to Palestinian movement and development. Due to US objections, the construction of housing projects in the E-1 area was suspended, but a new building for the headquarters of the West Bank division of the Israeli police was built there. Currently, this is the only Israeli building in this area.

PROVIDING SECURITY SERVICES TO BUSINESSES IN SETTLEMENTS

According to company publications and findings of the group 'DanWatch', G4S offers its security services to businesses in the illegal settlements in the West Bank and in the settlement neighbourhoods of East Jerusalem. These include providing security equipment and personnel to shops and supermarkets in settlements, including in the settlements of Modi'in Illit, Ma'ale Adumim, Har Adar and the settlement neighbourhoods of East Jerusalem.

Merav Amir and Dalit Baum are coordinators of 'Who Profits from the Occupation', a project of the Coalition of Women for Peace in Tel Aviv.

TRANSCRIPT OF JURY Q&A: MERAV AMIR AND DALIT BAUM

Michael Mansfield QC: There is a third angle on this, and that is bringing suits, civil suits, in the United Kingdom against G4 [*sic*: G4S], for obvious violations. Now, in order to do that, you've given us some information on what they are doing at the moment, irrespective of what they say in various letters. One of the objectives would be to identify an English director. Is there an English director? You mentioned there were three but I don't think you mentioned the English one.

Merav Amir: For what we know, because it's a private company – the Israeli branch is a private company, it doesn't have to disclose all of its board or anything, but the three directors that we know of: one is Danish, one is Greek and the third one is Israeli. Any of them may have British citizenship and that is worth checking but from the preliminary investigation that we had, these are the three directors of the company.

Cynthia McKinney: ... I was looking at that full body scanner. Now, it's all the rage in the United States right now because people don't want all of their private parts just, you know, displayed. And in fact what has happened is some private parts have been exposed ... The question I have, is that the same machine, or a similar machine?

Dalit Baum: It's exactly the same machine, it's the same provider: L3 Communications is an American corporation that produces them. The machine is called SafeView, which makes you feel maybe it's safe. But you have to remember that in the Occupied Territories maybe people have to cross checkpoints, maybe twice a day, to work and back, to school and back, and cross that machine twice a day. So, with all the concerns about privacy and showing private body parts, I would also ask about the safety of this apparatus.

CM: So the company name is L3 Communications?

DB: L3 Communications, yes. It's a public US company.

CM: And also, there is a concern for radiation?

DB: Yes.

CM: And that means that ... even the young children are going ...

DB: We don't have any information about that, but I just know that this is called SafeView, which makes me worried.

MM: ... You indicated that the Israeli company [Hashmira] is 90 per cent owned by Danish-British, do you know the split?

DB: Yes. It's 90.5 per cent owned by the British-Danish corporation G4 Securicor. And the rest of the percentage is privately held by Iga'l Shermister who is the CEO, the Israeli CEO and the original founder of Hashmira.

MM: And do you know: with regard to the 90.5, how much of that can be attributed to the British angle as opposed to the Danish?

DB: No, this was merged, it's one company. It's not a partnership, it's a British-Danish company and it's dually traded in the UK and in Denmark.

*   *   *

Elbit Systems

Shir Hever

The information that I present here is based on an array of sources which, despite its variety and scope, remains very limited. Elbit Systems is first and foremost a weapons company. Most of its products are intended for military use, and as such it is naturally a secretive company. Thus, most of the information available on the company originates in the company itself – through numerous press releases which are distributed through the Israeli press in Hebrew, intended mostly for the eyes of potential investors.

Two points should be made here. First, we have more access to information about Elbit because it is a privatised company, and a by-product of their search for investors is more advertising. Secondly, Elbit is far more quick to announce deals with Europe and the US, but rarely mentions the names of their customers when the customers are from Asia or Latin America (with the exception of Brazil and South Korea).[15] Elbit's financial statements reveal ties with Argentina, Australia, Brazil, Bulgaria, Canada, Columbia, Georgia, Romania – but even the financial statement sometimes refers to 'other customers' without specifying.[16]

GENERAL INFORMATION ABOUT THE COMPANY

Elbit was founded in 1967, when the aftermath of the Occupation created a business opportunity. The Israeli government refused to relinquish the Occupied Territories, and has increased government investment in military build-up in order to face the inevitable conflict that would ensue from the Occupation. In 1996, the company split into Elbit Systems Ltd and Elbit Imaging Ltd.

The company has been growing rapidly since the 1990s, and has been acquiring more and more companies as part of its strategy to merge and grow. In 2007, it was ranked the world's 37th place in growth rate of defence companies in the world by *Defense News*.[17]

In 2001–05, Elbit had revenues of $765–1,070 million annually, and a net profit of $1.07–0.8 million annually. Total shareholder's equity was between $378 million and $451 million.[18] In 2005, it employed 6,430 workers.

The company is worth today approximately €1.6 billion, and the net profit for 2009 was €88 million. In 2009, it reached a profit per capital of nearly 30 per cent. The CEO is Joseph Ackerman, the biggest controlling share is held by Michael Federmann.

Elbit is a multi-branch company with many subsidiaries. It owns Tadiran, one of Israel's oldest weapons manufacturing companies.[19] Other subsidiaries are Vision Systems International, which develops targeting systems for ground bombing,[20] Elisra which produces electronic warfare systems,[21] Elop which produces electro-optic systems for defence and homeland security purposes, Cyclone which produces metal structural parts for aircraft, Silver Arrow (UAVs), Opgal (thermal imaging), SCD (semiconductors), Ortek (perimeter security systems) and U-TacS, a British subsidiary operating the Watchkeeper programme.[22]

Elbit Systems has a subsidiary called 'Elbit Systems of America (ESA)', which does deals with the US Army to take advantage of US military aid money to Israel.[23] An important aspect of this is Elbit's contract with Lockheed Martin for developing helmets and other systems for the F-35 Stealth fighter.[24]

In 2009, Elbit bought Kinetics, a company which produces accessories for combat vehicles[25] and BVR, a company which produces training systems and simulators.[26] It then proceeded to purchase Shiron, a company specialising in broadband communications.[27] Elbit also purchased the Mikal group which focuses on producing artillery and armoured vehicles, in response to a trend among tank producers to develop the technology to upgrade their own tanks.[28] It also recently bought the Azimut company which develops surveillance and targeting equipment for military and civilian customers.[29]

Elbit also has a subsidiary called Elbit European Subsidiary based in Belgium. Elbit is traded both in the Tel-Aviv Stock Exchange and on the Nasdaq.

Table 5.1   Share of Elbit sales

| | Year ended 31 December | | |
	2003	2004	2005
Israel	29%	26%	29%
United States	37%	37%	37%
Europe	12%	13%	10%
Others	22%	24%	24%

The profits of Elbit Systems are closely tied to European customers. When in the second quarter of 2010, European countries ordered fewer UAVs, Elbit suffered a 17 per cent drop in sales.[30]

MODE OF OPERATION

Elbit's business model is built on very close relations with the Israeli military. It has close ties with specific units in the army, and begins recruiting them even before they are released from service.[31]

In addition to the soldiers, who help the company with combat experience and with an intimate knowledge of the needs of the military, the company works closely with Israeli institutions of higher learning: the Technion in Haifa, and also the Weizman Institute, both opened centres for electro-optic research with Elbit (and the Technion specifically trains students to work in Elbit). The Technion also gave an honorary PhD to Joseph Ackerman. Michael Federmann, chairman of the board of directors of Elbit and its biggest shareholder, is also a member of the board of governors of both the Weizman Institute and the Hebrew University. The Weizman Institute initiated with Elbit a program to train high-school pupils in electro-optics in Elbit factories. Elbit also sponsors the Atidim programme for academic reserve soldiers.

Once Elbit develops a system, the company first gives it to the Israeli army to use. Once the Israeli army makes an order, it is much easier to market the system to other armies as well. The systems are sold to customers on the basis of a sequence of contracts. The clients buy the equipment, but Elbit offers to renew and improve it after several years with a follow-up contract.

Elbit is a major supplier for the Israeli Air Force. For example, it provides training airplanes for air force cadets[32] and flight simulators for F-16 planes.[33] It also provides equipment for other branches for the Israeli army. For example, it provides fire control and electric gun and turret drive systems to Israel's main battle tank, the Merkava, that is used against civilian populations, and for Israel's 'Digital Army' programme that was used in the war of 2006.[34]

Elbit provides electronic equipment for land forces and air forces, and has done so for many countries, including several European countries.[35] Elbit also deals with intelligence equipment, providing products for both Israeli and international customers.[36] Elbit's targeting systems, especially night-vision equipment, is also widely distributed around the world (for example, to the US).[37]

Elbit is very famous for its unmanned aircrafts which are used by the Israeli military but also by many other countries, including the UK. Elbit cooperates with the French Sagem company and the British Thales company in producing and marketing UAVs.[38] These UAVs are used in Afghanistan.[39]

The Hermes 1500, for example, is capable of carrying a payload of 350 kg, has a range of 200 km (or double if it does not return), and can stay 24 hours in the air. As such, it could also be considered as a missile. Elbit UAVs were used by Turkey in the Kurdish areas where the government is committing war crimes.[40]

Elbit also provides many products for the civilian market. For example, it provides a system to protect against ground-to-air missiles for commercial flights, but the system greatly increases the aircraft's fuel consumption.[41] The system is already operative in some El-Al planes.[42]

Elbit became a major player in the 'Homeland Security' market in the last decade, producing airport and seaport security systems, border control systems (including databases on passengers), coastal control systems, electronic fences, surveillance technologies, UAVs for police, and so on.[43]

Some Elbit technologies are adapted for non-military use, such as for medical procedures.

INCENTIVE FOR WAR

Elbit is a classic case of a company that profits from war, with a vested interest in conflict, terror and fear.

During the recent global economic crisis, Elbit's profits soared while most of the companies around the world suffered heavy losses. In the third quarter of 2008, as the world was just struck by the global economic crisis, Elbit's gross profits jumped by 121 per cent to $78.3 million, and their net profits jumped by 35 per cent to $35.5 million.[44] It had another 34.5 per cent increase in net profit in the first quarter of 2009.[45]

But Elbit is not indestructible. The company's rapid expansion through mergers is fuelled by credit, and the credit is collected through the stock market by selling stocks and bonds. In 2009, the Norwegian pension fund decided to divest from Elbit as a result of their ethical policy, and because Elbit provides equipment for the separation wall in the West Bank (which was declared illegal by the International Court of Justice in the Hague in 2004). This decision was followed by similar decisions by Swedish and Dutch pension funds. In May 2010, Deutsche Bank decided to divest from Elbit as well. This decision was not a moral decision as it was with the pension funds, but a business decision based on the bank's strategic assessment that Elbit is about to lose many investors, and as a result to lose market value.

The example of South Africa proves that divestment can eventually force a company to respect international law, and Elbit seems no less vulnerable to such pressure.

Shir Hever is an economist at the Alternative Information Centre in Jerusalem, and author of The Political Economy of Israel's Occupation, *Pluto Press, 2010.*

TRANSCRIPT OF JURY Q&A: SHIR HEVER

Mairead Maguire: Can we just say that Jamal Jumma' from Palestine [coordinator of the Stop the Wall Campaign who had originally been due to speak with Shir Hever], we're very sorry that he has been denied permission [for a visa to enter the UK]. We wish him all the best. And that the Russell Tribunal will look at this problem that when we invite people to come to give testimony, they are not allowed out of their country. This should not exist in the twenty-first century ... I would like to know about the diamonds and drones connection here. We know that diamonds constitute [a proportion] of Israeli exports and there are both gem and industrial diamonds. I would like to ask you, please Shir, if you would address the question: how are industrial diamonds essential for Israel's armament industry, in particular in laser technology for the drones and for the surveillance equipment?

Shir Hever: Well, a lot of that information is not disclosed to the public. Israel's diamond exports are indeed quite significant especially considering the fact that Israel has no raw diamond deposits, all the diamonds are imported into Israel ... If you look at the net export – which means the value of exported diamonds minus the value of imported diamonds – it's not as a significant an export for Israel as others and in fact it's not Israel's biggest export, contrary to what might seem from just the aggregate number.[46] The role of the diamond industry in Israel's security industry is not quite clear, but what we can say (and that also following the fact that Israel has a very large part of its economy dedicated to defence and security and militarism) is that every time Israel exports a diamond and every time somebody buys diamonds that w[ere] exported from Israel, some of that money ends up in the Israeli military. So the financial connection is quite there. And recently I've tried to make a calculation of how much that would be, and overall the Israeli diamond industry contributes about $1 billion annually (it's a very rough estimate) to Israel's military and security industry, to prisons, to the wall of separation and so on.

Ronnie Kasrils: ... It's a follow-up on the diamond issue. Very pleased this has come up. And certainly those who presented earlier on the financial system should also take note and we might require further information. But I note from your written report that the connections between Elbit and the rest of the world, are basically South and North America, and parts of Asia. I want to come to the issue of Africa: the blood diamond issue. I'm not going to mention specific African states', Central and West Africa, connections with the Israel military. It's been noted that in those countries there's developing military assistance, these are countries that have very little to pay with – the blood diamond is an issue. We need to look into this further. And the question following on the chairperson's question to you is that specific link: it's international, I'm raising the African angle ... I'm really raising the flag in term of how very important this is. And, by the way, some of these African countries are ones that in the past benefited from solidarity action internationally and at a certain stage were very pro- the Palestinian struggle. Now I'm being objective here: I'm just wanting to get a picture of what is happening here. And the blood diamond issue is a very evil issue as we all know.

SH: Well let me give you a very brief comment on that. In Israel, every officer of a rank of colonel or higher can almost automatically receive a permit from the Ministry of Defence to trade in arms. And the arms trade industry in Israel ... is of course very connected to the arms production industry, but it's not the same. Elbit is mainly an arms production industry, and the arms traders may buy Elbit equipment and sell to African countries in exchange for raw diamonds – which would definitely qualify them as blood diamonds – but they might just as well use equipment from other companies, not necessarily Elbit. So we should make a clear separation here. Israel is a member of the Kimberley process. Now actually this year, Israel was elected to be the chair country of the Kimberley process to avoid trade in blood diamonds and I think that's problematic because the Kimberley process forbids the trading of diamonds from conflict areas, and I would definitely say that Israel is a conflict area.

Cynthia McKinney: ... The question I have relates to the drones that are killing – that are being used by the United States, and killing people in Pakistan. Are those drones manufactured by an Israeli company do you know?

SH: Well, once again, governments rarely advertise which particular weapon they use was bought from which particular company, when they talk about their operations – which they rarely do. So I do know that a lot of Israeli companies are involved in that, that Elbit, for example, is very well connected with Lockheed Martin which produces drones as well. There is also another Israeli company called Aeronautics and several others that also produce drones and drones components. So even if specifically the Hermes 1500 is not used in Pakistan or Afghanistan (and I just don't know – it might be), then components produced by these companies might definitely be used. But since the British Army is also deployed in Afghanistan and on the border of Pakistan, and they are using the Watchkeeper programme (the Watchkeeper programme we know does utilise Elbit products) so at least when it comes to the British Army, we do know that these drones are used.

CM: ... Why do we have a war on terror? Why do we have these wars and the destruction that goes along with it and these people are making profits?

SH: Well, this is a much bigger question than I can possibly begin to answer here. But I wouldn't be quick to say that all wars are a result of greed, in a direct way. I think greed plays a very important component. And the people who profit from war definitely contribute to the fact that we experience so many wars. I think that human beings are usually more complex than just formulas and their decisions are based on varied reasons and so we shouldn't be quick to reduce people to a very simplified form.

I do think that the United States aid to Israel (that's a topic that was raised before) plays a very important role here because the US aid to Israel is actually a subsidy to weapon companies in the United States, because Israeli citizens don't enjoy it: the fact that there are more deadly airplanes above their heads gives them no further security. And so one thing which should be mentioned is that the lobby within the United States of AIPAC [American Israel Public Affairs Committee] (the pro-Israeli lobby) seems to wield a lot of power and some people develop these theories as if AIPAC is actually in control of the United States – which I don't agree with – but Lockheed Martin has a lobby [a] hundred times bigger than AIPAC. Why would the United States president – the United States president would probably be uncomfortable giving talks to Lockheed Martin and saying 'we will promote your interests' – that wouldn't look so good. But if he goes to AIPAC and says 'The US is an eternal ally of Israel', that is OK within US politics and the end result is that Lockheed Martin takes the profits.

John Dugard: ... One understands that as a result of the Gaza flotilla, Turkey has terminated its relations with Israel and this has had an impact on the purchase of drones. Does this send out a message to the company that it has to take into account the illegality of Israel's operations?

SH: Well first of all, it should be mentioned that Elbit has been producing UAVs for Turkey for many years, and Elbit also mentioned that these particular UAVs were used by Turkey in its south-eastern border. Let's not close our eyes to the war crimes committed by Turkey against the Kurdish population as well, for many years. And then, of course, Turkey made no moral objections about the use of UAVs against civilians. But now that Turkey has made some reduction in its relations with Israel, and some slow-down (I wouldn't say even a complete stop) of its military relations with Israel, this does affect military companies and Elbit included. But I don't think that Elbit is the company that would later go to the Israeli government and say 'you shouldn't attack civilians on the flotilla' because, after all (actually the opposite is the result, because after the attack on the flotilla, weapon companies – I don't know which ones, they didn't identify themselves but Elbit might have been one of them) proposed new technology that the Israeli army could have used in order to avoid the flotilla embarrassment by using more sophisticated weaponry. That's the sort of logic that is being used.

*   *   *

The Cases of EDO/ITT and Raytheon
Paul Troop

I was defence counsel in two criminal cases that raised issues related to the activities of commercial companies in Israel/Palestine. Both of these cases were directly linked to the Israeli attack on Gaza between December 2008 and January 2009.

In Derry, Northern Ireland, on 12 January 2009, a number of individuals entered the premises of Raytheon UK, a subsidiary of the US arms manufacturer Raytheon Corporation. They were unable to access the main premises. They were subsequently asked to attend the police station to be interviewed. When interviewed, they said that they believed that Raytheon UK were assisting the Israeli military to commit war crimes and damage property in Gaza and that they intended to enter the company premises to cause damage and thereby prevent those crimes and that damage. They were subsequently prosecuted for various offences including burglary.

In Brighton, England, on 17 January 2009, a number of individuals entered the premises of EDO/ITT, a subsidiary of the US arms manufacturer ITT Corporation. They were able to gain access to the premises and caused substantial damage. They were arrested and interviewed by the police. When questioned, they also said that they believed EDO/ITT were assisting the Israeli military to commit war crimes and damage property and that they were acting to prevent those crimes and that damage. They were subsequently prosecuted for offences including, in particular, criminal damage.

It is important to note that in these cases, the courts were determining the criminal liability of the individual accused to the criminal standard of proof, that is, beyond reasonable doubt. The trials were also primarily examining what the accused believed the companies to be engaged in, rather than what the companies were in fact engaged in. The witnesses for the companies in both cases denied that they were supplying weapons to or assisting the Israeli military. However, as part of their defences, the individuals in both cases provided extensive evidence as to why they believed the companies to be assisting the Israeli military. Counsel for the accused put this case to the witnesses for the companies and cross-examined the witnesses on this basis.

The accused in both cases relied upon three defences available in English and Northern Irish law. These were: (1) lawful excuse pursuant to section 5(2) of the Criminal Damage Act 1971 and its Northern Irish counterpart; (2) the use of reasonable force in the prevention of crime under section 3 Criminal Law Act 1967 and its Northern Irish counterpart, and (3) the common law defence of necessity.

At a preliminary stage in the Brighton case, the prosecution sought to persuade the judge to rule that the defences were unavailable.

However, the judge refused to make such a ruling. The primary reason, as set out by the House of Lords in the case of *R* v *Wang* (2005) 2 Cr App R 136, was essentially that it is the role of the jury to determine the facts and if there is some evidence supporting the defence, the judge should leave this to be determined by the jury.

In both cases, the accused provided extensive evidence as to their knowledge about what was happening in Gaza and the activities of the companies in question.

Following a trial between 18 May 2010 and 4 June 2010, the jury in Belfast Crown Court acquitted the individuals who had been charged with burglary relating to the Raytheon UK premises. Other individuals were convicted of other offences relating to the protest that had taken place at the same time.

Following a trial between 7 June 2010 and 2 July 2010, the jury in Hove Crown Court acquitted the individuals who had been charged with burglary related to the EDO/ITT premises.

Paul Troop is a barrister practising in human rights and civil liberties law, covering both domestic and international work.

TRANSCRIPT: PAUL TROOP INTRODUCTION

Paul Troop: Good afternoon. I better start off by introducing myself. I'm a barrister and I practice, amongst other things, international criminal law and criminal defence. But I should also clarify two particular points because I don't, unfortunately, think the introduction that I've been given is entirely accurate. And this is something which the jury may want to want to examine a little bit more closely.

But the introduction is that 'I will discuss recent court cases against UK-based arms manufacturing companies EDO/ITT and Raytheon.' Now much as some may wish this situation to have been the case, unfortunately it hasn't been the case and actually the truth of the matter is that the cases that I've been involved in have been defending individuals who have been prosecuted for causing damage to those arms companies.

So that's the background which I'll give to you. The second thing I'll say is that I was the lawyer, or one of the lawyers, that was involved in both of these cases and we also fortunately have one of the individuals who was one of the defendants, not my client, but one of the individuals – Chris Osmond. He is much, much more familiar with the information concerning the companies because it's not something which is terribly transparent. But in terms of experts I think he can provide more expertise than I could so he will speak after me … .

TRANSCRIPT OF JURY Q&A: PAUL TROOP

Mairead Maguire: Thank you very much Paul. Well, very interesting and being from the north: Belfast, it's interesting to me because the Derry campaign was of greater interest to many of us. The irony of the fact that we had just come out of over 30 years of violent ethnic-political conflict and many of us were trying to take the arms out of Ireland. We should then receive one of the largest arms manufacturers in the world to come into Derry as a foothold into Ireland.

So the connections between what was happening in Raytheon for the future of Ireland – because we don't want Ireland to become a militarised, armed country, hosting arms manufacturers. So I would like to – and Raytheon is no longer in Derry, so there's many interesting points here, we could talk about in the right to protest non-violently, the role of civil community in actually challenging these corporations in the arms race, all that.

But, there was one – I would like to ask you one question. One of the points that the campaign used was the fact that Derry had a – council, city council – had an ethical investment policy. And how would that help people campaigning against these corporations and multinationals in the arms race. How local councils having ethical investment policies – how does that help and is it a tool that could be used?

Paul Troop: Well I should say that my expertise is really in the area of law rather than campaigning. But I think matters like that were very relevant to the trial. Because if you are going to go to some lengths that are as extreme as going into a factory and causing hundreds of thousand pounds worth of damage, you can't just do it on a whim, and you can't just take the law into your own hands. The law is quite strict. You have to show that you have exhausted every other potential remedy.

So in both of the cases, the individuals showed that they had peacefully campaigned, they'd protested, they'd raised it with their politicians, they'd sought to have these policies applied, they'd sought to find out what the company was doing, they had tried to complain to the police and get the police to investigate. And essentially they had exhausted every other possible non-violent route that was available to them.

So when it came to cross-examination by the prosecution, it was very difficult for the prosecution to point to something else that these individuals should have done, in terms of taking a reasonable course of action.

M. Maguire: Thank you Paul. And we have a question here from Lord Gifford and then Michael. Michael?

Michael Mansfield QC: This is a question, Paul, I am afraid without notice, but I'm sure if you feel unable to answer it you will say so. It's because of something you said, in other words that we as a jury have to consider whether companies like this should be prosecuted or indicted is the word you used. Mairead just said, you know, what are the methods of challenge? And we are interested in corporate responsibility. Now I also know that you have been involved in efforts to arrest, get arrest warrants for members of the Israeli military when they are nearly set foot in the United Kingdom. However they were pre-empted by other forces at work.

However, given your familiarity with this. The question really is this – and we haven't really dealt with it head-on, so far. And it's the question of obtaining prosecutions, arrest warrants, in relation to corporate responsibility for war crimes. Now are you, do you feel in a position to deal with this?

PT: Well essentially, it's the other side of the coin of these protest cases. Because one of the things, which we had to do, in terms of establishing the defence for the individuals, was to show that the individuals within the UK who were working for these companies could be committing criminal offences. Because you cannot have a defence until you can point to a belief that there was a criminal offence being committed that you were acting to prevent.

I have been involved together with a number of other people in teams which have been seeking arrest warrants for individuals, some of which have been Israeli military individuals who have come to the United Kingdom. The difficulties in terms of prosecuting individuals within the UK are slightly different, obviously. And the reason for that is that where someone from Israel, or other countries, comes to the United Kingdom there's quite a narrow range of offences, which you can pursue them for. And secondly, the basis on which you can pursue them for is also very narrow because there are only certain offences which you can seek an arrest warrant for somebody when they are in the United Kingdom.

In relation to individuals who have companies in the United Kingdom, the offences are much greater. Because there's not just the ones where you can pursue suspected individuals for under the Geneva Conventions Act but you can also pursue them under the International Criminal Courts Act which is a much, much wider range of offences. And also it's much easier to show that the individual has jurisdiction, because they don't just need to be in the country, they can be a citizen, they can be residing there, the test is much, much wider.

So the difficulties of pursuing, or the potential difficulties of pursuing, an individual in the company tend to be more evidence-based. So collecting the evidence to show that in fact they were assisting individuals in another case. And also political, because for obvious reasons – although of course, as we know, pursuing an Israeli general is also a political hot potato. Pursuing commercial individuals and members of companies who are supposedly making profit for that company is also a political issue. But, in theory, you could ask the police to investigate, you could ask the Crown Prosecution Service to prosecute or you could bring a private prosecution yourself.

MM: Just one follow-up. If the – yes you can bring a private prosecution. If the public authority refuses to do so, are there methods of judiciary reviewing in the decision not to?

PT: Yes there are. The difficulty in judiciary reviewing a public authority in terms of the decision in whether or not to prosecute is that the courts give a huge amount of discretion to the prosecution whether or not to prosecute. And it's only where they come to decisions such as effectively that they will never prosecute, in any case – which I suspect may be the case in relation to Israel/Palestine. If effective, that's what they are doing, then you can judiciary review that. And in theory, it is possible to judiciary review but it is difficult because there's such a wide margin of discretion, which is given to the prosecutor. The historical protection against that has always been the private prosecution. Or historically was the private prosecution. Which is at least if the prosecutor isn't going to do it, or the state isn't going to do it, then the individual can do it. As we are seeing, there are moves afoot to at least limit the extent to private prosecutions in relation to arrest warrants. Whether that can be extended to other cases, if the individuals try and bring private prosecutions, we will have to see.

M. Maguire: I would like to ask Lord Gifford here to say a few words because Lord Gifford was actually on the defence team of one of the individuals who entered Raytheon in Derry. And I would love him to tell us a little bit about that please.

Anthony Gifford QC: Very quickly. I think that the importance to our deliberations here of Paul's evidence and the experience of these cases is that it helps us to give any guidance that may be important to members of the community who find that they have a subsidiary of a major corporation, which is complicit in war crimes, crimes against humanitarian law. What do you do? And the answer is not, as Paul has said, to go straight in and smash up their property. I would never counsel that. Two things. One, as he has said, all peaceful means – all means by way of demonstration, asking questions, writing letters, should be attempted. Secondly, the material from the company's own websites can sometimes be devastating in a propaganda – in a propaganda on our side. Our jury watched Raytheon's own boastful propaganda as to how precise and destructive its missiles were. And I think that is probably what turned the scales.

*   *   *

The Campaign Against EDO/ITT
Chris Osmond

MILITARY COMPONENTS

EDO MBM in Brighton own the intellectual property rights for the Israeli VER-2 bomb rack, the Ejector Release Unit 151 and the Zero Retention Force Arming Unit. The VER-2 bomb rack is in use by Israel, manufactured by Elbit. Paul Hills, EDO's managing director, has admitted that EDO in Brighton is responsible for the design activities for the VER-2.

The ERU 151 is an ejector component used in conjunction with the VER-2. The Zero Retention Force Arming Unit is the trigger unit for the VER-2 (stored inside the ERU 151). Until 2007, EDO MBM's website said that the company was actively manufacturing the VER-2 and that it was used by the Israeli Air Force.

THE EDO DECOMMISSIONERS

People have been campaigning against EDO MBM/ITT since 2004. This has included weekly demonstrations, direct action, legal complaints and attempting to persuade the local council to condemn EDO – see <www.smashedo.org.uk>.

On 17 January 2009, as the bombs rained down on Gaza, six people entered the EDO factory. They threw computers and filing cabinets out of a first-floor window and took hammers to machinery used for weapons production. Their aim was to disable the war machine and to take action against those who profit from the aerial bombardment of Gaza. During January 2009, the Israeli army launched an attack on the civilian population of Gaza. Over 1,400 people were killed, including over 300 children. Schools and hospitals were targeted.

Before entering the factory, they had recorded videos stating their intention to decommission the factory to prevent war crimes.

It is widely accepted that Israel committed war crimes against the people of Gaza. The arms companies who knowingly supplied the weapons to enable the invasion to happen are complicit in those crimes. The six people who took part in the action were on trial for conspiracy to commit criminal damage. They argued that they had lawful excuse to disarm the factory because EDO are complicit in war crimes committed by the Israeli Air Force during Operation Cast Lead.

The trial of the decommissioners began on 7 June 2010 and ended on 2 July, with all defendants being found unanimously not guilty by the jury. The jury had heard a five-day cross-examination of EDO's managing director, evidence from the defendants, expert evidence and eyewitness accounts of Israel's massacre.

THE EVIDENCE IN THE TRIAL

During the trial, EDO denied supplying Israel, claiming that the ZRFAU was manufactured in the US. It is the defendant's case that this was a lie. However, EDO did admit that they were the point of contact for the equipment and were the design authority, responsible for qualifying the installation of the components, that is, telling customers how to fit them onto a bomb rack. This, even on EDO's own account, makes them complicit in Israeli war crimes.

The company also admitted that they did not have export licences, despite transferring technical data on the ZRFAU. Transfer of military technical data requires an export licence. A case is being prepared for an investigation by HM Revenue and Customs on this point.

THE F-35 AND THE FRCS

In 2009, ITT, EDO's parent company, announced that the factory in Brighton would be manufacturing a component of the F-35, the Field Replaceable Connector System (FRCS). This was to be supplied to Lockheed Martin in the US.

The FRCS was invented in Brighton by two employees of EDO MBM and has been patented in the US, UK and Israel. It is also used on F-16s.

In October 2010, Israel signed a deal to buy 20 F-35s from Lockheed Martin, for $2.8 billion. The F-35 Joint Strike Fighter will replace the F-16 as Israel's main attack weapon.

Sources inside Lockheed Martin confirmed that the F-35s bound for Israel would include the EDO FRCS.

SOURCES

Websites last accessed 31 March 2010

- EDO Corp ZRFAU promotional document, preserved on Archive.org <web.archive.org/web/20070927214113/ http://www.edocorp.com/documentation/ZeroRetention-ForceArmingUt.pdf>
- EDO promotional document, preserved on Archive.org <web. archive.org/web/20040401120233/http://www.mbmtech. co.uk/br.html>
- Testimony of David Jones. Managing Director /of EDO MBM Technology Ltd. 7 December 2005. Appeal of Gittoes, Marcham, Sacca, A20050031/36/41. Lewes Crown Court (Sitting in Hove). Transcript provided by appellant.
- 'Lucas in B-2 weapons launch study', *Flight International*, 14 February 1990.
- EDO MBM Website 2003-07 Pylon Ancillaries page, preserved on Archive.org <web.archive.org/web/20031008125120/ http://www.mbmtech.co.uk/pa.html>

- EDO MBM Bomb Racks page removed in 2004, preserved on Archive.org <web.archive.org/web/20031215082036/www.mbmtech.co.uk/br.html>
- Decision Notice FS50180838, Information Commissioner's Office, 15 December 2008 <www.ico.gov.uk/upload/documents/decisionnotices/2008/fs_50180838.pdf>
- Confirmed by legal representatives for DBERR and ICO in Information Tribunal case EA/2009/0002. Telephone Directions Hearing, March 2009.
- David Miliband, statement to the House of Commons, *Hansard*, 21 April 2009.
- 'ITT awarded contract for F-35 Joint Strike Fighter Weapon Release Systems', ITT press release, 12 October 2009.

Chris Osmond is a campaigner against EDO, a researcher for Corporate Watch and was a defendant in the EDO decommissioners trial.

TRANSCRIPT: CHRIS OSMOND INTRODUCTION AND CONCLUSION

Chris Osmond: I've been asked to be brief. Thanks for listening to me. I'm going to explain some of the details about how EDO were complicit in supplying the Israeli military. I've been campaigning against EDO MBM in Brighton for nearly six years now, since 2004. There's been a popular campaign in Brighton involving thousands of people, which has included demonstrations, acts of direct action, lobbying of our local council, handing in complaints to the police.

And on the 16th of January 2009 after Israel had been engaging in the massacre in Gaza for two-and-a-half weeks, a group of people from Bristol turned up on my doorstep and said they wanted to get in the way of EDO's supply of weaponry to the Israeli military and I gave them some support in breaking into the EDO factory. And we were, as Paul said, tried for conspiracy to cause criminal damage and acquitted this year.

I'd just like to say my thanks really to those six people who had the bravery to get in the way of the Israeli war machine back in January 2009 and particularly to Elijah Smith who spent almost two years in prison on remand before being acquitted for the action …

[Summing up] I want to ask the tribunal two things: the [Smash EDO] campaign is complaining to Her Majesty's Revenue and Customs Department in relation to illegal exports and exports without a licence from EDO, and I'd ask the tribunal to make representations in support of the complaint. And also to everybody in the room: I'd say that it's the actions of ordinary people, of individuals, that are the light at the end of the tunnel in the struggle against Israeli apartheid and occupation. Not the actions of representatives or politicians, but the actions of people like us.

*   *   *

European Union R&D Subsidises for Israeli Security Actors
Ben Hayes

The EU is funding numerous Israeli corporations that profit directly from the occupation of Palestine. These funds take the form of research and development (hereafter R&D) grants awarded by the European Commission under the European Union (hereafter EU) Seventh Framework Programme for Research (hereafter FP7).

FP7 runs from 2007–13 and has an indicative budget of €50.5 billion. Nine specific research themes are prioritised in FP7, including a new European Security Research Programme (hereafter ESRP). All full participants in FP7, including Israel, make a contribution to FP7 based on their gross domestic product.

The ESRP has an annual budget of €200 million. Although this submission focuses primarily on Israel's participation in the ESRP (in line with Statewatch's mandate to monitor civil liberties in the EU), it should be noted that many of the other eight FP7 themes have an important security component (particularly nanotechnology, space, transport, energy, information and communications technology, and social science). Additional EU funds for security-related R&D – for which Israel is also eligible – are available under a dedicated Critical Infrastructure Protection programme, from EURATOM (the European Atomic Energy Community), the €1.8 billion EU fund for the 'Management of Migration Flows', and for components and applications of the Galileo (satellite navigation) system.

Israel participates in FP7 on an equal footing with the EU member states under the terms of an EC-Israel Association Agreement dating back to 1995 (last updated in 2004). In per capita terms, no non-EU country has received more from the FP7 programme than Israel. As the European Commission has observed, the EU is now second only to the Israel Science Foundation in Jerusalem as a source of research funding for Israeli academics, corporations and state enterprises.

According to European Commission records, Israel has participated in more than 2,300 EU-funded research projects in the last ten years. By way of comparison, researchers in the Occupied Palestinian Territories feature in just 55 EU projects.

The ESRP is unlike other parts of the FP7 programme in so far as it has the twin objectives of both funding innovation in security-related R&D and enhancing the EU's 'industrial competitiveness'. In essence, this means subsidising the development of the nascent European Homeland Security industry so that it can compete in an increasingly lucrative and global market place.

Unlike other aspects of FP7, the ESRP is managed by the European Commission's Directorate General (hereafter DG) for Enterprise and Industry (as opposed to DG Research). Extensive research by Statewatch has documented the way in which corporations – particularly those from the defence and security industries – have been able to shape the ESRP to their advantage (see Appendix 1).

The Counter-Terrorism Bureau of the National Security Council of the state of Israel was among the 'stakeholders' invited to participate in the European Security Research and Innovation Forum (an informal, EU-sponsored group tasked with identifying priorities for the ESRP).

To date, the details of 90 ESRP contracts have been released under the FP7 programme. Since FP7 promotes cross-border research, almost all of these awards are to multinational consortia. Of the 90 ESRP projects funded to date, Israeli companies and institutions are participating in 19. Of these 19 projects, Israeli entities are leading six. By way of comparison, only four out of the 27 EU member states (France, the UK, Germany and Sweden) lead more ESRP projects than Israel. The table in Appendix 1 details Israeli entities' involvement in the ESRP.

The ESRP projects in which Israeli entities participate concern counter-terrorism, border control, surveillance technology, homeland security and the emergency services. Some of this R&D concerns highly controversial elements and techniques of the global 'war on terror', including mass-intrusive surveillance, repressive border controls, the use of 'drones' (also known as unmanned aerial vehicles) and 'counter-radicalisation' strategy.

Among the Israeli companies that feature in the aforementioned ESRP projects are Israel Aerospace Industries (a state-owned manufacturer of 'drones'), Aeronautics Defense Systems (another 'drone' manufacturer specialising in 'networked warfare'), Motorola Israel (producer of 'virtual fences' around Israeli settlements), Elbit

Systems (one of Israel's largest private military technology firms, responsible for segments of the 'separation wall' around Jerusalem), Verint Systems (one of Israel's biggest homeland security exporters specialising in workplace surveillance, CCTV and wire-tapping facilities) and Ernst & Young Israel. See Appendix 1 for further information.

SOURCES

- Ben Hayes, 'Should the EU subsidise Israeli Security?', *European Voice*, 18 March 2010.
- Ben Hayes, 'NeoConOpticon: The EU Security-Industrial Complex', *Transnational Institute/Statewatch*, 2009.
- NeoConOpticon Blog – Israel <neoconopticon.wordpress.com/tag/israel>
- Briefing paper: 'Security Cooperation between the EU and Israel', Quaker Council for European Affairs, 2010.
- Alejandro Pozo Marín, 'Spain-Israel: Military, Homeland Security and Armament-Based Relations, Affairs and Trends', Centre d'Estudis per a la Pau/Justícia i Pau, 2010.
- Dave Cronin, 'Factsheet: How Israeli arms companies benefit from EU science funds', *Irish Palestinian Solidarity Campaign*, 2009.
- Ben Hayes, 'Israel's participation in EU R&D Framework Programmes: Importing Homeland security, exporting R&D subsidies?', *Transnational Institute*, 2009. Available on request.
- European Commission Security Research website <ec.europa.eu/enterprise/policies/security>.

Ben Hayes is a security policy expert for the civil liberties organisation Statewatch.

TRANSCRIPT OF JURY Q&A: BEN HAYES

Cynthia McKinney: I was trying to write down these projects and I'm glad to know that they're in the annex here so I'll study that. But did I understand you correctly to say that there is a €20 million project for autonomous land war controls?

Ben Hayes: Land *border* controls.

CM: Land *border* controls. And then there's an additional €14 million project for land and sea border drones.

BH: Absolutely, yes.

CM: So now: who is the EU afraid of?

BH: [Laughs] Well if you read European Union policy documents, as I unfortunately do for a living, you will see that the EU presents terrorism, organised crime, but particularly illegal immigration, so called, as the greatest threat facing the European Union today. And obviously a lot of us in this room might take very different positions. But I'd just like to say something if I may about the TALOS project that you mentioned. Because when this got funded, remember this 20 million for combat robots and drones for border control. And I rang up a contact I have very close to the security research programme. And I said, 'I cannot believe that you funded this. How on earth did it get through your ethical guidelines?' And the response that I got was, 'You should have seen the original proposal. There were electro-magnetic shock weapons on these combat robots. And we told them that these had to go before the proposal could be funded.' But that is very much the kind of research and development that we are talking about here.

John Dugard: ... Something that has not been touched on by this tribunal is the involvement of Israeli universities in military research. And I think your research shows very clearly that several Israeli universities are deeply involved in military research. Is that correct?

BH: That is certainly the case. Obviously the submission focuses on the corporations. But you will see the Technion Institute, which very much has a close relationship with Elbit Systems. You will see that's a name that crops up very often in terms of EU security research. Ben-Gurion University, the Hebrew University of Jerusalem: they're all in there. It's very much a sort of, a marriage of academia, corporations and what they call end-users, which are the security services and so on.

JD: Thank you.

Mairead Maguire: I would like to ask a question about the connection between this research and the funding for it, much of which happens in the settlements as well as Israel proper. I would like to ask you, is there a connection between what's happening here and NATO? We're all concerned about what's happening in NATO and Europe, a militarisation, literally, of Europe. America has six nuclear weapons in European states. [*Sic*: The US has nuclear weapons in six European states.] Germany currently wants rid of the Americans off of Germany. But America won't comply. So the whole growth of NATO and military force, and we know that Israel is interested in becoming a member of NATO. Can you please kind of, speak to what is the connection between the technological advancements being used by the money out of Europe that Israel is using and where's the connection between Israel's policies and NATO?

BH: Well I think there's two things happening. The first thing that's very obvious is that defence and arms companies have seen a potential decline in profits and recognised equally that homeland security is going to be a huge, massive global industry. And you will even hear arms company executives use phrases like 'Security is the new defence.' In respect to NATO, what you can see happening really is an outdated military alliance jumping on what are effectively crimes – organised crime, terrorism, illegal immigration, even things like climate change – to justify its existence for the next decades to come.

The final thing, I think that's related to this is – and this was touched on by a previous speaker – so much of this agenda is being set by the corporations. You know, you really have the EU saying 'Well, should we have a security research program? What should it look like?' And then you have this huge conflict of interest where corporations are invited to set the objectives for the research programme, then apply for the funding on offer, then use the stuff they develop in terms of the research and sell it back to the very member states that use the taxpayer budget to fund the research in the first place. And I'll stop there.

6
Witness Recall

Editor's note: The final part of the final day of the London session was used to bring back several witnesses to answer further questions to the jury. The following is a complete transcript, with only minor editing. Some portions were originally spoken in French.

Stéphane Hessel: This final session will begin with questions addressed by certain members of the jury to experts for whom they still have questions. Which members of the jury wished to hear an expert? … Would Mr Franssen please be kind enough to return to the stand? Thank you.

Pierre Galand: The question put to Mr. Franssen is 'It seems that in Belgium, there has been a reaction against Dexia by public institutions, communities, provinces and cities. Is he able to give us any information on that matter?'

Mario Franssen: … I shall address myself rather more to the public, because it's a question that is linked to campaigns. And so the public is more involved.

The first thing I would like to say is that there is an important element that, up to the present, has contributed to the fact that the Dexia campaign has, nevertheless, had quite a bit of success, and that is organisation. Right at the start of the campaign, the choice was made to try to organise people around the campaign as much as possible, and around our demand that Dexia should break all ties with the Occupation.

Now, there are various levels to the campaign, and they have allowed people to get involved. A bank as large as Dexia needs quite a large response. That is why we have developed a platform, which is interesting, because it allows organisations to join us. There are now 78 different organisations in Belgium that have rallied to the platform. These are solidarity groups, municipalities of the campaign of Belgium all around the country, these are political parties, NGOs and other diverse companies.

And these organisations can do different things, and the popular level is the most important level that we have. We did the signing of petitions, we did the actions in front of Dexia branches, manifestations, etc. But you also have to be creative and I want to mention one specific thing we did: every company has its complaint line. So what we did, we mobilised 50 people who did during one week, called every hour with the same list of questions to the complaints line. Wednesday afternoon, it was already a nice discussion that volunteers could have with this people there because they start to know the campaign also very well and they were very happy that we called because usually they don't have anything to do, they said. But we could manage to find some other friends to join us so it was not a problem. So the popular level is very important to do.

Second, and this is specific for companies as Dexia, was our work towards the shareholders and the shareholders in this case, the different political levels in Belgium and there I think also is a specific option we took. We didn't go against the shareholders as such, we didn't confront them as being responsible of everything that's happened with the bank and what they did in the settlements. We tried to convince them to take a stand against what the bank was doing in the settlements. So we opened up possibilities that these shareholders, if it was the national governments, the local governments to ask questions in parliament, but also to vote motions asking the bank not to continue these policies because they were shareholders.

Second option was to try to get some members of the board at our side. Different groups of shareholders are not satisfied with what's happening in the Dexia bank and what they are doing in the settlements. The Christian Workers Movement is one of the shareholders and we know that the militants of this organisation do not really agree with what the bank is doing in the settlements. So instead of opposing them and confronting them as being responsible, we opened up the debate with them and see what they can do, which political weight they can bring in the campaign.

And last but not least, we also tried to talk to Mr Jean-Luc Dehaene, Pierre Mariani and also Stefaan Decraene [who] is the CEO of the Dexia Belgium branch. We managed more or less to get in contact with them but it was not really a discussion as I explained this morning.

But there is more. Everybody can be a shareholder of a private company and one share is enough to attend a general assembly. So think about it: the Dexia share in the stock option in Belgium today is three point something euros. You can manage to obtain one. It's not a big investment and I want to make a call already now also for the people watching on the net: buy a share of Dexia and we invite you the second Wednesday of May in Brussels to join us to the General Assembly. Usually 70 to 80 people are present. We want to be more.

The third thing about this type of international companies is the international aspect of campaigning and I heard many examples here of possibilities: Ahava, G4 Security, etc., etc. They are multinationals which means they are active in multi-countries so this opens up opportunities. For Belgium, France and Luxembourg which are the home markets of Dexia, it was pretty easy to find contacts but also I would advise to read strategic papers of the different companies. For Dexia, for example, in 2014, all the growth they want to make, they will make it in Turkey. Turkey is, for [the] financial sector, one of the growing markets. Belgian banks are there, Spanish banks are there, everybody is there and Dexia wants to through its 99.8 per cent controlled bank (the DenizBank) to grow largely. So we also made contacts with groups in Turkey and the first press statement was published a few weeks ago there.

Now, I will turn back a little bit to the jury because the fourth is the legal aspect of course. For us, as a campaign and I want to stress – I'm only here as a spokesperson, we're 78 organisations – it's the principal stand we take. We cannot agree that a Belgian company is involved in the Occupation. If we have a legal basis to prosecute, yes or no, it doesn't really matter. But, I think for many experts who brought our cause before the jury here, we wonder and we want to see if it's possible to have some legal action done and I'm really – and many, I think, are looking forward to the conclusions and see if we also on a legal basis, we can find means to work together and link up the campaigning with the legal aspects and introduce legal aspects into campaigning.

SH: … Would Mr Hilary please be kind enough to approach? Thank you. You have the floor.

PG: We would like to ask Mr Hilary the following question: War on Want is subject to a British law called the Charity Law. Nevertheless, we have heard today that the director of War on Want has taken a very clear position on issues that involve ethics and politics. We are astonished to see that many English NGOs use the cover of the Charity Law in order not to have to take a stand on the rights of the Palestinian people. Could he tell us what is this difference?

John Hilary: ... So, in terms of the question and the issue of Charity Law as it applies to War on Want. We are a charity and for those who do not come from the UK, this brings certain advantages in terms of tax and benefits: that we can take donations from members of the public and augment those donations by 28 per cent through a certain aspect of UK law. On the other hand, it means that we are regulated by Charity Law and we are regulated by the Charity Commission. And the Charity Commission in the UK takes a particular line on those charities who campaign on Palestine. We do have the right to campaign on a range of different things. This have been established over many, many years and many important struggles – particularly at the time of apartheid South Africa when we stood up in the struggle on the front-line states. And many of the different charities like War on Want were involved in trying to expand the opportunities for campaigning and political campaigning especially.

So we do have the right to campaign but War on Want knows that for many other NGOs, many other charities, in the UK, that right to campaign becomes problematic when it comes to Palestine. That is partly because they feel nervous, perhaps, around the issue and about accusations of anti-Semitism which are wildly used by many of the Zionist groups in this country and indeed by the Israeli embassy which has written to us on several occasions, accusing us of anti-Semitism.

But also many of the Zionist groups have learned how to use the structures of the Charity Commission to cause problems for charities in this country. And so they will write in to the Charity Commission accusing us of having infringed our charitable status by continuing the campaigning on behalf of the Palestinian people. And I think this is one of the reasons why some other NGOs feel nervous again about taking too strident a position, or too precise opposition as you put it very clearly.

War on Want has always seen as one of our roles to try to push back the barriers of what it is generally understood to be perfectly permissible for charities to do. So we meet with the Charity Commission when we are called to them to defend our statements on Palestine and we try and push back against the Zionists who use those structures to call us into question in that respect. And I think that is one of the roles which my board of trustees has identified as important for War on Want to keep pushing back and not to be cowed by the use of this criticism. And again, once more to refer to the report which we put out on boycott, divestment and sanctions: it was deliberately done to be able to show other charities that you can explicitly call for BDS as a charity – there is absolutely nothing wrong in doing that. And if I may just add one little thing as to how sometimes this can work.

In January of last year, at the time of the Operation Cast Lead and the attacks on Gaza, War on Want joined an open letter which was published in the *Guardian* here in the UK, calling for a suspension and an immediate hold to any upgrade in the EU-Israel relations. If you remember that time, this diplomatic and economic upgrade between the EU and Israel was very much on the agenda and was being pressed forward by many of the EU members states. And so we wrote our name on the bottom of one of these letters in the public domain and it went out and was published. The next day, we had a phone call from one of the other charities in the UK which said: 'Are we allowed to do that as charities?' We said: 'absolutely, no question about it.'

They then the next day started round the other charities and got them to sign up to a position saying 'no to the upgrade of EU-Israel relations' and that was then put before the Foreign Secretary when we met with him. We could sit there – the others didn't want to raise this – but we could sit there with the Foreign Secretary and say: 'Everybody in this room is against your position of upgrading EU-Israel relations.' And as a result of getting those others in the room – because War on Want's strength in this respect is not sufficient perhaps to turn the mind of the Foreign Secretary – with the other bigger NGOs, the bigger charities, we did manage to get him to change his position. So that is partly why we consider this is worth doing and partly why I think it's useful for this message to go out to other charities and other NGOs that they do not have to be scared of a Zionist movement which is in retreat.

SH: We have, I think, a third one. Oh, a question, yes, please would you stay? A question from a member of the jury. Go ahead.

Cynthia McKinney: A little bitty question. Mr Hilary, I noted that in your testimony the Apache helicopter was one of the helicopters that the US transferred over to Israel. Was that the helicopter that was used to attack the *Mavi Marmara*?

John Hillary: That – I don't know if that was the Apache helicopter and there will be other people, I'm confident, in the room who will maybe be able to give you that information. The Apache helicopter is a fighter aircraft supplied by Boeing and which has been used, certainly as an aggressive assault weapon in Gaza, in Lebanon and many of those other situations. Whether it is the same helicopter from which the commandos came down ... [audience member speaks] Black Hawk, is the word from the audience.

CM: And it's made by: who? Who makes the Black Hawk?

JH: We think maybe Lockheed.

SH: ... First of all, we have received three replies from the various corporations to which we have posed questions. Three replies, you remember. Perhaps I'll ask our coordinator, Pierre Galand, to tell us which those three companies were. Mr. Galand?

PG: The most important response was from the Netherlands pension fund PFZW. The other replies were from Veolia and ... G4 Security. What we have not said, Mr President, what we have not had the chance to say, is that we have also received a letter from a fourth correspondent, the president of the European Commission.

SH: Ah: the president of the European Commission.

PG: The President of the European Commission reaffirmed the principles that currently guide the commission in terms of humanitarian law and international law. He confirmed the decision taken by Europe in December 2009 to reaffirm the 1967 borders, that Jerusalem is the capital of both states, and that Europe is opposed to the whole colonisation process. And finally – it's quite amazing in view of the fact that he never replied to us when we put to him the Barcelona conclusions – he said 'I take this opportunity to wish you good luck with the proceeding of your conference.'

SH: Thank you for your reply. We recall that it was at Barcelona, seven months ago, that we addressed ourselves very directly to the European Union and its members, and we continue to consider them as bearing a large part of the responsibility for the situation in Palestine. I shall now ask the chamber: are any of the members here present representatives of one or other of the corporations or companies to which we addressed our recommendations? If there is anyone, could he please take the floor ... The silence is our answer to that question.

I'm sorry, because I think it's essential that the Russell Tribunal on Palestine should be an even-handed tribunal and should not allow itself, in particular, to be carried away by the emotion produced by the testimonies that we have heard, although that's difficult. We cannot listen to only one voice. We must be aware that on the other side there are entrenched interests that have to be taken into consideration. Israel's enormous need for security, in view of what took place in past centuries, when that security was not always respected, is something that must be taken into account. Nevertheless, it is true that over these two days that we have spent together – and I must first thank the coordinator and his team for having made those two days – I'm sure you'll agree with me, very interesting. We have been able to gain an understanding of several issues linked to what was the basic purpose of this second session, namely, to understand the violations and complicities which are incumbent upon corporations. That is to say, private or semi-private international companies, but not the states which are in each case behind those companies.

It will be difficult for us in our conclusions to distinguish between what the companies, banks, arms companies and financial companies whose problems have been mentioned over the past two days are really responsible for and what is caused by not just the Israeli government and the Israeli army, of course, but also by the states which underpin those companies and corporations and who are often the instigators of their action.

This is the task that we will have to undertake over the next few hours and which will, I hope, lead us to present to the press tomorrow a report that indicates the points on which the jury has reached agreement. I have forgotten to say that the members of the jury are totally independent and that each one of them must be taken into account.

I don't want to conclude without telling you how important it is, when dealing with a problem such as the one that concerns us, to know that progress is being made. What the United Nations Secretary-General is doing with the Global Compact and by appointing Mr Roger Plant as Special Representative on Business and

Human Rights is a beginning. There are others, about which we've heard over these two days. However, those beginnings will have no chance to become realities in the future – and for real progress to be made in protecting the Palestinian people and ensuring that it accedes to the state to which it, in common with all other peoples, has the right – unless each one of us uses his energy to pursue the mechanism which provides real hope for underpinning that major operation, namely, BDS, boycott, divestment and sanctions. BDS is now internationally recognised as legitimate and cannot be considered by any government as some form of discrimination. In no case must we allow ourselves to be intimidated by propaganda that is trying to make the struggle for the freedom of the Palestinian people appear to be anti-Semitic. That word should be banished once and for all from our vocabulary. We are in favour of the Palestinians having a people [*sic*: state] and we are in favour of the requirements for reaching that position being examined by the Russell Tribunal as part of its continuing humanitarian work inspired by Bertrand Russell, man of this country, and by Ken Coates, the loss of whom several weeks ago we deplore [note: it had actually been several months ago]. This action must be continued and I invite you all to take stock of all that you have heard on this last day, and make good use of it in helping us to move forward. Thank you. [Audience applauds].

PG: Thank you. Thanks to the president of the tribunal for those very interesting words about what we have achieved. As you know, we will end this second session of tribunal hearings and the jury will withdraw. The jury will withdraw, and within the next hour-and-a-half, it will go into session in order to draw up the conclusions of this meeting. As the president has told you, we will be hosted tomorrow by Amnesty, where we will meet the press and publish the conclusions of the tribunal.

We will also very quickly tell you those conclusions, because we think they will help each of you in the work that we do to ensure that we live in a just world, where the rights of every people to live in dignity and independence are recognised.

I should also like to tell you that we have already begun negotiations and I thank those friends who have come here from South Africa, because the theme of the third session of the Russell Tribunal on Palestine will be 'Is the crime of apartheid applicable today to Israel?'

That session will take place in 2011. We can't give you the exact dates yet, but we are convinced that the work in which we are engaged must be carried on, and that the third session will indeed take place, you may be sure of that. We are asking that all the national committees that have helped us so far should immediately start working to publicise the outcome of this second session and carry on the work which has made it possible for us to meet here today. It is on the basis of that citizen's effort that the tribunal can exist and will continue to exist.

I thank you for coming and wish you every success with your future action as experts, as witnesses, as national committees, as associations, as NGOs. Your work will permit us to create, little by little, that vast citizen's movement that, at the time, allowed us to stand by the people of South Africa, and, with the unions, the churches, the big associations and the big NGOs, finally bring an end to what is truly a crime against a people, the crime of depriving a people of the right to freedom and the right to have its own state. Thank you all and thank you to all the members of the jury.

7
The Jury's Findings

The following statement was released to the media, and read out by the jury at the concluding press conference of the Russell Tribunal on Palestine. The press conference was held at the Amnesty International Human Rights Action Centre in Shoreditch. The statement served as the interim conclusions of the tribunal until the jury's detailed findings were published in January 2011. You can download the full findings (55 pages long, plus annexes) from the website <www.russelltribunalonpalestine.com>.

CONCLUDING STATEMENT, RUSSELL TRIBUNAL, LONDON, 22 NOVEMBER 2010

Public Statement of the Russell Tribunal on Palestine following the conclusion of the London Session on corporate complicity in Israeli violations of international law

The Russell Tribunal on Palestine, London session took place at the Law Society, 113 Chancery Lane, London, WC2A1PL on 20–21 November 2010.

Over the past two days, the tribunal heard compelling evidence of corporate complicity in Israeli violations of international law, relating to: the supply of arms; the construction and maintenance of the illegal separation wall; and in establishing, maintaining and providing services, especially financial, to illegal settlements, all of which have occurred in the context of an illegal occupation of Palestinian territory.

It is clear from the evidence of witnesses that this conduct is not only morally reprehensible, but also exposes those corporations to legal liability for very serious violations of international human rights and humanitarian law. What distinguishes the present situation from others in which international action has been called for, is that in this case both Israel and the corporations that are complicit in Israel's unlawful actions are in clear violation of international human rights and humanitarian law.

The first session of the tribunal, held in Barcelona in March 2010, found the EU and EU member states complicit in Israeli violations of international law, including the illegal construction of the wall in Palestinian territory; systematic building of illegal, exclusively Jewish, settlements on occupied Palestinian territory; the illegal blockade on Gaza, and numerous illegal military operations against Palestinian civilians, particularly during Operation Cast Lead in Gaza (December 2008–January 2009), which constitute war crimes and/or crimes against humanity.

Further, the Russell Tribunal notes that the international community is clearly in agreement that Israel is in flagrant disregard of its international obligations, and further notes with deep regret that this wholly unsatisfactory and unacceptable state of affairs has been allowed to continue. None the less, Israel's continued impunity and disregard of its state obligations as a member of the United Nations and bound by the UN Charter, has set it apart from the rest of the international community. Accordingly, the Russell Tribunal draws to the attention of all corporations complicit in Israel's grave violations that their continued business activities place them on the wrong side of international opinion, morality and law. This clearly places both Israel and the corporations in a position in which they are undermining the very integrity and credibility of international law and the institutions that underpin it.

The main questions the jury considered in London were:

- Which Israeli violations of international law are corporations complicit in?
- What are the legal consequences of the activities of corporations that aid and abet Israeli violations?
- What are the remedies available and what are the obligations of states in relation to corporate complicity?

Accordingly, in answering these questions, the tribunal's full findings from the London session, which will be available at the beginning of December 2010, will both summarise the key evidence that it heard about corporate complicity and identify specific legal and non-legal consequences and remedies. The tribunal has noted the failure of states to take appropriate action to put an end to Israel's violations and illegal conduct, despite the requirements of international law, or to hold to account corporate complicity in Israeli actions, which has prompted civil society to step in and take action to bring about policy changes that respect human rights and international humanitarian law. This includes a very wide range of actions in support of the Palestinian call for boycott, divestment and sanctions (BDS). Corporations play a very decisive role in enabling Israel to commit war crimes and crimes against humanity. These corporate activities can, and have been, the subject of citizens' movements that the Russell Tribunal received evidence about; they include boycotts, shareholders holding corporations to account, divestments by pension funds of investments tainted by illegality, and actions that continue to put corporations in the spotlight with the purpose of bringing about change in corporate culture. In the Israeli context, civil society is taking effective action to enforce the law. Therefore, the Russell Tribunal calls on states to protect the rights of all those who initiate or take such lawful BDS actions. Twelve corporations and the EU were invited to participate in the London session but all declined. Letters were received from three corporations and the EU, which were entered into evidence. They will be annexed to the tribunal's final conclusions of the London session. The Russell Tribunal's conclusions conclude its findings as to the potential legal liability of several corporations, including the following:

- **G4S**, a multinational British/Danish corporation, supplies scanning equipment and full body scanners to several military checkpoints in the West Bank, all of which have been built as part of the separation wall, whose route was declared illegal by the ICJ in its Advisory Opinion of 9 July 2004. G4S also provided scanners for the Erez checkpoint of Gaza. G4S operates in settlements, providing equipment for prisons for Palestinian political prisoners and for installations of the Israeli police in settlements.
- **Elbit Systems**, a leading Israeli multinational, has an intimate and collaborative relationship with the Israeli military in developing weapons technology first used by the Israeli army in its active combat operations, before marketing and selling the technology to countries worldwide. For example, Elbit supplied the unmanned aerial vehicles (UAVs, otherwise known as drones) that were extensively and illegally used in the Gaza conflict. Despite this, the British Army has recently awarded Elbit a joint contract worth over $1 billion for the development of the next generation of UAVs (known as the Watchkeeper programme). The British corporation UAV Engines Limited, a wholly owned Elbit subsidiary, will produce

the plane's engines. A serious concern regarding the use of drones relates to their indiscriminate nature. This is illustrated by the fact that, for every alleged combatant targeted by drones, ten civilians die. The Norwegian government's pension fund divested from Elbit Systems as a result of this complicity in human rights violations.

- **Caterpillar**, based in the US, supplies specifically modified military D9 bulldozers to Israel, which are used in: (i) the demolition of Palestinian homes, (ii) the construction of settlements and the separation wall, and (iii) in urban warfare in the Gaza conflict; in all cases, these bulldozers cause civilian deaths and injuries, and extensive property damage not justified by military necessity.
- **Cement Roadstone Holdings**, an Irish multinational corporation, purchased 25 per cent of the Israeli corporation Mashav Initiative and Development Ltd, which in turn wholly owns Nesher Israel Cement Enterprises Ltd, which is Israel's sole cement producer, supplying 75–90 per cent of all cement in Israel and occupied Palestine. This cement is used, amongst other things, for the construction of the illegal separation wall.
- **Dexia**, a Franco-Belgian corporation, finances Israeli settlements in the West Bank via its subsidiary Dexia Israel Public Finance Ltd.
- **Veolia Transport**, a French corporation, is involved in the construction of the East Jerusalem Light Railway. Veolia also operates bus services to illegal Israeli settlements as well as landfills where settlements dump their garbage on Palestinian lands.
- **Carmel-Agrexco**, an Israeli corporation, is an exporter of agricultural produce, including oranges, olives and avocados from the illegal settlements in the West Bank. It also exports Palestinian products which are mislabelled as 'made in Israel'.

The tribunal heard evidence that G4S, Elbit Systems and Caterpillar all acknowledge and actively boast in their promotional material about the use of their equipment during the Gaza conflict, which unlawfully inflicted loss of life, and extensive and serious damage on Palestinian civilians and their property. Civil claims against the above corporations, brought by victims of their complicity, are possible in the countries where those corporations are domiciled or have a significant presence; corporations and corporate actors can be subject to criminal prosecution for breach of domestic law (for example, money laundering and/or concealment) and/or for the commission of international crimes, including the pillage of natural resources. In many countries, domestic law incorporates international law, including international humanitarian and human rights law. This is without prejudice to universal jurisdiction, or the jurisdiction of the International Criminal Court. The full conclusions of the tribunal's London session will provide detailed examples of such potential litigation, and also highlight and encourage civil society/BDS actions that can achieve corporate accountability. The tribunal was impressed by the range and depth of the evidence given during the sessions. The tribunal is extremely grateful for the time, generosity and courage of the witnesses, particularly those that took part at considerable personal risk. The Russell Tribunal will hold two more sessions in the next two years. The third session, to be held in South Africa, will consider the applicability of the crime of apartheid to Israel. After the fourth session, it will publish its full conclusions. The jury of the Russell Tribunal was composed of the following members:

- Stéphane Hessel, Ambassador of France, Honorary President of the Russell Tribunal on Palestine, France,
- Mairead Corrigan Maguire, Nobel Peace Laureate 1976, Northern Ireland,
- John Dugard, Professor of International law, former UN Special Rapporteur on Human Rights in the Palestinian Territories, South Africa,
- Lord Anthony Gifford QC, UK barrister and Jamaican attorney-at-law,
- Ronald Kasrils, writer and activist, former government Minister, South Africa,
- Michael Mansfield, barrister, President of the Haldane Society of Socialist Lawyers, United Kingdom,
- José Antonio Martin Pallin, emeritus judge, Chamber II, Supreme Court, Spain and
- Cynthia McKinney, former member of the US Congress and 2008 presidential candidate, Green Party, United States.

Afterword

Asa Winstanley and Frank Barat

The next step for the Russell Tribunal on Palestine is the third international session in South Africa (see below). After that, two more sessions are planned. The fourth session will take place in the United States, focusing on US and UN complicity with Israeli violations. The final session will take into account all previous conclusions and issue a set of final recommendations. This last session will put into perspective all previous sessions and ask the question: 'What is the goal of Israel in denying the Palestinians their right to self determination?'

BOYCOTT, DIVESTMENT AND SANCTIONS (BDS)

As at the Barcelona session, a lot of attention was paid over the course of the London tribunal to the campaign of boycott, divestment and sanctions. BDS is a strategy that, in 2005, a broad coalition of Palestinian civil society groups formally endorsed. You can read the full list of endorsing Palestinian organisations at <www.bdsmovement.net> – the website of the BDS National Committee (BNC). The aim is to target institutions that benefit from the occupation with BDS campaigns until Israel:

1. ends the occupation of all Arab lands it occupied in 1967;
2. recognises the right of the Palestinian citizens of Israel to full equality, and
3. recognises the right of Palestinian refugees to return to their original homeland.

In the full London findings, the tribunal advised individuals and organisations to adopt BDS strategies in order 'to secure compliance of corporations with international human rights and humanitarian law standards' (p. 54). The BNC endorsed the findings of the London session.[1]

THE THIRD SESSION OF THE RUSSELL TRIBUNAL ON PALESTINE

The third session of the Russell Tribunal on Palestine will take place in November 2011 in South Africa. It will deal with the applicability of the crime of apartheid to Israel in regards of its treatment of the Palestinians in the Occupied Palestinians Territories (OPT) and in Israel itself.

Experts and witnesses from all over the world will be invited to testify in front of an eminent panel. Topics covered will include the Bedouins and the unrecognised villages, house demolitions, access to education, health, jobs, natural resources, the separation wall and the system of bypass roads, the Galilee and the creation of Jewish-only towns, Israel's legal system and its new laws, Israel's military courts and many other subjects.

HOW TO HELP THE RUSSELL TRIBUNAL ON PALESTINE

The Russell Tribunal on Palestine is a citizens' initiative that is sustained by contributions from individuals, associations, organisations and solidarity movements. Its independence relies on the great variety of volunteers, material and financial help it receives.

The tribunal is organised by a network of National Support Committees (Spain, United Kingdom, Ireland, the Netherlands, Belgium, Luxembourg, Germany, France, Italy and Portugal). Thanks to them, the first two sessions of the tribunal were a success in terms of audience impact audience and media attention (see the website for media coverage and pictures).

The tribunal's conclusions provide a legally grounded body of arguments, an important tool for those who seek to ensure respect for the rule of international law, and the rights of the Palestinian people.

If you want to get involved, please join a National Support Committee, or create one in your country.

International Secretariat of the Russell Tribunal on Palestine
115 Stevin St, 1000 Brussels, Belgium
Tel/fax: 00 32 (0)2 2310174
Mobile/cellphone: 00 32 (0)479 12 95 32

Contacts
General Coordinator: Pierre Galand
Coordination in Brussels: Virginie Vanhaeverbeke <trp_int@yahoo.com>
Coordination in London: Frank Barat <russelltribunaluk@gmail.com>

<www.russelltribunalonpalestine.com>

Account no.: IBAN BE92733038712023 Bic KREDBEBB
Donate online: <www.russelltribunalonpalestine.com/en/support-us>

Appendix I
Israeli Participation in the European Security Research Programme (ESRP)

Project	Title	Theme & key deliverables	Israeli participants	Total EU funding**
TASS	Total Airport Security System	Surveillance – 'multisource labyrinth fusion logic enabling situational and security awareness of the airport anytime and anywhere'	*Verint Systems Ltd,* * *Elbit Systems Ltd, Israel Airports Authority, Ernst & Young Israel*	€8.98 million
ESS	Emergency Support System	Security control system – 'suite of real-time data-centric technologies which will provide actionable information to crisis managers during abnormal events'	*Verint Systems Ltd,* * *Aeronautics Defense Systems Lt., Magen David Adom (emergency services), Ernst & Young Israel*	€14 million
OPARUS	Open Architecture for UAV-based Surveillance System	UAVs/Drones – development of 'unmanned air-to-ground wide area land and sea border surveillance platforms in Europe'	*Israel Aerospace Industries*	€11.88 million
TALOS	Transportable autonomous patrol for land border surveillance	Border control – 'inform the Control and Command Centre and an intruder about her/his situation, and will undertake the proper measures to stop the illegal action almost autonomously with supervision of border guard officers'	*Israel Aerospace Industries*	€12.9 million
SEABILLA	Sea Border Surveillance	Border control – 'a solution that can be implemented at national and EU level to increase effectiveness, pool resources and address Maritime Security and Safety challenges; for world competitiveness of EU industries'	*Correlation Systems Ltd*	€9.84 million

SAFIRE	Scientific Approach to Fighting Radical Extremism	Counter-terrorism – 'improve fundamental understanding of radicalization processes and use this knowledge to develop principles to improve [the implementation] of interventions designed to prevent, halt and reverse radicalization'	Israeli International Counter-Terrorism Academy	€2.91 million
SAFE-COMMS	Counter-terrorism crisis communications strategies for recovery and continuity	Counter-terrorism – 'a crisis communications manual, and series of training modules'	Bar Ilan University*	€1.09 million
PREVAIL	Precursors of explosives	Counter-terrorism – developing chemicals to render common ingredients in home-made explosives unusable for this purpose	TECHNION (Israeli Institute of Technology)	€3.34 million
EUSECON	A new agenda for European security economics	Homeland Security – 'building new analytical and conceptual insights on the most pressing research needs in this field'	Hebrew University of Jerusalem	€2.36 million
FESTOS	Foresight of evolving security threats posed by emerging technologies	Homeland Security – 'continual scanning of the unfolding technology landscape for potential security threats'	Tel Aviv University* Efp Consulting Ltd (a specialist FP7 consultancy based in the UK and Israel)	€1.23 million
PROTECT RAIL	Railway-Industry Partnership for Integrated Security of Rail Transport	Homeland Security – 'define, research and develop solutions in terms of architectures, technology deployment'	Elbit Systems Ltd	€13.11 million
RIBS	Resilient Infrastructure & Building Security	Homeland Security – 'design of effective and viable integrated security measures aimed at protecting infrastructures without impacting on their business dynamics'	TECHNION (Israeli Institute of Technology)	€3.32 million
IDETECT 4ALL	Novel intruder detection and authentication optical sensing technology	Surveillance – 'alerting technology for surveillance and intruders detection inside and in the surrounding of Critical Infrastructures'	Motorola Israel, CAL Cargo Airlines Ltd, Arttic Israel Company, Azimut Technologies Ltd	€2.29 million
ISTEMIS	Integrated system for transport infrastructures surveillance and monitoring by electromagnetic sensing	Surveillance – "information and images of infrastructure status to improve decision support for emergency and disasters stakeholders"	Tel Aviv University	€3.11 million

* Denotes project leader ** Total EU funding for entire project/consortium

Appendix II
Formal Responses from Companies

 EUROPEAN COMMISSION
EXTERNAL RELATIONS DIRECTORATE GENERAL

DIRECTORATE Middle East, Southern Mediterranean
Near East

Brussels, **1 2 NOV. 2010**
ER.F3/AMB/ak D(2010) **SYB-2010-AA1729**

Russell Tribunal on Palestine
115 Rue Stévin
B 1000 Brussels
Belgium

The Organising Committee of the Russell Tribunal on Palestine,

Thank you for your invitation to the President of the European Commission Barroso to participate in the session of the Russell Tribunal that will be organized at the end of November. He has asked me to reply on his behalf.

Regretfully, the President of the European Commission will not be able to be participate in the second international session of the Russell Tribunal on Palestine.

The EU attaches the utmost importance to the respect of International Human Rights Law and International Humanitarian Law. In its last statement of 21 September, the Middle East Quartet reiterated its call on all parties to respect International Humanitarian and Human Rights Law.

As mentioned by President Barroso during his meeting with Palestinian Prime Minister Fayyad in July, the EU stands firm on its full support to the goal of two states, Israel and Palestine, living side by side in peace and security, as part of a just and comprehensive peace. Our strong commitment and support for a just negotiated solution has also recently been reiterated to President Abbas and Prime Minister Netanyahu by High Representative Ashton during her visits to the region.

I take this opportunity to wish you good luck with the proceedings of your Conference.

Yours Sincerely,

Ilkka UUSITALO
Head of Unit

Commission européenne/Europese Commissie, 1049 Bruxelles/Brussel, BELGIQUE/BELGIË - Tel. +32 22991111
Office: CHAR - Tel. direct line +32 229-60413 - Fax +32 229-91045   ilkka.uusitalo@ec.europa.eu

188

Dear Russell Commission

This is our statement in response to your invitation to take part in the Commission's proceedings this weekend:

The Middle East peace process is at a delicate stage. We believe it should be left to the principals involved to try to make progress. We do not believe this weekend's hearings of the Russell Tribunal on Palestine, well-intentioned as they no doubt are, will help this process. We have therefore decided not to engage with the Tribunal or respond to the statements it has made to the media, except to state that G4S seeks to enhance security worldwide by offering high quality services to commercial organisations, individuals and governments. Our policy is always to comply with national law in any jurisdiction in which we operate.

Regards

Michael Clarke
Public Affairs Director
G4S plc

+44 7872 158833

www.g4s.com

Le Secrétaire Général

Russel Tribunal on Palestine
Pierre GALAND
115 rue Stevenin
1000 Brussels – Belgium

Paris, 8th November 2010

Dear Sir,

Thank you for your letter.

Veolia Environnement, which operates in more than 70 countries, is a leading player in the environmental services sector. Veolia Transport, a subsidiary of Veolia Environnement, entered into the Jerusalem Light Rail Project in the aftermath of the Oslo Accord, when there was a prospect of a peaceful settlement to the Israeli-Palestinian conflict. We believed then and we believe now, that this project will provide a real contribution to the improvement to the lives of all sections of the population. We have always made it very clear that unless there was to be equal access by all, we would withdraw from the project.

At all times we have sought to obey International Law and we have stated that if it were ruled by a properly constituted judicial court that we were in breach of International Law, then we would withdraw. We therefore did not oppose the decision by the French courts that they had jurisdiction and we always made it plain that we would abide by their decision. In the event the process has taken much longer than we had hoped and it has been Veolia who has been pressing the court to come to its consideration and verdict.

The changed circumstances in the region have also made managing this project ever more complex and polemical. At the same time, Veolia has been approached by a transport company and has decided to initiate the divestiture of its interests in the project, subject to fulfilling its contractual obligations.

In light of these circumstances, we do not find it appropriate to participate in your session at the present time. The story of these events illustrates just how difficult it is to deliver essential public services and thus to seek to contribute to a better living environment in disputed areas.

Yours sincerely,

Olivier Orsini
General Secretary

Veolia Environnement
Siège social : 38, avenue Kléber • 75799 Paris Cedex 16 • France
tél. +33 (0)1 71 75 01 26 • fax +33 (0)1 71 75 03 72
www.veolia.com

Société anonyme à conseil d'administration
au capital de 2 486 811 960 €
403 210 032 RCS PARIS

PENSIOENFONDS
ZORG & WELZIJN

Date
12 November 2010

Our reference
PFZW2010-057

Subject
Russell Tribunal

Russell Tribunal on Palestine
Attn. Mr. Pierre Galand
115 Rue Stévin
1000 BRUSSELS
Belgium

Contact person
J.W. van Oostveen

Phone number
+31 30 277 5575

Dear Mr. Galand,

In response to your letter dated October 18th, 2010 regarding the London session of the Russell Tribunal on Palestine on corporate complicity, I wish to inform you that we respectfully decline the opportunity to provide a statement at the tribunal in London. Please do find enclosed a written statement clarifying our position.

The Board of Stichting Pensioenfonds Zorg en Welzijn (PFZW) is deeply concerned about the ongoing conflict between Israel and Palestine, and the consequential long time occupation of Palestinian territories by Israel. It is further concerned about ongoing violations of international law in this context and about possible complicity in such violations by companies that are active in Israel and the occupied territories.

The enclosed statement sets out how PFZW is determined to attempt within its policy framework to use its influence as a shareholder in these companies by addressing the above concerns and to try to make a modest contribution towards the common goal of achieving a lasting and peaceful resolution to this complex conflict situation in the Middle East.

Thank you for your attention to this letter and enclosed statement.

Yours faithfully,

Hans Alders
Chairman of the Board Stichting Pensioenfonds Zorg en Welzijn

Enclosed: Statement PFZW to Russell Tribunal on Palestine

Statement PFZW to the Russell Tribunal on Palestine

1. Profile of Stichting Pensioenfonds Zorg en Welzijn (www.pfzw.nl)

Stichting Pensioenfonds Zorg en Welzijn (hereafter referred to as PFZW) is responsible for the pension policy and pension assets of over 2.2 million current and former employees in the care and welfare sector. The pension fund is the owner of the assets, which at the end of September 2010 amounted to EUR 97 billion. PFZW has outsourced the administration of the pension scheme and the management of the pension assets to PGGM (www.pggm.nl).

PFZW has been active in the field of responsible investment for over 20 years. It is the pension fund's belief that this way of investing contributes to a high and stable return in the long term. PFZW's first activities on responsible investment date back to 1985. The pension fund has since been involved in the establishment of the "Principles for Responsible Investment (PRI)". This is an initiative taken at the invitation of the United Nations with a large number of international institutional investors. The PRI offer an aspirational framework for investors to take account of environmental, social and corporate governance factors. The PRI has now been signed by over 800 parties managing total assets in excess of $22 trillion (www.unpri.org). PFZW's activities with regard to responsible investment are internationally recognized. Also, for three years in a row the pension fund came first in a benchmarking exercise of Dutch pension funds with regard to their approach to responsible investing (www.vbdo.nl).

2. Investment policy

PFZW is responsible for the financially sound administration of pension assets. The financial future of pension fund's beneficiaries and their families partly depends on the returns achieved on these pension assets. PFZW therefore aims to generate stable and above-average returns by means of an innovative investment policy.

PFZW applies an investment policy that is appropriate for the pension liabilities of the fund, with a risk-return profile ensuring an adequate and stable cover ratio. PFZW determines this investment policy with the support of PGGM.

As a result of this investment policy PFZW invests across the globe in a wide range of asset classes, including for example listed equity, bonds, private equity, hedge funds, real estate and infrastructure.

2.1   Listed equity
In line with its investment beliefs PFZW has in place a benchmark-based strategy for investments in listed equity (i.e. in shares of companies listed at stock exchanges around the world). In order to generate the highest net returns for the pension fund's beneficiaries, while considering the high costs of active management, a 'Sophisticated Matching Approach' is applied to closely track a selected benchmark of listed companies. In other words, there is no active stock picking involved. With the exception of the companies on the Exclusions List (see below), PFZW could invest in all companies that are included in the benchmark that is being tracked.

1

Statement PFZW to the Russell Tribunal on Palestine

Currently PFZW invests in over 4000 companies worldwide. It is important to understand that, with the exception of the Listed Real Estate portfolio and the Responsible Equity Portfolio, individual selection of listed companies for investment does not take place. This is solely determined by the benchmark that is being tracked.

3. Responsible Investment Policy

The PFZW Responsible Investment Policy emphasises the strategic importance of responsible investment. Responsible investment is an integral part of the pension fund's investment policy and investment beliefs. It is PFZW's aim to apply the Responsible Investment Policy to all investment categories.

PFZW defines responsible investment as consciously taking account of the influence of environmental factors, social factors and good corporate governance in all investment activities. These three aspects are also referred to as ESG factors. PFZW expects the focus on ESG factors to impact the risk and return of the pension fund's investments, enabling PFZW to continually achieve a high and stable return.

The key points of the Responsible Investment Policy are:
- active backing for the conviction that financial and social returns can go hand in hand;
- exploiting sources of return in cases where the influence of ESG factors plays an important role;
- representing shareholders actively to contribute to the quality and continuity of companies;
- expressing the pension fund's identity in terms of the limits of the investment policy and choosing specific focus areas on the basis of that identity;
- encouraging partners in the financial sector to practise responsible investment; and
- accountability with regard to targets, activities and results in the field of responsible investment.

3.1 Focus areas
As a reflection of the pension fund's identity, attention is focused on the following specific areas:
- Controversial weapons;
- Human rights and labour rights;
- Climate change;
- Health; and
- Good corporate governance.

These themes were adopted after extensive consultations with the beneficiaries of the pension fund and various social organisations.

3.2 Responsible investment activities
For the implementation of its policy, PFZW specifically and exclusively selected asset manager PGGM Investments. As part of this implementation PGGM Investments undertakes the following activities:
- ESG Integration into existing investment processes;
- Focussed ESG Investments;
- Exclusions;
- Voting; and
- Dialogue with companies (engagement)

Statement PFZW to the Russell Tribunal on Palestine

The approach to exclusions and engagement will be discussed below. The PGGM website or their Responsible Investment Annual Report can be consulted for more detailed information regarding the other activities of PGGM[1].

4. Exclusions Policy

Criteria whereby PFZW will not invest in certain companies have been in place since 1985. These criteria have been adjusted over time.

4.1 Controversial weapons

Since 2007, PFZW has excluded companies which make or trade in controversial weapons. These are weapons of mass destruction (nuclear, chemical and biological weapons) and weapons with a significant risk of (civilian) casualties during and/or after the military conflict (anti-personnel mines, cluster bombs and depleted uranium ammunition). Currently, 34 companies are being excluded from investments because of their involvement in the manufacturing of and/or trade in these controversial weapons. The PFZW website can be consulted for the full list of excluded companies[2].

4.2 Government bonds

In 2008 the Exclusions Policy was amended to include a provision on government bonds. Government bonds of five countries were excluded at the end of 2008. These include Iran, Myanmar (Burma), North-Korea, Somalia and Sudan. Government bonds (including inflation-linked government bonds and other debt securities – without any predefined purpose – of central and local government bodies) of these countries are excluded from investment. The exclusion does not apply to other investments in these countries.

4.3 Human Rights: Exclusion as a last resort, engagement as the preferred approach

In addition, PFZW regards it as a basic tenet of its identity that the companies in which the pension fund invests respect human rights and labour rights. Experience shows that there are high-risk countries and high-risk sectors in which violations of human rights are relatively frequent and in which companies can become involved. PFZW expects companies operating in these countries and sectors to have human rights policies, programmes and reporting systems in place.

PFZW does not in principle directly exclude such companies from its portfolio if these programmes are lacking, but prefers a role as active shareholder by firstly pursuing an engagement approach. On the pension fund's behalf PGGM Investments will enter into a dialogue with a company to improve the situation (end the violations if persistent) and to avoid any such violations in the future, for example by establishing satisfactory human rights policy, programmes and reporting.

---

[1] http://www.pggm.nl/About_PGGM/Investments/Responsible_Investment/Responsible_Investment.asp

http://www.pggm.nl//Images/10-3538%20PGGM%20VB%20Jaarverslag%20UK-02-LoRes_tcm21-165939.pdf

[2]

http://www.pfzw.nl/about_us/Investments/Responsible_Investments/Activities/Exclusions_of_listed_compan ies/Exclusions_of_listed_companies.asp

Statement PFZW to the Russell Tribunal on Palestine

If the engagement does not prove to be successful within a specified period – in other words, if a company fails, for example, to establish a policy and/ or remains frequently involved in new violations of human rights – the company will be excluded after all. Exclusion is explicitly regarded as a last resort (ultimum remedium), i.e. in case of problematic *behavior* PFZW prefers to first use its power to influence change.

Exclusion may then be the result of a company failing to move in the desired direction or completely failing to respond to specific engagement on the part of PGGM Investments. Recently, the Indian mining company Vedanta Resources and its daughter companies were added to the pension fund's Exclusions List, when PGGM Investments' dialogue with them did not bring about sufficient change in the company's environmental and human rights practices. In 2008, the Chinese oil company PetroChina was excluded because they were unwilling to seriously discuss human rights concerns related to Sudan.

5. Engagement

The dialogue with the companies in pension fund's investment portfolio (engagement) is outsourced to PGGM Investments. PGGM Investments has the following engagement approach in place. Engagement takes place within the context of the concept of active ownership. The PGGM Listed Equity Ownership Policy[3] can be consulted for a detailed explanation of this concept.

Subject to the Responsible Investment Policy, the engagement focuses on corporate governance, human rights, climate change and health. Within these focus areas, specific spearheads for engagement are defined.

Periodically a list is compiled of companies on which PGGM Investments will focus their engagement efforts. To compile this engagement focus list, the following selection criteria are applied:

- The size of the investment within the equity funds and segregated accounts managed by PGGM Investments;
- The relative stake in the company and relative voting power;
- The expected impact on the ESG issue due to PGGM Investments' efforts;
- The expected contribution to long term value creation for PGGM Investments' clients.

5.1   Human Rights
For engagement in the area of human rights, the entire portfolio is carefully screened by external data providers to identify those companies in the pension fund's portfolio that may face allegations of or are involved in human rights violations. This information is then used to prioritise companies the engagement efforts will focus on. Stakeholder concerns are explicitly considered in this process.

---

[3] http://www.pggm.nl//Images/10-3454%20PGGM%20Investments%20Listed%20Equity%20Ownership%20Policy_tcm21-165337.pdf

Statement PFZW to the Russell Tribunal on Palestine

Every engagement project has concrete objectives and timelines. This enables for adequate assessment whether the objectives have been achieved. Experience indicates that engagement projects take considerable time, typically 2-3 years to achieve their objectives. Where possible and appropriate PGGM Investments endeavors to inform the pension fund's beneficiaries and other stakeholders on the progress of the engagement projects, for example in the Responsible Investment Annual Report mentioned before or the quarterly reports on Active Ownership (in Dutch only)[4].

6.   PFZW's current exposure to companies active in the Occupied Palestinian Territories

The letter PFZW received from the secretariat of the Russell Tribunal on Palestine states that PFZW invests in 27 companies involved in corporate activity in the Occupied Palestinian Territories. The letter however does not disclose the source of this information.

For this statement it is assumed that this number was derived from the analysis of the PFZW portfolio (dated 31-12-2009) by the Israeli organization Who Profits as included in a report published by the Dutch organization Werkgroep Keerpunt on their website in February of this year[5].

While the publicly available information on the pension fund's portfolio[6] is updated once a year, the portfolio changes continuously as a consequence of investment decisions and benchmarks changes. Currently , PFZW invests in 13 companies identified on the list by Who Profits as being involved in corporate activity in the Occupied Palestinian Territories. The total amount of assets invested in these companies is almost €323 million (the average investment in these companies being close to € 12 million). This amounts to about 0.3% of total assets under management. The ownership percentage in these companies varies from 0.59% to 0.01%.

Due to a recent change in one of the benchmarks that is tracked for the pension fund's listed equity investments, PFZW is no longer invested in any of the Israeli companies mentioned on the list by Who Profits.

4

http://www.pggm.nl/Over_PGGM/Investments/Publicaties/verslagen_en_documenten/verslagen_en_docum enten.asp#0

[5] http://www.werkgroepkeerpunt.nl/dossier.php

6

http://www.pfzw.nl/about_us/Investments/Transparancy/Overview_of_Investments/Overview_of_Investmen ts.asp

Statement PFZW to the Russell Tribunal on Palestine

7. Engagement with regard to companies active in Occupied Palestinian Territories

The situation in the Middle East and particularly in the Occupied Palestinian Territories deeply concerns the Board of PFZW and has therefore been the topic of various board discussions with the pension fund's external ethical advisors[7] over the past few years.

Also, a small number of beneficiaries as well as other stakeholders, notably Werkgroep Keerpunt and nederlands palestina komite, have indicated to PFZW that the investments in companies that are active in the Occupied Territories, are of concern to them.

In response to these concerns, PFZW has asked PGGM Investments to develop an engagement approach with regard to these companies. This engagement approach focuses on those companies
* that contribute to sustaining the occupation (for example banks providing loans to finance Israeli settlements in occupied territory);
* whose products or services are directly associated with the occupation or suppression (for example a company allegedly providing custom-made bulldozers involved in the destruction of Palestinian homes);
* that contribute to activities that can be seen as in direct violation of international law (for example companies involved in a controversial tram way).

The starting point for the engagement is fact finding. PGGM Investments asks the companies to provide detailed information on for example policies and systems in place to identify and avoid the risk of being in violation of international law and what specific efforts have been undertaken to avoid or mitigate these risks. Where applicable, companies are asked to indicate how they ensure that there is equal access to their products or services.

In addition, information is gathered from different sources and experts to provide further input to these engagement efforts and the decision on the final outcomes, which may or may not be the decision to exclude the company from investments.

8. Concluding remarks

Finally, the Board of PFZW wishes to emphasize that it is deeply concerned about the ongoing conflict between Israel and Palestine, and the consequential long time occupation of Palestinian territories by Israel. It is further concerned about ongoing violations of international law in this context and about possible complicity in such violations by companies that are active in Israel and the occupied territories.

PFZW is determined to attempt within its policy framework to use its influence as a shareholder in these companies by addressing the above concerns and to try to make a modest contribution towards the common goal of achieving a lasting and peaceful resolution to this complex conflict situation in the Middle East.

---

[7] Ethical advisors to PFZW are Prof. C. Flinterman, Mr. C. Homan and Mr. R Willems.

Notes

All web links checked 31 March 2011.

INTRODUCTION

1. 'Legal Consequences of the Construction of a Wall in the Occupied Palestinian Territory', International Court of Justice, 9 July 2004; available at <www.icj-cij.org>.
2. Jean-Paul Sartre, inaugural statement at the Russell Tribunal on Vietnam, 1967.

1. THE LEGAL FRAMEWORK RELEVANT TO CORPORATE CONDUCT

1. Cited in John Ruggie, 'Clarifying the Concepts of "Sphere of influence" and "Complicity". Report of the Special Representative of the Secretary-General on the Issue of Human Rights and Transnational Corporations and other Business Enterprises', UN Human Rights Council (A/HRC/8/16), pp. 18–19, 15 May 2008.
2. Cited in 'Economic, Social and Cultural Rights, Commentary on the Norms on the responsibilities of transnational corporations and other business enterprises with regard to human rights', Economic and Social Council/Commission on Human Rights, (E/CN.4/Sub.2/2003/38/Rev.2), pp. 5–6, 26 August 2003.
3. John Ruggie, 'Protect, Respect and Remedy: a Framework for Business and Human Rights. Report of the Special Representative of the Secretary-General on the issue of human rights and transnational corporations and other business enterprises', UN HRC, (A/HRC/8/5), pp. 8–9, 7 April 2008.
4. Ibid., p. 18.
5. 'Report of the Secretary-General on the implementation of Security Council resolution 1625 (2005) on conflict prevention, particularly in Africa', UN Security Council (S/2008/18), p. 5, 14 January 2008.
6. *Prosecutor* v. *Furundzija* (IT-95-17/1-T Judgment of 10 December 1998), paragraph 235.
7. Draft code of crimes against the peace and security of mankind, Article 2, paragraph 3(d). Report of the International Law Commission on the work of its 48th session, 6 May-26 July 1996 (A/51/10).
8. Ruggie, 'Clarifying the Concepts of "Sphere of influence" and "Complicity"', p. 15.
9. E. David, *Elements of international and European criminal law*, Brussels: Bruylant, 2009, §3.2.44.
10. Ibid., §12.2.33.
11. Scotland and Northern Ireland have separate legal systems.
12. Considerations of criminal liability are excluded from this paper; see Daniel Machover and Paul Troop, and so on.
13. The case of *Jones* v *UK* and *Mitchell & Ors* v *UK* (Application Numbers: 34356/06 and 40528/06) is currently pending before the European Court of

Human Rights. This is a challenge to the principle of State Immunity in the context of allegations of torture. If that claim is successful, then there may be the possibility of English courts entertaining private law claims against Israeli officials accused of torture, albeit under carefully prescribed circumstances.

14. *R (Saleh Hasan) v SS for Trade and Industry* [2008] EWCA 1311 (hereafter 'Hasan'). Saleh Hasan, a Palestinian living in the West Bank and operating in conjunction with al-Haq, filed a claim requesting the UK government to clarify its position on its arms-related licensing agreements with Israel. In particular, the claim sought to require the UK government to reveal how it satisfies its own criteria that material sold under these agreements is not used in the commission of human rights abuses in the Occupied Palestinian Territories.

15. *R (on the application of Al-Haq) v Secretary of State for Foreign and Commonwealth Affairs [2009] EWHC 1910 (Admin)* (hereafter 'Al-Haq'). Al-Haq, a Palestinian human rights organisation, sought judicial review of the UK government's failure to comply with four key obligations under customary international law arising from Israeli breaches of peremptory norms of international law: (1) to denounce and not to recognise as lawful situations created by Israel's actions; (2) not to render aid or assistance or be otherwise complicit in maintaining the situation; (3) to cooperate with other states using all lawful means to bring Israel's breaches to an end, and (4) to take all possible steps to ensure that Israel respects its obligations under the Geneva Conventions.

16. *Al-Haq*, paras 41–6. In *Al-Haq*, the Court determined the subject matter of the claim to be: (1) the 'condemnation of Israel' (paras 41, 53) and (2) to direct the UK government's foreign policy (paras 46, 51). It ruled that it was not competent to decide whether Israel is in breach of its international obligations (para. 41).

17. *Kuwait Airways Corp v Iraqi Airways Corp* (No 5) – [2003] All ER (D) 225 (Jan).

18. The court was not satisfied in this case because there was no authoritative judgment on Operation Cast Lead.

19. *R (Abbasi) v Secretary of State for Foreign and Commonwealth Affairs* [2002] EWCA Civ 1598.

20. *Al-Haq*, para. 42.

21. *R (Gentle) v The Prime Minister & Others* [2006] EWCA Civ 1689 at para. 26.

22. *Al-Haq*, para. 54.

23. Ibid.

24. Parliamentary Joint Committee on Human Rights, 'Any of our business? Human Rights and the UK private sector', First Report of Session 2009–10, Volume I: Report and formal minutes, HL Paper 5-I, HC 64-I (16 December 2009) at p. 67.

25. Ibid.

26. EU Public Procurement Directive, Clause 149.

27. There is a challenge to the application of state immunity from civil suit in the context of torture currently pending before the European Court of Human Rights – *Jones v UK* and *Mitchell & Ors v UK* (Application Numbers: 34356/06 and 40528/06) – but even if that appeal is successful, it is most unlikely to establish any form of universal civil jurisdiction for claims against foreign states in England and Wales.

28. Brussels and Lugano conventions 1968 and 1988 incorporated into UK law by the Civil Jurisdictions and Judgments Act 1982 as amended. Now substantially

superseded by EC Regulation (EC) 44/2001 of 22 December 2000, which has direct effect in the UK.

29. [2002] EWCA Civ 877. The case was referred to the European Court of Justice; see footnote below.

30. *Owusu* v *Jackson* [2005] 2WLR 942 (ECJ), paras 37–46. See also opinion of the Advocate General, 14 December 2004.

31. Civil Procedure Rules ('CPR'), 6.20(8).

32. CPR, 6.20(8).

33. CPR, 6.20(3).

34. CPR, 7.3.

35. Regulation (EC) No 864/2007 on the Law Applicable to Non-Contractual Obligations' ('Rome II') [2007] OJ L199/40 (hereafter 'Rome II'). Since Rome II is a Regulation, it is directly applicable in the UK; there is no requirement for implementing legislation and inconsistent legislation is disapplied.

36. *Phillips* v *Eyre* (1870) LR 6 QB 1 (Exch Ch) 28–29.

37. Rome II, Article 1(1). Note subparagraph (d), which states 'non-contractual obligations arising out of the law of companies and other bodies corporate or unincorporated regarding matters such as the creation, by registration or otherwise, legal capacity, internal organisation or winding-up of companies and other bodies corporate or unincorporated, the personal liability of officers and members as such for the obligations of the company or body and the personal liability of auditors to a company or to its members in the statutory audits of accounting documents'.

38. Rome II, Article 3.

39. Articles 5–9 provide for specific cases: product liability, unfair competition, environmental damage, intellectual property and industrial action.

40. Rome II, Article 4(1).

41. Rome II, Article 23 provides that 'habitual residence' of companies and other bodies, corporate or unincorporated, shall be the place of central administration. Where the event giving rise to the damage occurs, or the damage arises, in the course of operation of a branch, agency or any other establishment, the place where the branch, agency, or any other establishment is located shall be treated as the place of habitual residence. Subparagraph 2 provides that the habitual residence of a natural person acting in the course of his or her business activity shall be his or her principal place of business.

42. Rome II, Article 4(2).

43. Rome II, Article 4(3).

44. Rome II, Article 14(1)(a); note also Article 14(1)(b), which allows a pre-event choice of law where all the parties are pursuing a commercial activity and the choice of law agreement has been 'freely' negotiated.

45. This provision has caused the most controversy; for example, (i) Rome II only provides for law/rules to apply but the process of assessing damages is often determined by practice not law; and (ii) the distinction between substance and procedure is preserved, Article 1(3) provides that Rome II does not apply to procedure and evidence, which may cause difficulties in assessing quantum.

46. PIL(MP)A, Article 11(1).

47. PIL(MP)A, Article 11(2).

48. This wording suggests that the general rule may be displaced in relation to individual issues in a case rather than the whole case. This was the position at common law before the PIL(MP)A.

49. *Boys* v *Chaplin* [1971] AC 356.

50. *Kuwait Airways Corporation* v *Iraqi Airways Company and Others* [2002] UKHL 19, [2002] 2 AC 883, [168].
51. *Salomon* v *Salomon & Co Limited* [1897] AC 22.
52. *Trustor* v *Smallbone (No 2)* [2001] 1 WLR 1177 (ChD).
53. Sarah Joseph, *Corporations and Transnational Human Rights Litigation* (London: Hart Publishing, 2004), p. 130.
54. *Adams* v *Cape Industries* [1990] Ch 433 (CA Civ) at 539.
55. *Smith Stone and Knight* v *Birmingham Corporation* [1939] All ER 116 (KB).
56. TLR 10 November 1995, 579.
57. Joseph, *Corporations and Transnational Human Rights Litigation*, p. 130.
58. This was in part the basis of the claim before the House of Lords in *Lubbe* v *Cape Plc* [2000] 1 WLR 1545 and more recently in *Gurerrero & others* v *Montericco* [2009] EWHC 2475.
59. See Ian Cobain, 'British mining company faces damages claim after allegations of torture in Peru', *Guardian*, 18 October, 2009 and *Guerrero* v *Montericco*, cited above.
60. Contracts (Rights of Third Parties) Act 1999; Chitty, *Contracts* (29th edn), 18-084-7 (n. 91).
61. Available at <www.oecd.org/daf/investment/guidelines>.
62. The reference to human rights is however, somewhat vague in that it refers to the fact that corporations should 'respect the human rights of those affected by their activities consistent with the host government's international obligations and commitments': para 2(2).
63. See 'The UK National Contact Point For the OECD Guidelines for Multinational Enterprises', Department for Business, Innovation and Skills, October 2009. Available at <www.bis.gov.uk>.
64. For further information, see <www.bis.gov.uk/nationalcontactpoint>.
65. Composed of representatives of relevant government departments and four external members nominated by the Trades Union Congress, the Confederation of British Industry, the All Party Parliamentary Group on the Great Lakes Region of Africa, and the NGO community. I am the external member nominated by the NGO community.
66. UK National Contact Point For the OECD Guidelines
67. Available at <http://www.bis.gov.uk/files/file47341.pdf>.
68. Parliamentary Joint Committee on Human Rights, 'Any of our business?', pp. 62 and 90.
69. See Twenty-eighth Report of Session 2005–06, 'Legislative Scrutiny: Fourteenth Progress Report', HL Paper 247/HC 1626, paras 1.1–1.19.
70. Ruggie, 'Protect, Respect and Remedy'.
71. UN Human Rights Council, Resolution 8/7, 18 June 2008.
72. Report of the UN Special Representative of the Secretary-General on the issue of human rights and transnational corporations and other business enterprises, John Ruggie, 'Business and Human Rights: Further steps toward the operationalization of the "protect, respect and remedy" framework', UN Doc. A/HRC/14/27 (9 April 2010) (hereafter 'Ruggie 2010 Report').
73. Report to the United Nations Human Rights Council, by Professor John Ruggie, 30 May 2011 <http://www.business-humanrights.org/SpecialRepPortal/Home/ReportstoUNHumanRightsCouncil/2011>.
74. Ibid., at para. 82.
75. Panel of Eminent Persons, *Protecting Dignity: An Agenda for Human Rights*, December 2008 <www.udhr60.ch/agenda.html>. See also Manfred Nowak and

Julia Kazma, *A World Court of Human Rights, Swiss Initiative to Commemorate the 60th Anniversary of the UDHR Protecting Dignity: An Agenda for Human Rights* (June 2009) and Manfred Nowak, 'The Need for a World Court of Human Rights', 7(1) *Human Rights Law Review* (2007) 251–9.

76. War crimes include wilful killing, torture, inhuman treatment, wilfully causing great suffering or serious injury, extensive destruction or appropriation of property not justified by military necessity, unlawful deportation or transfer or displacement of the civilian population and intentionally directing attacks against civilian populations. They also include property offenses such as pillage and unlawfully destroying or seizing property. Gross human rights abuses that constitute international crimes are genocide, slavery, torture, extrajudicial execution and enforced disappearance.

77. For the breach of fiduciary duty claim, only the political question and act of state defences apply.

78. Court of Appeal, Criminal Chamber, 14 December 1999, soc. Spie Citra: Criminal Law Bulletin, No. 306; Court of Appeal Reports, p. 430; Criminal Law 200, Comm. No. 56, RJDA 1999, No. 351; Bull. Joly 2000, §145, obs. J.-F. Barbièri, solution implic.

79. Court of Appeal, Criminal Chamber, 13 March 1891: Bull. Crim., n° 66 – 7 September 1893: Criminal Bulletin., n° 252 – 30 April 1908: S. 1908, 1, p. 553, note A. Roux – 2 July 1932: Gaz. Pal. 1932, 2, p. 532 – CA Lyon 27 December 1892: DP 1894, 2, p. 254 – T. Corr. Paris, 11 April 1983: Gaz. Pal. 1983, 2, p. 372, note J.-P. Doucet.

80. Cf. especially R. Beraud, Omission, punishable, JCP 1944, éd. G, I, 433 – A. Chavanne: op. cit., no. 71ff. – Note ss CA Bourges, 16 February 1950: JCP 1950, ed. G, II, 5629.

81. Court of Appeal, Criminal Chamber, 4 March 1964: JCP 1964, ed. G, IV, p. 57 – 29 March 1971: Criminal Bulletin, No. 112.

82. Cf. in particular Court of Appeal, Criminal Chamber, 25 January 1962: Criminal bulletin no. 68; Rev. sc. Crim. 1962, p. 749, obs. A. Légal.

2. CORPORATE ACTIVITIES IN AND AROUND ISRAELI SETTLEMENTS

1. See our 'The Cellular Companies and the Occupation', *Who Profits Newsletter*, August 2009. Available at <www.whoprofits.org>.

2. Alternative Information Centre, Bulletin II, July 2005.

3. From various sources and publications.

4. Sophie Crowe, 'Israel's Toxic Chemical Factories Giving Cancer to West Bank Residents', *Palestine Monitor*, 17 November 2010.

5. Ibid.

6. Sarah Irving, 'Palestinian women settlement workers' plight', *Electronic Intifada*, 1 May 2009.

7. Case C-386/08, Judgment of 25 February 2010.

8. TUC, Congress 2010, Composite motion C18 Palestine. Available at <www.tuc.org.uk>.

9. Israel Ministry of Foreign Affairs, 'Jerusalem: Urban Characteristics and Major Trends in the City's Development, Part II: Economic and Urban Development', 5 January 1997. Available at <www.mfa.gov.il>.

10. [Israel] Prime Minister's Office, 'PM Sharon's Statements at the Ceremony for the Signing of the Light Train Agreement', 17 July 2005.

11. Orient House [the PLO's Jerusalem office] press release, 'Israel to Confiscate More Land in Occupied East Jerusalem for the Light Rail', 11 July, 2001. Available at <www.orienthouse.org>.

12. Amira Hass, 'Palestinians to Arab states: You can stop Jerusalem light rail', *Ha'aretz*, 17 November 2009; Abe Selig, 'Palestinian boycott calls won't hinder Jerusalem light rail construction', *Jerusalem Post*, 23 November 2009.

13. Adri Nieuwhof, 'Veolia whitewashes illegal light rail project', *Electronic Intifada*, 26 August 2010.

14. 'Veolia Environnement', Who Profits company profile: <www.whoprofits.org>.

15. Karolien van Dijck, 'Public transport and political control: empirical study of the CityPass project on the West Bank', University of Ghent, 2008–09 (unpublished).

16. Nir Hasson, 'Officials slam "racist" Jerusalem light rail survey', *Ha'aretz*, 23 August 2010.

17. Diakonia press release (translation by AIC), 'Veolia Publishes Discriminatory Ad for Jerusalem Light Rail', 27 August 2010.

18. 'Veolia – Taking out Israel's Trash', Corporate Watch blog, 31 March 2010 <www.corporateoccupation.wordpress.com>.

19. 'Still doing Israel's Dirty Work: Veolia's Tovlan landfill in the Jordan Valley', Corporate Watch blog, 12 July 2010.

20. Report of the Special Representative of the UN Secretary-General on the issue of human rights and transnational corporations and other business enterprises, UN Human Rights Council, A/HRC/8/5, 7 April 2008.

21. The Ireland-Palestine Solidarity Campaign website is <www.ipsc.ie>.

22. 'CRH Code of Conduct', available at <www.crh.com>.

23. The CRH website is <www.crh.ie>.

24. Nesher Israel Cement Enterprises Ltd website is <www.nesher.co.il/new_site/en/>.

25. Project Clean Hands website is <projectcleanhands.wordpress.com/category/crh/crh-photos>.

26. Amnesty International news release, 16 June 2004.

27. Nesher Israel Cement Enterprises Ltd: <http://www.nesher.co.il/en/index.htm>.

28. Who Profits, 'Nesher Israel Cement Enterprises', <http://www.whoprofits.org/Company%20Info.php?id=637>.

29. 'Legal Consequences of the Construction of a Wall in the Occupied Palestinian Territory', International Court of Justice, 2004. Available at <www.icj-cij.org>.

30. UN Office for the Coordination of Humanitarian Affairs (UN OCHA), 'The Humanitarian Impact of the Barrier: Four years after the advisory opinion of the International Court of Justice', July 2008. Available at <www.ochaopt.org>.

31. The Universal Declaration of Human Rights. Available at <www.hrweb.org/legal/undocs.html#UDHR>.

32. Ibid.

33. Report by the Divestment Task Force of the New England Conference of the United Methodist Church, 2010. Available at <www.neumc.org/pages/detail/375>.

34. John Ruggie, 'Protect, Respect and Remedy: a Framework for Business and Human Rights', UN HRC, (A/HRC/8/5), 2008.

35. 'OECD Guidelines for Multinational Enterprises', 2008. Available at <www.oecd.org>.

36. Ibid.

37. CRH Code of Conduct.

3. TRADE AND LABELLING OF ISRAELI SETTLEMENT GOODS

1. These elements of the crime have been deduced from case law on pillage, particularly the trials held by the Nuremberg Military Tribunals of German industrialists after the Second World War and from the International Criminal Court 'Elements of Crime' which codifies the offence.

2. Natural resources will be considered state-owned immovable property, where national laws provide that natural resources belong to the state. Natural resources are 'immovable' because extensive work must be done to extract them from the land.

3. Ahava's CEO disputed that the company extracts minerals from occupied territory, in a written response he made to the allegations of the advocacy group Code Pink. There appears, however, to be objective evidence that Ahava's extraction of resources takes place near to the settlement of Kalia, in the occupied West Bank (<www.stolenbeauty.org>).

4. Information obtained from Who Profits and from Ahava's website <www.ahava.co.il>.

5. Ahava, meaning the company itself or its representatives, depending on the mode of criminal responsibility asserted.

6. The matter requires further research in order to be determined.

7. Note by the Secretary-General, 'Economic and social repercussions of the Israeli occupation on the living conditions of the Palestinian people in the occupied Palestinian territory, including Jerusalem, and of the Arab population in the occupied Syrian Golan', UN Doc. A/61/67 and E/2006/13 (3 May 2006), pp. 12–13, para. 47.

8. R. Falk, 'Situation of human rights in the Palestinian territories occupied since 1967', UN Doc. A/63/326, 25 August 2008; COHRE (2008), 'Submission to the Goldberg Committee regarding violations of the human right to water and sanitation in the unrecognised villages of the Negev/Naqab'.

9. Hilo Glazer, 'Palestinian Child Labour in Jordan Valley Israeli Settlements', Kav LaOved report, 6 June 2009. Available at <www.kavlaoved.org.il>.

10. 'GF Group s'investit à Sète en accord avec l'exportateur israélien de fruits et légumes Agrexco (marque Carmel)', *Chambre de commerce franco-israélienne*, 26 February 2009.

11. Statistical Abstract of Israel, Central Bureau of Statistics, Issue 2007-No. 58, Tel Aviv, August 2007.

12. Falestine Hurriyah, 'The Agrexco Seven: Day one', *Indymedia UK*, 24 January 2006.

13. Agrexco Agricultural Company Ltd: Transaction report for the period 10/04–12/04 (see annex).

14. Agrexco Agricultural Export Company Ltd: Letter from the management to French customers, 15 March 2010 (see annex).

15. See the websites <www.jordanvalleysolidarity.org> and <corporateoccupation.wordpress.com>.

16. Euro-Mediterranean Agreement establishing an association between the European Communities and their Member States, of the one part, and the State of Israel, of the other part, signed in Brussels on 20 November 1995 (OJ 2000, L 147, p. 3). Entered into force on 1 June 2000.

17. *Brita* Judgment, Court of Justice of the European Communities (CJEC), 25 February 2010.

18. Statement by Phyllis Starkey on the EU-Israel Trade Agreement, Hansard, 27 January 2010.

19. See her website: <www.nicolekiilnielsen.eu/526>.

20. CJEC, 7 December 1993, *Huygen*, C-12/92, ECR I-638, paragraph 27.

21. CJEC, 9 February 2006, *Sfakianakis*, C-23/04 to C-25/04, ECR I-1265, paragraph 38; CJEC, 14 May 1996, *Faroe Seafood*, C-153/94 and C-204/94, ECR I-2465, paragraphs 24 and 25.

22. CJEC, 14 November 2002, *Ilumitrónica*, C-251/00, ECR I-10433, paragraph 74.

23. Writ of summons for summary proceedings before the Créteil Commercial Court against Carmel-Agrexco (see annex).

24. Ahava Dead Sea Laboratories official web site <www.ahava.co.il>.

25. Michal Lev-Ram, 'Turning Dead Sea Mud Into Money: Transcending Politics and Ecology, an Israeli Cosmetics Firm Goes Global', *Fortune Small Business*, 10 December 2009. See <money.cnn.com>.

26. Fourth 1949 Geneva Convention, Section III. Article 49, 'The Occupying Power shall not deport or transfer parts of its own civilian population into the territory it occupies.'

27. Information on the company's ownership structure found in the database of Who Profits.

28. Adalah, Interactive Map and Database on the History of the State of Israel's Expropriation of Land from the Palestinian People: <www.adalah.org/features/land/flash>.

29. *Mara'abe* v *The Prime Minister of Israel*, HCJ 7957/04, Israel Supreme Court, 15 September 2005. Available at <www.unhcr.org>.

30. Resolutions 446, 465 and 484.

31. 'Applicability of the Geneva Convention relative to the Protection of Civilian Persons in Time of War, of 12 August 1949, to the Occupied Palestinian Territory, including Jerusalem, and the other occupied Arab territories', UN General Assembly resolution, (A/RES/58/97), 17 December 2003.

32. US State Department, 'Israel and the occupied territories: Country Reports on Human Rights Practices', 4 March 2002. Available at <www.state.gov>.

33. EU-Settlements' Watch, 11 February–31 July 2002. Available at <www.consilium.europa.eu>.

34. 'Legal Consequences of the Construction of a Wall in the Occupied Palestinian Territory', International Court of Justice, 9 July 2004. Available at <www.icj-cij.org>.

35. ICRC, 'Conference of High Contracting Parties to the Fourth Geneva Convention: statement by the International Committee of the Red Cross', 5 December 2001.

36. Meirav Crystal, 'Holland to Probe if Ahava Products Made on Occupied Land', *YnetNews.com*, 18 November 2009.

37. Jamie Welham, 'Pro-Palestinian Protesters Claim Covent Garden Store Ahava are Mislabelling Products', *West End Extra*, 27 August 2010.

38. Katie Bird, 'Sephora Taken to Court Over Products from Israeli Brand Ahava', *Cosmetics Design Europe*, 28 May 2010.

39. Liel Liebovitz, 'Pink Panthers: Why the Antiwar Group CODEPINK has Targeted an Israeli Cosmetics Company', *Tablet Magazine*, 27 August 2009.

40. Donald Macintyre, 'Palestinians barred from Dead Sea beaches to "appease Israeli settlers"', *Independent*, 14 June 2008.

41. 'The Prohibited Zone: Israeli Planning Policy in the Palestinian Villages in Area C', Bikomon report, 2008.
42. Ralf Beste and Christoph Schult, 'EU Eyes Exports from Israeli settlements', *Business Week*, 14 June 2009.
43. Euro-Mediterranean Agreement establishing an association between the European Communities and their Member States, of the one part, and the State of Israel, of the other part, 20 November 1995 (the EU-Israel Association Agreement), OJ 2000 L 147/3.
44. *Brita*, Case C-386/08, 25 February 2010.
45. Beste and Schult, 'EU Eyes Exports from Israeli settlements'.
46. ASA Council, 9 April 2008 (48887); 15 July 2009 (95205); 14 April 2010 (114921).
47. Reclame Code Commissie, 27 September 2010 (2010/00360). This ruling of the Dutch advertising regulator was later overturned on appeal (after the initial submission of this paper).
48. Directive 2005/29/EU of the European Parliament and of the Council of 11 May 2005, OJ L 149/22, Unfair Commercial Practices Directive, see Articles 6 and 7.

4. THE FINANCIAL SERVICES SECTOR

1. 'Financing the Israeli Occupation: The Direct Involvement of Israeli Banks in Illegal Israeli Settlement Activity and Control over the Palestinian Banking Market', Who Profits report, October 2010.
2. See also Adri Nieuwhof and Guus Hoelen, 'Major Dutch pension fund divests from occupation', *Electronic Intifada*, 12 November 2010.
3. ICJ, Corporate complicity and legal accountability, 2008.
4. UN Special Representative of the Secretary-General on the Issue of Human Rights and Transnational Corporations and other Business Enterprises on the corporate responsibility to respect human rights.
5. Hague Regulations IV (1907), articles 43 and 55 and Geneva Conventions, Common Article 1.
6. This provision violates Article 2(2) of the ICESCR and Articles 4(1) and 26 of the ICCPR as well as the Convention on the Elimination of Racial Discrimination of 1965.
7. <http://www.whoprofits.org/Newsletter.php?nlid=59>.

5. THE SECURITY INDUSTRY AND THE WAR INDUSTRY

1. *SIPRI Yearbook 2010: Armaments, Disarmament and National Security*, Stockholm International Peace Research Institute, July 2010.
2. 'Elbit Systems to supply Skylark 1 UAV to France's Special Forces', Elbit Systems press release, 24 March 2008.
3. 'The Arms Trade Between EU Member States and Israel', Quaker Briefing Paper, October 2010.
4. 'Caterpillar: The Alternative Report', War on Want, March 2005.
5. 'Profiting from the Occupation: Corporate complicity in Israel's crimes against the Palestinian people', War on Want, July 2006.
6. The Israeli Committee Against House Demolitions, 'Statistics on House Demolitions (1967–2010)'. Available at <www.icahd.org>.

7.   B'Tselem, 'Through No Fault of Their Own: Israel's Punitive House Demolitions in the al-Aqsa Intifada', November 2004. Available at <www.btselem.org>.

8.   Jeremy Sharp, 'U.S. Foreign Aid to Israel', Congressional Research Service, 16 September 2010, p. 24. Available at <www.fas.org>.

9.   The text of the MOU is available at <endtheoccupation.org/downloads/2007israelusmou.pdf>.

10. The text of the declaration is available at <ccrjustice.org/files/Corrie_WeinbergDeclaration_10_05.pdf>.

11. Data compiled from Department of Defense Section 655 Reports, obtained by the Federation of American Scientists through a Freedom of Information Act (FOIA) request. The reports are available at <www.fas.org/programs/ssp/asmp/factsandfigures/government_data_index.html#655>.

12. Data compiled from tables available on the Statistics page at <www.btselem.org>.

13. For more detailed descriptions and legal analysis of human rights abuses committed by Israel with Caterpillar bulldozers, see 'Israel's Human Rights Violations Facilitated by the Use of CAT Bulldozers', available at <www.endtheoccupation.org/article.php?id=1178>.

14. Shuki Sadeh, 'Danish company halts equipment supply to West Bank in wake of public protest', Ha'aretz, 15 March 2011.

15. Yuval Maoz, 'Elbit Systems Will Provide Airborne Electronic Warfare Systems for Korea for 7 Million Dollars', The Marker, 8 February 2009.

16. Securities and Exchange Commission, 'Form 20-F: Annual Report Pursuant to Section 13 or 15 (d) Of the Securities Exchange Act of 1934 – Elbit Systems LTD.', Securities and Exchange Commission, Washington, DC, 2006.

17. Ora Koren, 'Defense News: Elbit Systems in 37th Place in Rapid Growth Rate of Security Companies in the World', TheMarker, 7 September 2008.

18. Securities and Exchange Commission, 'Form 20-F: Annual Report Pursuant to Section 13 or 15 (d) Of the Securities Exchange Act of 1934 – Elbit Systems LTD.', Securities and Exchange Commission, Washington, DC, 2006.

19. Rotem Sela, 'Tadiran Communications from Elbit Systems Group Won a Contract for 127 Million Dollars to Provide Tactical Systems', TheMarker, 5 May 2008.

20. Vadim Sviderski, 'Elbit System's Subsidiary will Provide Boeing Products for 80 Million Dollars', TheMarker, 11 May 2010.

21. 'Elbit Systems will Provide an Asian Customers Electronic Warfare Systems for 147 Million Dollars', TheMarker, 24 March 2010.

22. Securities and Exchange Commission, 'Form 20-F'.

23. Yoram Gabizon, 'Elbit Systems Won a Contract Worth 68 Million Dollars from the U.S. Army', TheMarker, 13 October 2010.

24. Yuval Maoz, 'Elbit Systems Will Provide Head Systems for the F-35 Plane for 541 Million Dollars', TheMarker, 16 June 2009.

25. 'Elbit Systems Buys the Remaining Stocks of Kinetics for 100 Million Dollars', TheMarker, 7 April 2009.

26. Natan Sheva, 'Elbit Systems to Buy BVR For 34 Million Dollars', TheMarker, 20 July 2009.

27. Natan Sheva, 'Elbit Systems Signed a Deal to Buy the Shiron Communication Company According to a 16 Million Dollars Value', TheMarker, 8 January 2009.

28. Yoram Gabizon, 'Elbit Systems Bought Gilat's and Naftali's Mikal for 90 Million Dollars', TheMarker, 2 September 2010.

29. Yoram Gabizon, "Elbit Systems is Buying Azimut According to a Company Value of 210 Million NIS', *TheMarker*, 25 January 2010.

30. Yoram Gabizon, 'Elbit Systems Will Set Up a Joint Enterprize in the UAV Field with She French Segem', *TheMarker*, 16 September 2010.

31. Securities and Exchange Commission, 'Form 20-F'.

32. Vadim Sviderski, 'Airport Extends Elbit Contract for Snunit Training Planes for 20 Million Dollars for 10 Years', *TheMarker*, 22 February 2010.

33. Tal Levy, 'Elbit Systems Provided a Simulator for the Sufa Plane of the Airforce', *TheMarker*, 6 March 2010.

34. Securities and Exchange Commission, 'Form 20-F'.

35. Dutch Ministry of Defense, 'Contract Award Notice Goods – Battlefield Management System', 28 September 2010.

36. Yuval Maoz, 'Elbit Systems will First Provide Intelligence Systems for a Foreign Customer: The Deal is Estimated to be Worth 9 Million Dollars', *TheMarker*, 17 June 2008.

37. Yoram Gabizon, 'Elbit Systems Won a Contract for 45 Million Dollars for the U.S. Army – Will Upgrade Night Targetting Systems for Helicopters', *TheMarker*, 26 October 2010.

38. Yoram Gabizon, 'Elbit Systems Will Set Up a Joint Enterprise in the UAV Field with She French Segem', *TheMarker*, 16 September 2010.

39. Yael Pollack, 'Elbit Systems will Provide a European State Hermes 450 UAVs for 20 Million Dollars', *TheMarker*, 7 July 2008.

40. Ora Koren, 'IAI and Elbit Stopped a UAV Deal with Turkey for 180 Million Dollars', *TheMarker*, 14 June 2010.

41. Zohar Blumnkrantz, 'Disagreement between the State, El-Al and Elbit Delays Protecting Planes', *TheMarker*, 10 August 2010.

42. Zohar Blumenkranz, 'Israel will Purchase an Elbit System to Defend Passenger Planes from Shoulder Missiles', *Ha'aretz*, 24 June 2009.

43. Securities and Exchange Commission, 'Form 20-F'.

44. Yuval Maoz, 'Elbit Systems Won Contracts to Upgrade Planes and Helicopters in Europe Worth About 80 Million Dollars', *TheMarker*, 17 December 2008.

45. Yuval Maoz, 'Elbit Systems Continues to Show Strength: Net Profit Jumped in the Quarter by 34.5% to 43.3 Million Dollars', *TheMarker*, 20 May 2009.

46. According to the Israeli Central Bureau of Statistics (2009). Israel's total diamond exports that year were worth about $5.9 billion, comprising almost 14 per cent of Israel's total commodity exports, and about 9.2 per cent of Israel's total exports.

AFTERWORD

1. 'BNC endorses findings of London session of Russell Tribunal on Palestine on corporate complicity', BNC statement, 30 November 2010. Available at <www.bdsmovement.net>.

Index

Compiled by Sue Carlton

Page numbers in **bold** refer to photographs